# STONE TOOLS AND SOCIETY

Working Stone in Neolithic and
Bronze Age Britain

## Mark Edmonds

B.T. Batsford Ltd, London

© Mark Edmonds 1995

First published 1995

All rights reserved. No part of this publication
may be reproduced, in any form or by any
means, without permission from the Publisher

Typeset by DW Design, London
and printed in Great Britain by
Butler and Tanner, Frome

Published by B. T. Batsford Ltd
4 Fitzhardinge Street, London W1H 0AH

A CIP catalogue record for this book is available from the British Library

ISBN 07134 7141 7

# Contents

# List of Illustrations

5

## List of Illustrations

# Preface and Acknowledgements

The last few years have witnessed a series of developments in the perspectives that we bring to bear on the study of the past. Archaeologists are being encouraged to reflect upon the conditions under which they attempt to understand past societies, and to explore the problems that accompany the translation of material remains into narratives about people and history. Nowhere are these shifts of perspective more evident than in the field of material culture studies. Over the last few decades, our views on the nature and significance of past material culture have undergone various transformations. In particular, we have begun to question the idea that notions of practical utility or adaptation are sufficient to capture the many dimensions of the prehistoric tools and other artefacts that we recover today. In the wake of these debates has come an acknowledgement that attention needs to be given to the 'social life of things' and to the part that artefacts may have played in shaping the identities and positions of people in the past.

Stimulating though much of this debate has been, there is a sense in which it has remained somewhat abstract. If this is the case within material culture studies as a whole, it is particularly true of stone tool research in Britain. This is somewhat surprising given that stone tools and their associated waste assemblages are perhaps the most durable, and in some cases almost the only classes of data that students of prehistory have at their disposal. While many important studies have been undertaken, we are still some way from an understanding of how the production, use and deposition of stone tools was caught up in the broader flow of social life and social change in the past. The discussions contained in this book represent a small step in the direction of that understanding. Working at a very general level, it attempts to show how many of the tools that we recover today may have carried a wide range of connotations and values. Following traditions of working and using stone from the Neolithic to the beginning of the Middle Bronze Age, it attempts to show how the cultural biographies of some of these tools may have been caught up in the broader web of contemporary social and political relations.

Inevitably, any work of this nature carries with it a number of problems. Almost by definition, general narratives gloss over the local and particular detail that comes with more focused studies. As a result, they can create a spurious sense of unity which is at odds with the images derived from more detailed research. Indeed, it is worth acknowledging that the very concept of 'Prehistoric Britain' carries with it a series of assumptions which may have little relevance for our understanding of the conditions under which people lived at that time. Just as these basic assumptions need to be recognized, so we must also acknowledge that biases arise from other sources. The historical development of archaeology in Britain is far from balanced. Our knowledge of some areas is exceptionally rich, reflecting nearly two centuries of fieldwork. Other regions have only recently seen anything like the same amount of attention and it is difficult to resist the temptation to 'fill in the gaps' by extrapolation from one area to another. Although the thematic nature of this study provides some scope for avoiding these problems, it will be readily apparent that my resistance is low.

General accounts also carry with them a series of obligations. In the course of writing this book I have drawn upon research conducted by a large number of people, many of whom may not agree with the arguments developed here. The bibliography that appears at the end will provide the reader with an opportunity to follow up (and assess) many of these arguments in more detail. Equally, I have benefited from discussions, conversations, criticism and encouragement given freely by many colleagues and friends. In particular, I would like to thank the following for their direct and indirect influence on this book: John Barrett; Barbara Bender; Robin Boast; Richard Bradley; Anick Coudart; Chris Evans; Frances Healy; J. D. Hill; Koji Mizoguchi; Colin Richards; Niall Sharples; Marie-Louise

Sørenson; Julian Thomas and Sander Van der Leeuw. In addition, I am indebted to a variety of people who contributed illustrations or information. In particular, I am grateful to Gwil Owen at the Museum of Archaeology and Anthropology at Cambridge and Alison Sheridan at the National Museum of Scotland for their work on many of the photographs that appear here. Thanks must also go to Peter Dunn, Judith Dobie and Chris Jones for their excellent reconstruction drawings. I am also grateful to Peter Kemmis Betty, Sarah Vernon-Hunt and Charlotte Kilenyi at B.T. Batsford for their patience.

Last but not least, I would like to acknowledge a rather different sort of debt to 'Flint Jack'. During the nineteenth century, Flint Jack carved out a precarious existence fashioning artefacts and decorative items from flint with a dexterity that remains unmatched today. Often, he undertook these tasks at the behest of antiquarians and his demonstrations persuaded many people that stone tools were neither 'elf-shot' nor thunderbolts, but the products of a human hand. At the same time, he attempted to make a living by selling 'antiquities' to many local societies and county museums. What is clear from the records that survive is that curators often continued to pay for his products for some time after they realized that their antiquity was – to say the least – open to question. It seems that many were happy to do so because the artefacts that sprang from his hand were far 'superior' to the worn, broken and patinated examples found in fields and graves. In keeping with the idea that we fabricate stories about stone tools in accordance with the values and preconceptions of our time, I dedicate this book to him.

# 1 Squeezing blood from stones

Over four and a half thousand years ago in what is now south Dorset, someone took up a nodule of flint and began to work. He or she probably turned the lump of stone in the hand several times, familiarizing themselves with its weight and form, before raising a hammerstone and letting it fall to detach a flake.

With this first removal of flake from core, they continued to turn the stone, running their fingers across the dark, inner body of the flint and the coarse, off-white skin of the nodule. The platform or striking surface prepared, they began removing that outer cortex as the flakes sprang out like sparks from beneath the hammer. Now their fingers fastened onto ridges and scars as they casually trimmed the edges to create an angle for working. A dust like powdered glass coated their fingers, and small chips of flint joined the flakes and spalls that lay scattered on the ground around them.

Here they may have paused . . . bending to retrieve one of the larger flakes from the scatter that lay at their feet. Tracing its contours between finger and thumb, they may have considered the potentials it held before letting it fall a second time in favour of the parent stone and the task at hand. Gradually, the shifting tempo of hesitant working gave way to a more fluid rhythm as hand and eye relaxed to an accustomed edge. Carrying them forwards through the stone, the rhythm continued unbroken – the scatter on the ground slowly darkening as the last peninsula of cortex was removed. Even the slow rotation of the core kept time with the steady rise and fall of the hammer. Then, when it seemed as if they might have continued on until the stone in their hand had vanished, they paused and bent once more, placing the faceted core among the debris. Brushing the dust and splinters from their legs, they gathered up this loose assemblage and walked to where a small pit lay open, its mouth gaping in the freshly cut chalk. Leaning forward, they poured the stone

through the open mouth until it came to a clattering rest amidst the shards of a broken vessel, the fleshy jaw of a pig, and the still warm ashes from a fire. As they pulled the dark soil in from the edges of the pit, the smell of the ashes faded as first the jaw, then the flint, disappeared from sight. Rising again, they scattered the remaining soil across the ground, and turned away from the darkened circle.

Anyone with any flint knapping experience will tell you how difficult it is to describe the interweaving of action and thought that marks the making of a stone tool. As with many of the tasks that we routinely perform today, the act of working around a piece of stone involves a tacit negotiation of the material, in which hands, eyes, ears and expectations are all engaged. Knowledge of how to proceed and the intentions of the producer are constantly tempered by the conditions encountered as the raw material is transformed from its original state to a specific cultural form. This process resists conscious articulation. Indeed, it often proceeds most smoothly when the gestures and procedures that make up the act remain partly unconsidered or taken for granted (fig. 1).

In attempting to study of the results of this process – assemblages of prehistoric tools and waste – archaeologists have available a battery of techniques. These techniques allow us to 'read' the scars and ridges on the surfaces of artefacts and by-products and to grasp some of the material dimensions of tool production and use. We can determine the physical, chemical and mechanical properties of different stones, assessing the constraints and potentials that they create. Through experiments and morphological analysis, we can estimate how much waste will be produced during the making of a tool or the working of a core (fig. 2). We can specify what forms the waste flakes will take and the relative frequencies in which they are likely to occur. In exceptional cases, we can even refit flakes to

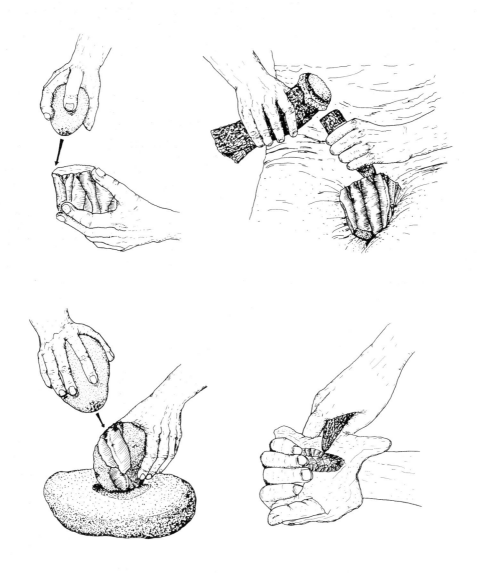

1 Although people could exercise a measure of choice, the manner in which different stones were worked and used in the past depended to a certain extent on their physical and mechanical characteristics. Materials such as flint and some volcanic rocks have a regular crystalline structure which allows them to be 'flaked' in a regular manner. Other materials such as granite possess a rather different structure. As a result, they can only be rendered into tools by the laborious process of pecking, grinding and polishing. Materials such as flint can be worked in a number of ways: by direct percussion with a stone, antler or wooden hammer; by indirect percussion using a hammer and a punch; and through the use of hammers and anvils. Flakes and core tools may also be 'retouched' through direct percussion or pressure flaking.

2 We can learn as much from the waste created during the making of tools as from the finished products. In the case of materials such as flint, the waste or 'debitage' created during tool production and use can be used to identify general 'reduction sequences' – the steps or procedures followed in transforming a lump of stone into a cultural artefact. Found in excavations or on the surfaces of ploughed fields, different classes of waste provide valuable information on the character and spatial organization of stoneworking.

their parent cores, creating complex three-dimensional jigsaws which allow us to capture particular episodes of working in more detail (fig. 3). To this list can be added techniques linking particular raw materials with their geological sources, and those which reveal how, and on what material, different tools were used.

Devoted as it is to the stone tools of Neolithic and Bronze Age Britain, this book would not be possible without these and other techniques. Indeed, the description of flintworking with which this chapter opened is itself derived from a refitting study. But as that passage also suggests, the issues that we face in dealing with these traces take us beyond questions of physical description. Certain techniques may allow us to

reconstruct the material specifics of this act and to explore some of the choices that were made in the creation and working of the core. But they do not provide us with a basis for understanding the cultural milieu in which that act was undertaken, nor the purposes that were served by the deposition of the entire assemblage in the ground.

Like the routines that shape much of our lives today, the tasks undertaken by people in the past would have provided a frame through which they might have come to recognize aspects of their world and themselves. The tools and waste that we recover would have been entangled in that world of social practice, providing cues for this process of recognition and interpretation. As such, the ideas that shaped their production and

11

3 A refitted flint core. Occasionally, closer analysis of waste material makes it possible to identify the 'grammar' or pattern of choices that people followed during particular episodes of stoneworking. This is often explored in the context of refitting – the reassembly of flakes and spalls around the core or artefact from which they were struck.

use would have stretched beyond problems of procedure to encompass concepts of the self and society. With the passage of time, however, these artefacts have become disentangled, only to be caught up in new frames as we try to 'make sense' of them in the present.

These two themes of description and interpretation are also intertwined in archaeological practice, so that it is not always clear where one begins and the other ends. As the title suggests, this book documents some of the principal categories of stone tool that were made, used and discarded in later prehistoric Britain. But at the same time, it is also concerned with the conditions under which those artefacts were brought into being. In particular it highlights the ways in which the production, use and deposition of stone tools played a part in maintaining or reworking the concepts of identity and authority that were recognized by people in the past. The remainder of this chapter serves as an introduction to some of the problems that surround our attempts to squeeze blood from stones. This brief discussion provides the point of departure for the chapters which follow.

## Approaches to prehistoric technology

For some time now, it has been accepted that the study of stone tools is synonymous with the study of technology. Commonly made and used in the execution of practical tasks, stone tools seem to sit comfortably within this general category, amenable to the forms of analysis and explanation favoured in technological studies. While its significance may have changed in keeping with broader shifts in our perspectives, the technological realm has long been granted a pre-eminent position in our accounts of the past. From the inception of the Three Age system through to more recent studies, it has often been cast in a major role: as a marker of cultures, as an indicator of evolutionary development and as a system that determines the character of society and stimulates change. Admittedly, we are now more reluctant to equate particular artefact types or assemblages with specific 'cultures', or with stages in grand evolutionary schemes. Moreover, we now acknowledge that while technologies and social relations are often inter-twined, there is little merit in the view that productive forces shape society in a strict and deterministic sense. Yet, at a practical level, much research continues to be guided by these long-standing assumptions regarding the significance of technology and the 'effects' that it has upon economic and social life.

In the study of stone tools, these assumptions are apparent in the priorities that are assigned to different avenues of research. More often than not, questions of function are given pride of place, as ever more detailed descriptions go hand in hand with general discussions of subsistence or 'food-getting' behaviour. Similar limits are often placed upon the treatment of the lithic scatters identified through fieldwalking and other forms of surface survey. For the most part, we tend to use these data to plot the location of settlements, taking these as reflections of broader economic regimes. These are obviously important questions to consider. Yet as new descriptive techniques are developed, or new applications are found for existing analyses, so it seems that the scale and scope of research becomes increasingly narrow and specialized. In short, we seem to leap from detailed descriptions of wear traces on tool edges to abstract models of subsistence and settlement that span vast tracts of space and time. Only rarely do we consider the problems that accompany movement between the two.

In a few cases, this emphasis upon description

has been rejected in favour of more explicit proposals regarding the conditions that may have shaped tool production and use. These studies have generally been based upon perceived 'regularities in technological behaviour' which are held to apply at all times and places, and here it is the adaptive significance of technology which is stressed. Particular attention is often paid to the efficiency of tools in the performance of tasks, and to the scheduling of tool procurement and production in relation to the availability of different resources. Under such a rubric, patterns of tool production, use and discard are generally cast as responses – adaptations which allow for group survival in the face of particular sets of ecological or social circumstances. Insofar as they stress the need for an explicit theorization of lithic studies, such approaches remain useful as tools with which to explore the phenomena that we study. Yet it is still possible to question the vast scales on which analyses are conducted and the assumptions upon which they are often based. Here again, the emphasis remains upon the functional dimensions of particular tools and techniques and the effects they may have had upon productivity and social organization.

Despite profound changes in our concepts, aims and techniques, our approaches to stone tools have remained rooted in a long-established tradition of enquiry. In keeping with this tradition, the technological system is generally seen as an arena which is somehow divorced from history and from lived experience. It is a realm where decisions are taken on the basis of an explicit and utilitarian logic and in which responses are made to largely external stimuli. More often than not, prehistoric technology is viewed as 'hardware' – placed between people and nature – which allows for the more or less efficient exploitation of particular resources by human groups. In effect, it is held as an objective field of past social life which presents relatively few problems for the contemporary observer. All that we appear to require for a satisfactory interpretation is detailed description and 'common sense'.

Of course it does not follow that the artefacts that we recover were not created and used in the execution of practical tasks. If functional analysis tells us nothing else, it does at least demonstrate that even unmodified pieces of stone could be employed for a wide variety of purposes. What is at issue is the belief that descriptions and 'common sense' are really all that are needed. Questions of function and productive efficiency may be important. But they do not provide a sufficient basis for capturing the broader roles that these objects may have played in past societies. This does not mean that our descriptive techniques are somehow flawed. They may have played their part in reaffirming a view of lithic technology as hardware, as much by their character as by their results, but they nevertheless remain vital. What needs to be reconsidered is the framework within which they are set.

# Material culture and social reproduction

This need for reconsideration has been addressed in recent studies of past and present material culture. Many of these studies start from the idea that our location in western society has an inevitable impact on our views of the past and how it may be studied. Perhaps the most basic point to be made is that our contemporary circumstances encourage a view of objects which denies their position in webs of social and political relations. Given the extraordinary volume of commodities that circulate today, and our tendency to discuss things in quantitative terms, this argument remains persuasive. Indeed, the prevailing view of technology as hardware provides a good case in point. What we often overlook, however, are the roles played by everyday objects in shaping our understandings of self and society.

Some aspects of this role are more easily identified than others. For example, we generally have no difficulty in recognizing the importance of insignia, uniforms and badges of office as cues for the classification of people according to their positions or roles within society. Motifs and costumes often carry complex and even abstract ideas regarding the authority vested in particular people, or the qualities, beliefs and histories that separate them from others. What is sometimes more difficult to grasp is the rather more subtle part played by material culture in

guiding our opinions and perceptions. Even a cursory glance at the totemic images produced by the advertising industry demonstrates the extent to which we endow many practical objects with ideas and values that extend far beyond their immediate utility. Just as these associations may influence our decisions as to what to buy, use or wear, so they also play a part in guiding our appreciation of other people. Visiting someone's house, we make remarkably rapid and sophisticated assessments of the furnishings and trappings that we encounter in different areas. How are the rooms furnished? What objects or paintings are displayed? Is the kitchen equipped with the latest styles of knives and cooking pots? Where they are acknowledged at all, the rapid judgements that we make on the basis of these readings may be explained away as a matter of taste or preference. But they remain crucial to the ways in which we come to think about or categorize other people in terms of their economic and socio-cultural identity.

At the same time, the routine use of material items also provides a medium through which we come to know ourselves. As Winner states:

. . . individuals are actively involved in the daily creation and recreation, production and reproduction of the world in which they live. As they employ tools and techniques, work in social labour arrangements, make and consume products and adapt their behaviour to the material conditions they encounter in their natural and artificial environment, individuals realize possibilities for human existence.

Put simply, tools may not determine the character of society, but they are nonetheless caught up in the process by which the social order is continually brought into being. As such, they are also resources that can be drawn upon when people attempt to question or rework aspects of the conditions under which they live. In our own society, anthropologists and sociologists have shown how concepts of personal and group identity are often carried through the clothes that we wear, the tools that we use and the trappings that we surround ourselves with. Brought together in the repertoires and routines that make up our lives, material categories simultaneously contribute to the shaping of our identities at a variety of levels. Often passing almost unnoticed, they help us to classify ourselves as members of particular age or gender sets and as people who occupy particular positions within broader socio-economic and political structures. They may also signify aspects of our identity as members of particular cultural groups or even nation states.

Similar ideas may also be taken on board through the spatial pattern of our daily lives. For example, recent studies in cultural geography have shown how the spatial arrangement of the urban environment is informed by (and helps to reaffirm) many of the social, economic and political divisions that cross-cut society. At a more localized level, the spatial order of many day-to-day activities may also lend itself to the maintenance of a variety of social categories and norms. For example, parts of a house may have practical and historical associations with different categories of person. Some rooms may have stronger links with women than with men, and even the tools or utensils that we associate with different tasks may carry ideas about specific divisions of labour and authority. Although we seldom think about these associations and may even laugh when they are brought to our attention, the routines and paraphernalia of these tasks may still play a part in defining our sense of place within the home and within a broader social order.

Similar observations have been made in very different contexts. For example, Henrietta Moore has shown how the organization of many day-to-day activities among the Marakwet of Kenya is both an expression and an outcome of distinctions drawn on the basis of age, gender and kinship. The artefacts and materials that are caught up in those activities are imbued with ideas related to traditional links between particular tasks and specific categories of person. Equally, among the Loikop (Samburu), the production and use of spears is intimately bound up with ideas about the qualities and roles that constitute adult male identity. Through their production and use, these artefacts simultaneously stand for particular social categories and provide a medium through which those categories are realized. Indeed, it is their very physical properties and applications which make these things 'good to think with' as well as good to use. These associations are often tacit and largely unconsidered. Yet through their continued use, artefacts guide people's understandings of the cultural and historical significance of their actions.

On this issue at least, there may be little to be gained from a rigid distinction between modern western and non-capitalist societies, past or present. Yet it may well be that the role of material items in social reproduction is all the more crucial where the separation of objects from people is far less marked. Under these circumstances, everyday objects might refer to particular tasks and divisions of labour, to persons or properties of persons, or to traditional concepts of affiliation, kinship and obligation. They may even serve as points of reference within broader belief systems. Smoothed with service and patinated with history, they may hold stories about the self and society which are understood or made familiar through social practice. As material metaphors or metonyms, they may also carry those stories into different areas of social experience. Brought into new contexts and into association with different objects or people, they may 'presence' specific concepts or values. This may be particularly important in the case of portable artefacts which can be – both literally and metaphorically – 'taken up'.

The complexity of the ties between the social and the material have recently been addressed in two studies of stone procurement and tool use. Among Australian Aboriginal groups in Western Arnhem Land, Paul Tacon has shown how the classification, procurement and use of stone is intimately bound up with ideas about the activities and personalities of ancestral beings. Raw materials may be regarded as the residues of dreamtime activities or even as the remains of ancestral beings, and they are commonly classified according to their aesthetic and spiritual qualities. These associations and values are drawn upon as people acquire and use stone, and as such, they provide powerful media through which concepts of place, kinship, belonging and even age and gender are negotiated. In a rather different vein, work in Irian Jaya by Pierre and Anne-Marie Petrequin has also shown how the timing and spacing of stone tool procurement and use may be keyed into broader concepts of kinship, personal identity and the ancestral past. In this case, even qualities such as colour, lustre, elegance and balance during use are caught up in the routine process through which certain tools come to stand for particular people or properties of people.

In effect, particular traditions of making and using things can be said to have political qualities. The social and historical relations that permeate any society will ultimately condition the values and associations that are attached to particular tools and tasks. As a result, the material culture that people make and use may serve to maintain elements of a consensus about the social order. At the same time, the associations carried by those objects and traditions are not fixed, nor are they determined by rigid rules. Rather, acts of making and using are guided by dispositions which are continuously drawn upon and modified. As people experience and act upon different aspects of the conditions under which they live, so they may alter the character and traditional associations of certain tasks or objects. Many of these changes may be gradual, unintended and unforeseen. They may occur at an almost unacknowledged rate, and changes in one sphere of social life may have consequences for the ways in which other features of society are understood. In other cases, however, the ideas carried by material items may be pulled into a sharper and more strategic focus. They may be referenced more explicitly in the protection of certain interests or in attempts to rework established lines of social and political authority.

This more active sense of drawing upon objects as symbols may be undertaken in a number of ways. For example, material symbols often play an important part in formal or ritualized activities. Thus the regalia worn or carried at state occasions conveys a complex set of messages concerning the status and identity of those who are permitted to attend. These objects serve as reminders of the deep historical roots which are supposed to underpin the authority of the participants and the qualities that separate them from those who can only watch. In other words, material symbols are often rather more than decorative paraphernalia. They may play a critical part in shaping the proper conduct and interpre-

tation of important social events. Aside from the pomp and ceremony of state occasions, many junctures in our lives are marked by the formalized use of material symbols. From the giving of wedding rings to the acquisition of tools at the end of an apprenticeship, symbols help to define the meaning and significance of those occasions and the status that they confer. With the conclusion of particular ceremonies, many of these objects become familiar – part of the gear that we routinely wear or use and seldom worthy of comment. Nevertheless, they continue to play a part in shaping our ideas about ourselves and the ways in which we are seen by others.

Just as many explicit symbols may continue to convey meaning long after they have become familiar, so everyday objects may occasionally be highlighted to mark the authority and influence of people. For example, even simple tools such as the trowel may be understood in different ways according to the context and character of their use. Routinely used by bricklayers and plasterers, they become worn, familiar and attached to particular people. As tools that are intimately associated with specific forms of manual labour, they may even signify some of the qualities that separate people on the basis of gender. Placed in the hands of a visiting dignitary at topping-out ceremonies (and sometimes engraved or made in unsuitable metals), they become an element in more formal statements. Among archaeologists too, the trowel can have redolences which are used to rank or classify individuals. During excavations it is quite common to hear humorous references being made to the character or condition of a person's trowel as if it provided an index of their experience and skill. Is the blade riveted or drop-forged? Is it pristine or worn through long hours of use? While they may not be taken all that seriously, assessments such as these (and thus the trowel itself) serve as common points of reference for the small groups working together on excavations.

Other examples can be found rather closer to home. Kitchen utensils can be displayed as reflections of the taste and 'cultivation' of their owners. Yet, at the same time, the significance of individual pieces can change according to the circumstances in which they are used. For example, in many English households, carving knives are routinely employed for a variety of tasks and are generally treated in much the same ways as other utensils in the cutlery drawer. Until recently, however, this mundane tool would be seen rather differently at Sunday lunch, where the sharpening of the blade and the carving and serving of the meat was conventionally undertaken by the (male) head of the household. Despite the fact that the knife (like many kitchen utensils) may have been more regularly used by women, it was nonetheless drawn upon to highlight or symbolize the traditional role and authority of the man within the family.

Dated though this last example may seem, it does highlight the sense in which the meanings attached to objects can slide in and out of focus and change according to context. In this case, the use of the knife and the act of carving and serving on a Sunday was in keeping with traditional models of identity and authority. Equally common are instances where everyday objects are drawn upon to mark a break with the status quo, or to express a sense of difference between individuals or groups. Although it has been cited so often that it is now little more than a cliché, the transformation of safety-pins by punks in the late 1970s shows how mundane objects can become what anthropologists sometimes call 'weapons of exclusion'.

A rather different transformation of significance can occur where things are moved from one system of meaning and value to another. Objects which are mundane and apparently devoid of any particular significance in one context may be viewed quite differently from the vantage point of a different culture. They may even become highly valued and their possession may come to be regarded as an expression of personal status and authority. In the wake of western expansion and colonialism, one of the more pervasive caricatures that circulated was the image of non-western societies who willingly parted with highly prized goods in exchange for 'trinkets' or the detritus of settlers and European traders. Often missed in those early accounts was the fact that these transactions carried objects between two very different 'regimes of value'. What was often more important for those receiving such trinkets was the symbolic capital that they accumulated, and the prestige and

renown that they gained through their ability to conduct dealings with westerners. Alongside other trade goods, some of the tokens given by westerners became status items. In some cases, their display and circulation became both a prerogative of those in authority and a medium through which that authority was achieved or contested.

This process of transformation is not only played out through the movement of objects from one place to another. The patina of age can also obscure or add to the traditional meanings of things. Archaic tools may become important motifs or symbols, and yesterday's rubbish can become a much sought-after collectable. Passed down from one generation to another, objects may be endowed with complex personal biographies. Even stone tools become entangled in new systems of meaning and value. Found in a field and placed on a mantlepiece, they may be valued for their perceived aesthetic qualities or for the sense that they evoke of a long-established human presence. Fought over in the competitive arena of the auction room, their acquisition can be an expression of the wealth and taste of the highest bidder. Placed in museum cases and in books such as this, they can even be used to define past communities according to principles that may have meant very little to them.

## Squeezing blood from stones

Strange as it may seem, these observations have some relevance for the study of stone tools. We need to retain an appreciation of the tasks to which particular tools were put and the material effects that they may have had; these questions remain vital. But we must also acknowledge that lithic technologies, like other traditions of making and using, were shaped by social and political relations and not just by practical demands. In other words, stone tools may have been as much a technology for social classification as they were a technology for the acquisition of particular resources. At the same time, we need to recognize that the ideas and values that may have been carried by particular tools or ways of working were probably far from static. Tacitly acknowledged for much of the time, their routine associations could be drawn upon in the maintenance of the social and political order or in the reworking of established lines of authority and obligation. Just as their significance may have changed over the course of history, so many tools may also have been understood in different ways according to the contexts in which they were encountered and the circumstances in which they were used.

These issues are important, but we must be wary of taking the position too far. There is little merit in arguing that people had the capacity to transform their world simply by changing the ways in which they made and used particular categories of object, since this would be to ignore both the broader conditions within which they lived and the often conservative qualities of material culture. When we look at the evidence from Neolithic and Early Bronze Age Britain, what is astounding is the sheer persistence of particular traditions of making, using and depositing artefacts. It may be no more than an imaginative conceit to assume that people in the past could easily break with the traditions and political realities of their time any more than we can today. Under these circumstances, it might be more profitable to ask how those realities were sustained through traditions of working and using stone.

This brings us to the question of how we might hope to grasp some of these issues through archaeological evidence. This is a difficult enough task in the study of living communities because material culture may be endowed with ideas which are difficult to articulate. The archaeological objects that we recover are disentangled from the social contexts within which they were produced, used and deposited, so what scope is there for addressing similar issues in the prehistoric past? Can we really say anything about the social dimensions of Neolithic and Bronze Age stone tools?

Here we need to recognize the implications of the idea that action on the material world is a medium through which social relations and cultural traditions are maintained or reworked. The cultural significance of particular sites, activities and objects is sustained through practice, and is thus 'made flesh' through the traces that we can observe today. Patterns of landscape and resource use, the character of sites and traditions

of making, using and depositing artefacts would have played an intimate part in sustaining a variety of ideas about people and their place within society and nature. It follows that chronological changes in the character and context of these phenomena are rather more than mute reflections of a process of social change that was going on elsewhere. They were themselves important media through which social relations were sustained or transformed through time. This does not mean that we can directly reconstruct the specific meanings of particular places or things. In any case, this would be to deny that objects can convey a constellation of practical, abstract and even contradictory connotations. What is perhaps more useful is a concern with the conditions under which meanings would have been given to people and things in the past. In other words, we need to ask how concepts of identity, kinship and political authority were sustained through forms of traditional practice which were sustained and reworked over several generations. This requires a dual concern with the subtle persuasion of day-to-day routines, and those more explicit or ritualized junctures at which ideas about the self and society were probably brought into sharper focus.

Not surprisingly, it is rather easier to ask such questions than it is to furnish answers. The archaeological record offers an extraordinary potential for an understanding of how past societies were maintained or transformed through space and time. But it is a document that has itself been worked and reworked in the course of history. Different societies drew upon or erased the traces of the past that they encountered and a variety of natural processes have taken their toll on the patterns that we observe. In the case of the periods and areas covered in this book, it is difficult to balance the two sides of the equation. For the most part, the material that we have is composed of the traces of formalized activities. Burials, ceremonial sites and deliberate deposits of artefacts dominate the picture, and our impressions of life in settlements remain blurred. We can move from specific moments of formal deposition to talk of broader settlement and mobility patterns. But it remains difficult to establish the particular character and conduct of activities within the settlements that were routinely constructed and used by extended families and other larger communities. This limits our insights into some of the most powerful contexts within which many of the values and principles which animated people's lives were probably taken on board. Although they may have been far from rigid, it is likely that the distinctions that separated people on the basis of age, gender and kinship were mapped out in the character and spatial organization of the activities that they undertook on a daily basis. While we can speculate on the ways in which people became accustomed to these distinctions, much remains obscure.

An abstract discussion of the links between material culture, social practice and society can only take us so far. Indeed, the explicit discussion of how objects may serve to shape social life almost contradicts the tacit and unconsidered manner in which this is often achieved. For that reason, it is better to argue through a body of material, exploring the different dimensions of material culture production, use and deposition in the context of specific case studies. At the very least, this requires a shift of focus. While it may offer a variety of descriptive and aesthetic rewards, we need to shift our attention away from objects *per se*, to explore relations between objects and their contexts. We cannot extrapolate all that we might wish to understand from the objects themselves.

A concern with the conditions under which people lived also requires us to consider the general characteristics of the societies that we study. In the sorts of small-scale societies with which we are likely to be dealing in the Neolithic and Bronze Age, distinctions and divisions are often drawn on the basis of age, gender, kinship and other forms of group affiliation. Many of these themes may find their expression in the organization of day-to-day tasks as well as in more formal contexts. Under these conditions, tensions commonly arise in the reproduction of relations between age grades, in the negotiation of kinship and trading ties, and in competitions within and between groups for particular material and symbolic resources. While we cannot draw direct analogies with the ethnographic present, these general observations indicate some of the themes or discourses that may have animated the production and use of material culture in the past.

It is with these themes in mind that we can begin to explore how stone tools may have been caught up in the fabric of Neolithic and Bronze Age social life. The chapters which follow take us from the beginnings of the Neolithic and the appearance of new tools for the classification of people, through to the Middle Bronze Age and a time when it seems that stone tools lost some of their importance as symbolic resources. This inevitably moves us beyond strict description, and no doubt some may judge this move unwise. But as Tim Ingold has argued in a rather different context:

> . . . even if we were to imagine our compilation of facts to be exhaustive (which is, of course, a practical impossibility), the history that we would have constructed would be a *dead* history; that is to say, an account of events that omits to mention the consciousness of those who lived through them.

We cannot assume that the simple documentation of 'things' will lead us in some straightforward manner to the human pattern of the past. On the contrary, a concern with the ways in which objects contributed to the creation of people as social beings inevitably draws us into the realm of interpretation.

# 2 Technologies of the Earlier Neolithic

Even a cursory glance at a geological map of Britain reveals the extraordinary variety of raw materials capable of being worked and used as tools. Within this mosaic of resources, quality is highly variable, and many stones are far from evenly distributed. The main sources of good-quality flint are located in the chalklands of southern and eastern Britain, although smaller deposits occur more widely in areas of clay-with-flints and in riverine and coastal locations. These flint deposits are augmented by a variety of metamorphic and igneous stone sources, both in their original geological contexts and as erratics carried by the glaciers. These range from the porphyry of Shetland through to the gabbros of Cornwall, and figure 4 offers no more than a broad sketch of some of the sources exploited during the Neolithic and Bronze Age (fig. 4).

As might be expected, these varied material conditions had a major impact on the tools and techniques found in different areas. What is surprising, however, is the extent to which particular technologies and artefacts are distributed in ways that do not respect the basic pattern of raw material availability. Some stone tools can be found at great distances from their points of origin, and certain forms seem to have been made in much the same ways for over fifty generations. Others seem to have been made and used for shorter periods and may only be found in certain parts of Britain. Tools range from simple flakes to highly elaborate retouched or polished forms and it is not always easy to understand their appearance in functional terms alone. Equally, while many tools appear to have been routinely discarded in the course of everyday life, some were treated with a measure of formality. Some even appear to have been deliberately broken up or thrown into rivers while others were maintained, reworked and reused over considerable periods of time.

How are we to understand these patterns? How do we move from objects recovered during excavations, or from scatters of stone thrown up in the wake of the plough, to establish the roles these various artefacts played in the past? As noted in chapter 1, we have an impressive battery of descriptive techniques at our disposal and these are, of course, crucial. But if we wish to speculate on the 'social life of things' we must also consider the broader conditions under which different stone tools were made, used and discarded. Nowhere is this more vital than in the case of the Earlier Neolithic. Traditionally associated with the appearance of farming and ceremonial monuments, the period also sees the emergence of new categories of artefact and novel conventions concerning the contexts in which some tools were made and deposited. Some of these developments appear to make sense as practical expressions of economic change. Yet it also seems that the significance of stone often extended beyond its immediate utility. Different artefacts and raw materials seem to have been invested with a variety of qualities and values and, as such, they may have contributed to the process by which people came to understand aspects of the world in which they lived. It is this question of how people were themselves 'made' through technology that concerns us here.

## Neolithic origins

The inception of the Neolithic in Britain has long been the subject of heated debate. Shifting between models of indigenous development and colonization during the fourth millennium bc, this debate has been made all the more complex by the lack of good radiocarbon dates for the horizon separating the Mesolithic from Neolithic. Further problems arise because this transition also marks the meeting point between different traditions of enquiry; the two periods have generally been studied by different groups of scholars, each with their own perspectives and priorities.

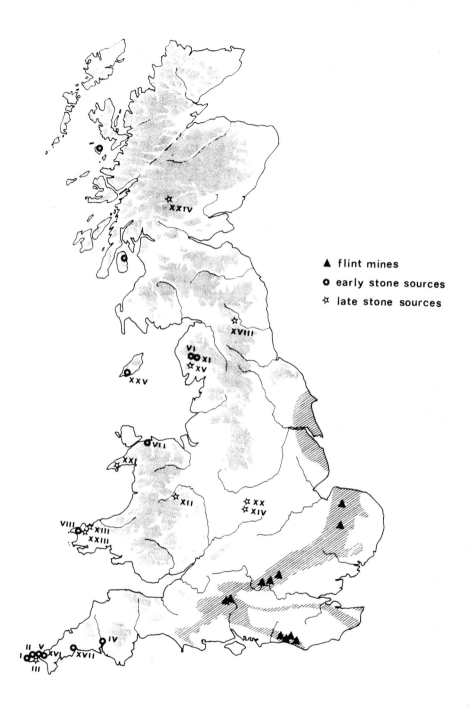

▲ flint mines
⊙ early stone sources
☆ late stone sources

4 Distribution of major raw material sources exploited during later prehistory. In any one area these materials would have been supplemented by a diverse range of locally available stones from riverine, glacial and other secondary sources. Numbers denote non-flint stone sources identified through petrological analysis.

21

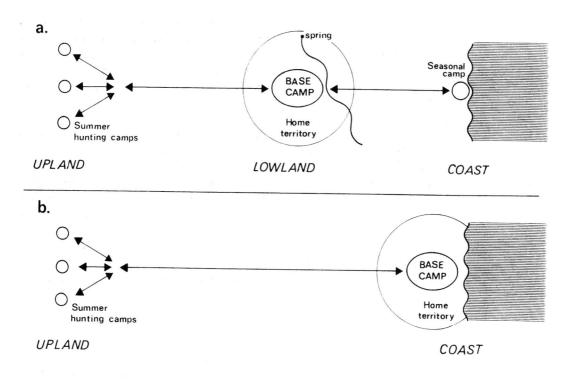

5 Model of Later Mesolithic land use in Britain. Despite the appearance of domesticates, it is possible that Earlier Neolithic settlement did not constitute a radical break with these long-established patterns of seasonal movement (after Darvill 1987).

This division of labour has become so entrenched that we often seem to forget that the two periods are, after all, analytical constructs. As a result, a measure of confusion still surrounds the appearance of what are commonly held to be the first farming communities in Britain.

This confusion has been compounded by the fact that our definitions of the term 'Neolithic' have been far from constant. Some accounts use the term to talk of definitive traits such as pottery production or farming that are independent of time and space. Others use it to denote a specific historical process, and it is by no means uncommon for people to shift back and forth between the two. Originally it was a label attached to a stage in a general evolutionary scheme, but the passage of time saw the term come to denote a cultural phenomenon, marked by a distinctive repertoire of artefacts and monuments, many of which have continental parallels. Talk of Neolithic cultures has, in its turn, given way to a view of the period as an economic enti-

ty, associated with a switch from hunting and gathering to food production.

This emphasis upon domesticates is important, but it may be misleading to view the transition as the point across which specialized hunters give way to settled farmers. In fact, the evidence suggests a rather more complex pattern, a process involving both continuity and innovation between what we define as two separate periods.

Together with excavation, the study of surface scatters of worked stone provides an insight into the character of Later Mesolithic settlement patterns. Evidence from a number of areas suggests that communities were already exploiting a wide variety of resources and modifying the landscape through limited woodland clearance during the sixth and fifth millennia (fig. 5). The period also saw a significant emphasis upon the seasonal movement of people between coastal or river valley settlements and a variety of upland locations. In the more open conditions established in upland areas of open country further to the north. Just as the emphasis upon elements of this broad spectrum appear to have varied from one region to another, so specific resources may have assumed greater or lesser importance with the passing of the seasons. By the same token, there is little to suggest that the Early Neolithic saw the establishment of wholly sedentary communities across the country to the degree that has often been assumed. Much of Britain saw only limited woodland clearance at this time, with many sites established in small clearings. Substantial houses are rare, and it seems that these small, dispersed communities maintained a measure of planned, perhaps seasonal mobility, dividing and recombining settlements at different times of the year. Although they may have encompassed areas that had seen only sporadic activity during the Later Mesolithic, these cycles of settlement and movement need not reflect a sudden and complete break with long-established traditions of landscape use.

This turn towards a rather more fluid conception of Early Neolithic subsistence would be uncontentious but for the fact that the economy has often provided the main source for our explanations of the period. More often than not, an assumed transformation in the nature of subsistence has been seen as the principal trigger for social change and as the material foundation upon which it was possible to construct the first major field monuments. This picture is not actually wrong, but, given the gradual nature of subsistence change in Britain, we must ask a basic question. Why is it that we see the rather more rapid appearance of tombs, pottery and novel classes of stone tool during the fourth millennium bc? One solution would be to fall back upon the traditional idea that these developments can be understood as the result of large-scale colonization from the Continent. Continental parallels for monuments and artefacts certainly exist, but this argument is difficult to sustain. It is probable that their appearance in Britain is largely the result of the indigenous adoption of materials and ideas encountered through networks of contact and communication that stretched between regions as far apart as Denmark, the Netherlands and the Atlantic coast of France.

The question that still remains is why communities in different parts of Britain should have taken these new materials and ideas on board at this particular time. Recent approaches to this issue have suggested that the Neolithic was as much a way of thinking about and ordering the social and natural worlds as it was an economic phenomenon. Domesticated resources may have already assumed a measure of economic importance, but equally vital was the fact that they were now harnessed within a framework of ideas concerning the character of social relations and the links between society, the ancestors and the natural world. Although they cannot be reduced to changes in subsistence, these new ways of thinking about the world had some of their roots in the character of everyday life. Wild resources remained important, but the shift to food production created the potential for changes in the manner in which relations between people were structured, in the perception of thresholds between culture and nature, and in conceptions of landscape and time. It may have been these potentials that were addressed through the construction and use of the first tombs and enclosures (fig. 8). Rather than being simple reflections of increased productivity or sedentism, these sites may have served as locales through which traditional ways of thinking and acting were reworked and redefined.

It is difficult to do more than speculate on the conditions under which these developments may have taken place in different areas. Some communities or broader groups may have assimilated aspects of this new material repertoire very rapidly, using them in the resolution of territorial disputes or other localized claims to access or authority over certain rights or resources. Part of the stimulus for these changes may have also arisen from adjustments in the character of the seasonal round, in particular, the new concerns and conceptions of place and pathway that accompanied the routine husbandry of cattle. Other groups may have become accustomed to the Neolithic rather more gradually, encountering the trappings of this material and symbolic order in their dealings with neighbours and relative strangers. Yet over the generations, through marriage ties and the creation of new bonds of kinship and affiliation, the boundaries of these

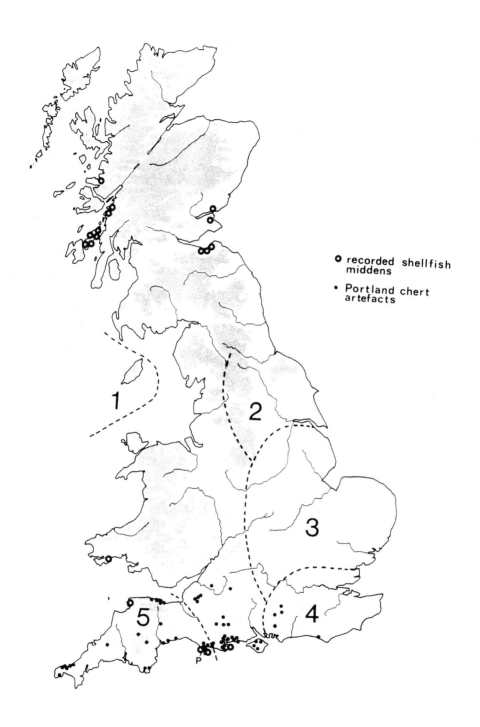

recorded shellfish middens

Portland chert artefacts

6 Suggested 'style zones' based on regional variations in microliths, and the distribution of shell midden sites and Portland chert artefacts (after Darvill 1987).

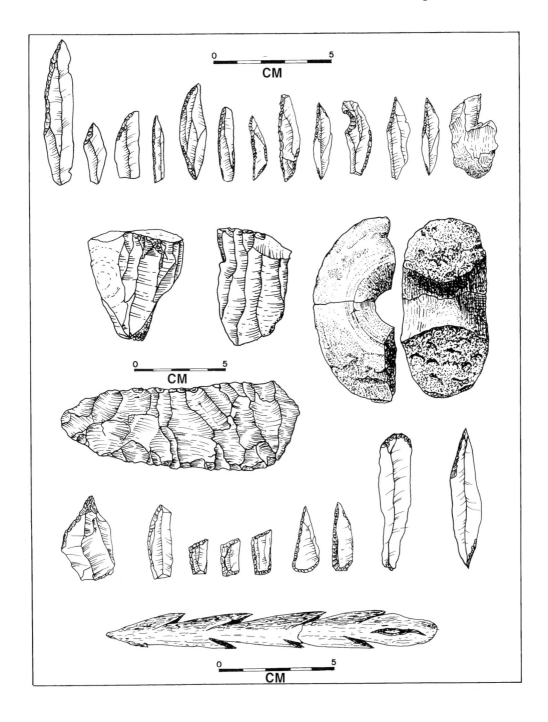

7 Later Mesolithic stone and bone tools: A and E microliths; B cores; C perforated implement; D flaked axe; F bone harpoon.

areas, groups may have been controlling or managing red deer herds through selective culling and the creation of areas suitable for browsing. The lithic assemblages which characterize sites from the sixth millennium onwards have generally been understood as an expression of this increased diversification. The microliths and blade cores which dominate Later Mesolithic sites have been taken to reflect the careful use of stone by mobile groups to produce composite tools with a variety of applications.

Regional variations in the character of microliths may also reflect the emergence of a measure of territoriality among Later Mesolithic groups (fig. 6). The simple flake and microlith assemblages of western Scotland can be contrasted with areas such as the Weald, East Anglia, the Pennines, the Midlands and the south-west. Each of these areas can be defined in terms of an emphasis upon particular microlith forms. This is particularly clear in the Weald, which is distinguished by the presence of 'Horsham points' with concave bases and invasive retouch. Whether these regionally specific traditions were recognized as such remains open to question. It is unlikely that differences in the ways in which people trimmed tiny bladelets provided the principal medium for explicit expressions of group identity, particularly since they were mounted (and more or less hidden) in composite tools. They may reflect no more than the existence of a consensus, sustained within and between particular communities regarding the 'proper' manner in which such artefacts were to be made. Nevertheless, the existence of regional traditions does at least suggest a recurrent relationship between particular communities and broad sections of the landscape. Similar links between people and land may also account for patterns on the North Yorkshire Moors, where lithic scatters in adjacent areas reflect the consistent use of quite different raw materials (fig. 7).

There is also evidence for broad networks of contact and communication between groups by the fifth millennium bc. In southern Britain, flint axes and adzes produced on the chalklands seem to have been circulated over much wider areas. The same may be true for the perforated sandstone 'maceheads' that have been recovered from Later Mesolithic contexts, and for artefacts of bloodstone produced on the Isle of Rhum. These patterns may be a product of broader cycles of movement, but they may also reflect exchange between different communities. Interaction between groups may also account for the dispersal of Portland chert into central and western England from its source on the south coast. For some, these patterns have been understood as pragmatic solutions to the problem of stone tool procurement. Where raw materials were in limited supply or of poor quality, people may have satisfied their needs through trade or exchange. These suggestions seem plausible enough. However, such transactions may have also been crucial for the formation of lasting ties between communities which extended beyond the more practical problem of obtaining stone. The negotiation of kinship ties and other bonds of affiliation may have been marked by the passage of stone artefacts from one group to another. These general observations may not take us very far. However, they do suggest that the landscape of Britain was already inscribed with social and historical significance prior to what we call the Neolithic. The landscape and its resources may have taken on associations with particular groups of people, and networks of contact and communication may have cut back and forth across the country. It remains difficult to specify the associations ascribed to particular places, or the means by which relations between groups found their expression. But for the purposes of this discussion, these patterns remind us that the sites, activities and artefacts that we generally take as markers of the Neolithic reflect the development or transformation of practices which had a long ancestry.

While generalizations should be made with caution, there is little to indicate that the beginning of the period witnessed a wholesale switch to settled agriculture. Rather, we see the emergence of a mosaic of activities with roots that extended far into the past. Small-scale 'garden plot' horticulture probably served as an adjunct to the husbandry of animals and the exploitation of a wide variety of wild resources by small, dispersed communities. Over much of southern Britain a particular emphasis appears to have been placed upon cattle, while sheep dominate

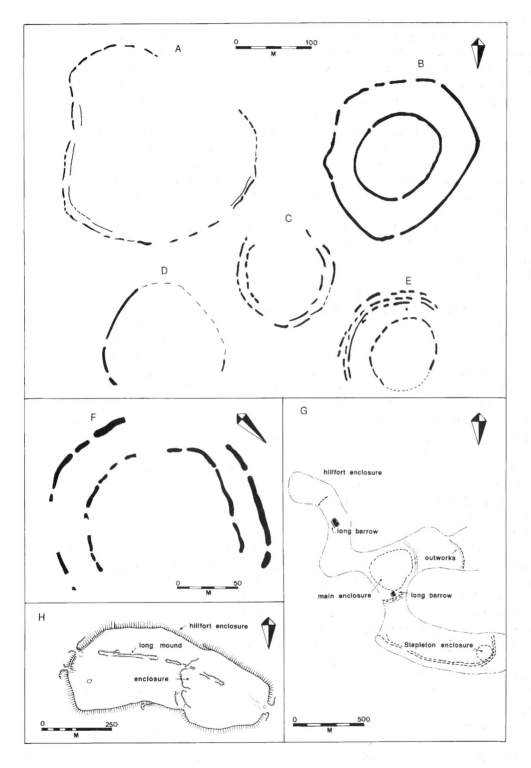

8 Causewayed enclosure plans: A Haddenham; B Robin Hood's Ball; C Great Wilbraham; D Etton; E Orsett; F Staines; G the Hambledon Hill complex; H the Maiden Castle complex.

9 Earlier Neolithic ceramics (drawn by Chris Jones).

different world views became more blurred. More and more people came to understand themselves through what we recognize as Neolithic practices and material symbols (fig. 9). Changes in the character of day-to-day activities and the seasonal round, the circulation of novel artefacts and the construction and use of monuments, may all have contributed to a redefinition of the connections between people and land and networks of social relations that had existed for many generations.

## The living and the dead

Evidence from Earlier Neolithic mortuary sites indicates some of the themes that may have animated people's conceptions of themselves and their world. In western Britain, the earliest sites are generally stone built. They include portal dolmens, rotunda graves, and simple passage graves whose distribution extends up to northern Scotland (fig. 10). In other parts of the country, early mortuary sites were made from earth and timber, often taking the form of a small, linear,

bounded area with a façade or forecourt. Variations on this theme have been found as far apart as Dalladies in Grampian, Street House in Cleveland, and Wayland's Smithy in Oxfordshire. Although the bodies of individuals have been recognized in a few cases, it is more common to find the disarticulated and/or cremated remains of a number of people in the interior of these sites (fig. 11).

Many of these earliest tombs were refashioned towards the end of the fourth millennium, and it is at this time that we see the widespread appearance of long barrows and long cairns. These more monumental mounds could be constructed over mortuary structures that had been in use for some time, but often the mound and its internal chambers appear to have been a single, planned entity. Many retain evidence for the provision of a forecourt or façade, and it seems that a number remained open and in use for several centuries. As with the earliest sites, it is possible to detect a measure of regional variability in the character and timing of long mound construction and use. Megalithic tombs predominate in the west and

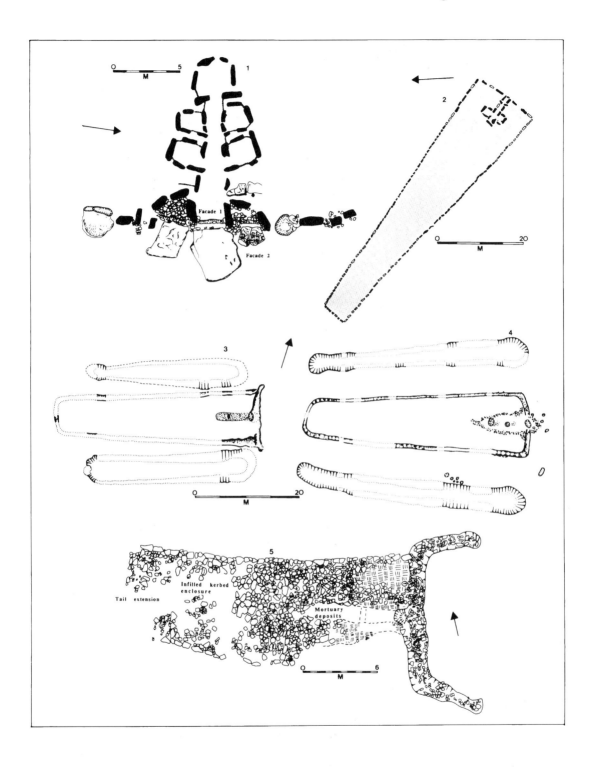

10 Earlier Neolithic mortuary sites: 1 façade and burial chambers at West Kennet; 2 Wayland's Smithy; 3 Willerby Wold; 4 Fussell's Lodge; 5 Street House.

11 The wooden structure found during excavations at Haddenham long barrow, Cambridgeshire. Made from a series of massive planks, this wooden chamber contained the remains of five people (Ian Hodder).

12 Portal Dolmen at Pentre Ifan (Julian Thomas).

north-east, and in much of Scotland large quantities of stone were quarried to create imposing cairns.

In eastern and southern England similar forms were achieved through the creation of large earthen mounds which could contain the disarticulated remains of up to fifty people. These remains were sometimes reorganized or rearranged to create piles of different skeletal elements. At times, the bones of different people could even be brought together to produce a composite 'body'. Further evidence for regional variation can be found in Yorkshire, where many long mounds were thrown up over large cremation trenches. This period also saw the development of a parallel funerary tradition in the north-east, involving the construction of round barrows. These were also erected over linear arrangements of disarticulated bone, but in a few cases deposits took the form of articulated bodies.

Although they differ from one region to another, these funerary practices generally reflect an overriding emphasis upon the collective. The weathering, mixing, reordering and removal of bones, and the deliberate firing of mortuary deposits, may all have contributed to a denial of the substantive individual in death, and to the creation of a more idealized member of an ancestral community. This process of transformation may have begun elsewhere, since some people may have been reduced to a bundle of bones prior to their incorporation in the houses of the dead.

There is no reason to suppose that the ancestors were any less important for communities during the Mesolithic; but by the late fourth millennium, their presence was harnessed or captured in tombs set at specific points within the landscape. Some of these places may have been invested with a particular significance by earlier communities. At Gwernvale in south Wales, a megalithic tomb constructed around a natural monolith sealed the traces of two or three small timber structures. As far as we can tell, these structures had been placed in an area that had seen considerable use during the

31

Mesolithic. Equally long and varied sequences of development can be seen at sites like Hazelton in Gloucestershire, while at Haddenham in Cambridgeshire or Kilham in Yorkshire, scatters of Later Mesolithic flintwork have been found beneath or close to tombs (fig. 12). A similar appropriation of places may have occurred at the Thickthorn and Woodford long barrows, which appear to have been built over flint extraction pits. Unbroken continuity cannot be assumed, but these associations suggest that certain tombs were constructed in order to harness or rework the cultural significance already ascribed to particular places.

These ancestral 'houses' may have become places of great spiritual and historical importance, but it may be misleading to think only in terms of their connections with funerary ritual. Like the churches of today, dealings with the dead may have been only one element in a wide range of rites and periodic ceremonies which took place in the shadow of these sites. We can begin by suggesting that inclusion in tombs may itself have been a privilege of position and kinship. Even if the contents of all known tombs are added together, we can only be dealing with a small section of the population. The remains of the absent majority appear to have been deposited or broken up and dispersed in a variety of contexts, from enclosures and isolated pits through to settlements. In these different contexts, the traces of the dead probably played their part in linking families to places, and as relics used in localized rituals, they may have helped to sustain the historical associations of particular day-to-day tasks. Many more may have been scattered to the winds, or treated in other ways that leave no archaeological signature.

The proximity of many tombs to settlement areas suggests that the simple presence of the

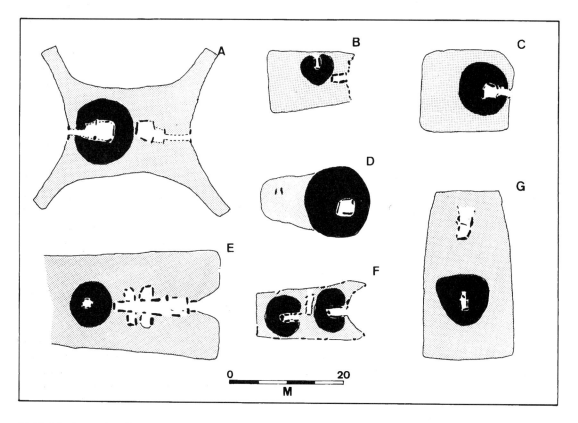

13 Multi-phase chambered tombs: A Tulloch of Assery, Highland; B Mid Gleniron II, Dumfries and Galloway; C Balvraid, Highland; D Pen-y-Wyrlod I, Powys; E Notgrove, Gloucestershire; F Mid-Gleniron I, Dumfries and Galloway; G Dyffryn Ardudwy, Gwynedd.

ancestors would have reinforced the ties between communities and the landscape in which they lived and worked. Indeed, the very act of constructing these tombs, perhaps over considerable periods of time, may itself have been a powerful medium for reinforcing these links. As powerful and perhaps dangerous forces, the ancestors may have been regarded as entities with the capacity to influence productivity and fortune, and it may have been these powers that were called upon at periodic gatherings. Often in prominent positions, tombs would have been seen and even encountered in the course of many everyday tasks. As familiar landmarks, they would have helped people to recognize both their physical position and their location in a social landscape composed of a patchwork of segmentary, perhaps lineage-based communities.

The character of particular tombs may have contributed to this process at a rather more detailed level. Some are aligned upon important lunar events and this may have added to their significance as the houses of the dead and as symbolically charged places. Moreover, despite the emphasis on the collective, the character and positioning of deposits may have marked distinctions that were important among the living. In the case of chambered tombs, interior spatial divisions would have directed the movement and attention of those who could enter, and thus the order in which particular deposits were encountered. Façades and forecourts would also have made it possible to differentiate between those who could participate in certain rites and those who simply watched. This last distinction is important, because it reminds us that the right to officiate at the rituals conducted at tombs may itself have been a privilege and source of authority (fig. 13).

At many tombs, the physical arrangement of bones may have been ordered on the basis of kinship, with individual families placed at different points. In others, piles of bones were structured around distinctions made on the basis of age and gender. Although the remains of males and females, and of adults and children, occur at many sites, they could be differentiated within the interior of particular tombs. In a few cases, the treatment of bodies may have taken a rather different character. Evidence from a number of

Severn-Cotswold and Clyde tombs demonstrates that the significance accorded to different skeletal elements may have varied, and in these contexts it is not uncommon to find separate clusters of long bones and skulls. A similar emphasis upon skeletal differentiation can be seen at West Kennet near Avebury. Such arrangements may have been changed from time to time, and in general, the early third millennium saw a gradual shift of emphasis towards adult males at many sites. Particular bones could also be removed from tombs, both to make room for new material and to circulate as relics among the living.

With the exception of the early round barrows in the north-east, direct associations between bodies and objects are rare and open to a number of interpretations. However, pottery is often concentrated within the area of the forecourt or façade, and together with pig bones may indicate that feasting was an integral part of the ancestral rites and other ceremonies conducted at many sites. The presence of animal remains within several tombs suggests that these ordered deposits could also refer to the ties between certain resources and categories of person. In southern Britain, the closest associations found inside tombs are with cattle. 'Head and hoof' burials have been recorded at a number of sites, and in certain Severn-Cotswold tombs, the bones of cattle were sometimes treated in the same ways as the bones of people. In effect, tombs appear to have provided a context in which links could be made between specific people and particular spheres of economic life. Nowhere is this clearer than at the Beckhampton Road long barrow near Avebury. In this case, cattle, not people, were one of the main deposits.

Just as these principles of order and association may have changed, so the form and significance of particular sites may have been adjusted from one generation to the next. As time passed they may have come to be regarded as familiar and permanent parts of the landscape, and this may have lent a sense of continuity and gravity to the ceremonies and rites played out under the gaze of the ancestors (fig. 14). The particular character and conduct of these ceremonies is difficult to determine. However, there can be little doubt that these periodic gatherings and feasts provided a powerful

14 Communities may have gathered in the shadow of their ancestral houses at various points in the annual cycle. While family heads or even shamans may have held sway over certain rites, entire communities were probably involved in many of these events. Perhaps people gathered to make offerings before the planting of corn, or before the cattle were taken to summer pastures. In accordance with custom, the addition of new bones and the rearrangement of old deposits would have drawn the attention of the participants to the ties that bound past and present generations. The co-ordination of successful ceremonies and feasts may have provided an important measure of the eminence and fortune of particular family heads.

context in which to idealize or strengthen the relationship between people, land and animals, and the lines of authority and distinction that ran within and between communities. Moreover, where proximity to the ancestors was an important source of authority, tombs and mortuary ritual would have provided a potent medium through which certain social categories and rela-

tions could also be reworked.

These observations are important, but they can only take us so far. The physical presence and episodic use of tombs may have had important consequences among the living. But we need to ask how particular concepts and relations among dispersed communities were actually grounded in day-to-day practice. As is so often the case, it is far easier to pose this question than it is to furnish answers. Many activities were probably undertaken by the majority of people in individual communities. Yet, like the functional divisions in many houses today, the timing and spacing of activities on settlements probably played an important part in reproducing distinctions that were drawn between people. Unfortunately, the absence of evidence for the organization of activities on Neolithic settlements means that this issue is difficult to explore. However, it is with this question in mind that we can consider the part that stone tool production and use may have played in sustaining some of the themes that shaped the construction and use of tombs. Just as those sites were not simply devoted to the burial of the dead, so traditions of working and using stone may have addressed issues which stretched beyond practical needs.

## Core themes

We can start by considering how basic traditions of stoneworking may add dimensions to the picture. Research in a number of areas has identified consistent patterns in the character and distribution of Earlier Neolithic assemblages. Dispersed across the landscape, many take the form of small, focused scatters of flakes, cores and tools. Where excavated, these scatters seldom produce features indicative of substantial structures. It is more common to find sites defined by the presence of bowl-shaped pits, many of which show signs of deliberate backfilling. No doubt other sites remain to be discovered in the bottom of river valleys or beneath colluvium, but these scatters support the idea that Earlier Neolithic communities retained a measure of routine mobility. The common association of Earlier Neolithic leaf-shaped arrowheads with Later Mesolithic surface scatters indicates that these patterns of movement often encompassed places that had been important in earlier times. This is particularly clear where deposits of stone provided sources of raw material in both periods, a pattern that has been demonstrated in the Fens by Frances Healy and on the Isle of Rhum by Caroline Wickham-Jones.

Given the durability of stone, these scatters may have contributed to the process by which the landscape itself took on cultural qualities. In the case of stone sources, which might be returned to on many occasions, knowledge of their location may have been sustained through oral tradition and through their associations with recognizable features and other activities. But just as scatters of stone mark the location of past activities for archaeologists, spreads of debris at other locales would have reminded people that their routines of movement also had a past. The presence of stoneworking debris in an overgrown clearing or area of coppice may have helped to define the connotations of that place, and may even have influenced the orientation of subsequent activities. Discarded cores and waste flakes may have carried associations related to the particular activities that had been undertaken in the past, or may simply have been recognized as rock that had been transformed by people. In other words, scatters of worked stone may have been subtle reminders that a particular place had a history.

The suggestion that scatters of debris could be recognized gains support from the character of stoneworking itself. For some time now, it has been accepted that traditions of making and using cores during the Earlier Neolithic possess a relatively high degree of resolution. We can identify distinctive categories of core, and a measure of regularity in the products of core working (fig. 15). These technological regularities are strong enough to allow scatters of flint to be assigned to the period even when there are no formal tools and all that remains is the material created during core reduction. This material often takes the form of narrow, and even parallel-sided flakes or blades of relatively regular thickness. This emphasis upon narrow flakes or blades is manifest in the character of the cores themselves. Their surfaces often retain parallel or sub-parallel ridges and scars, and they commonly possess one or two striking platforms. Given raw material constraints, this pattern is different in western and northern Britain, where it is more common to find cores reflecting bi-polar working. Nevertheless, these rather different forms also reflect a concern with the production of narrow flakes and blades.

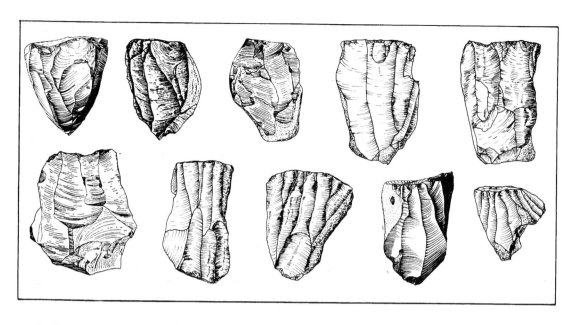

15 Earlier Neolithic single platform, opposed platform and bipolar cores.

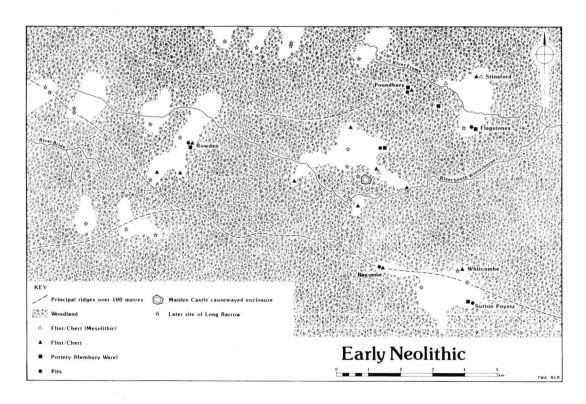

KEY

- – · – Principal ridges over 100 metres
- Woodland
- △ Flint/Chert (Mesolithic)
- ▲ Flint/Chert
- ■ Pottery (Hembury Ware)
- ● Pits
- ⬡ Maiden Castle causewayed enclosure
- ☆ Later site of Long Barrow

**Early Neolithic**

16 Changes in the landscape 1: the Earlier Neolithic landscape on the South Dorset Ridgeway (courtesy of Peter Woodward and the Trust for Wessex Archaeology).

Analysis of this material suggests that the process of core production and use was relatively structured or regular. Many cores and flakes retain evidence for the preparation and maintenance of striking platforms and a measure of precision in the placement of blows. This would have had a major impact upon the ease or success with which narrow flakes or blades could be removed in a regular and controlled manner. Moreover, many Earlier Neolithic assemblages contain evidence for the recovery or 'rejuvenation' of cores in the face of problems encountered during working. This suggests a concern with the maintenance of a good working angle between the platform and the face of the core, and an emphasis upon maintaining narrow flake or blade production itself. Where mis-hits, errors or irregularities in a core would have made such careful working difficult to sustain, it would still have been possible to remove rather more irregular flakes. No doubt this was an option that was often taken up, but the evidence indicates that an emphasis upon narrow flakes or blades was frequently maintained.

Here it is important to differentiate between the debris from core working and that created during the making of other types of tools, as this may introduce biases. For example, an Early Neolithic assemblage created during axe production will generally contain few narrow flakes or blades. Equally, we should recognize that these traditions were by no means rigid. Irregular or otherwise different core forms have been recovered from a variety of Earlier Neolithic contexts. These different sources of variability can usually be identified through technological and experimental studies. But even then, we have to ask why regularities in the form of cores and waste should exist at all and why they persist for as long as twenty to thirty generations?

This emphasis upon narrow flake and blade production reflects a measure of continuity with Mesolithic traditions. Although microliths are generally absent from fourth-millennium contexts, patterns of raw material procurement and core reduction in many areas indicate that more basic attitudes towards stoneworking may have persisted across the transition. These similarities may have their roots in the continued importance of seasonal cycles of movement, and it is

tempting to see Earlier Neolithic assemblages as a response to the conditions encountered by mobile communities (fig. 16). In other words, where people continued to move on a regular basis, there might be a premium on the careful use of good-quality stone to produce artefacts that were both multi-purpose and portable. One of the merits of regular flakes and blades is that they allow for the relatively efficient use of raw material, and they can be used as they are. They can also be reworked to create a variety of forms, and two of the commonest earlier Neolithic artefacts – endscrapers and serrated flakes – reflect just such a process.

This interpretation has its attractions, and it gains a measure of support from the fact that many of the elements in Earlier Neolithic assemblages are relatively small and easily carried. What remains puzzling is that while they are by no means rigid, these regularities in core technology are extraordinarily widespread. They cut across the regions defined by different traditions of mortuary practice and are maintained even where the nature of raw materials would have made blade or narrow flake production rather more difficult to achieve. They are even apparent in areas where flint was so widely available that people would never have had to walk very far in order to obtain all that they required. It is therefore possible that this tradition may have been shaped by the social conditions under which people learnt to work cores and make flakes.

At the very least, the ubiquity of narrow flake or blade cores on many Early Neolithic sites suggests that this was not an activity that was the preserve of specialists. While individuals may have been differentiated according to the level of skill with which they could manipulate stone, core working was something which was probably taught, observed and practised in most households. Subtle variations in procedure were followed in different areas, reflecting the impact of varied raw materials and the influence of the local context in which people became accustomed to working stone (fig. 17). Yet over the generations, through communal events, the creation of broader bonds of affiliation and the movement of people, this approach to flaking may have come to be widely accepted. As a practice with a very long history it may also have

37

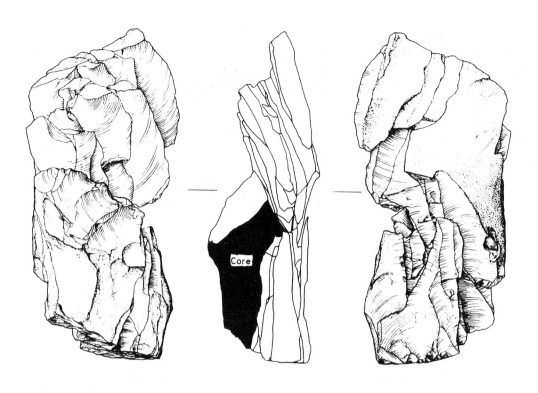

17 Refitted opposed platform core from Rowden, Dorset. Worked from either end, opposed platform cores reflect a knapping technique which integrates flake production with core maintenance (courtesy of the Trust for Wessex Archaeology).

been taken for granted, and as such, it may have offered quiet confirmation that disparate communities were linked by common ways of working stone.

Quiet though this confirmation may have been, we should recall that the associations of certain acts or objects may slide in and out of focus and may change according to context. There is evidence that even the simple action of working stone may itself have been an activity to which symbolic importance could be attached. Formal deposits of cores or knapping debris have been recognized at a number of tombs, including Thickthorn Down, Tilshead Old Ditch and Winterbourne Stoke 1. At Hazelton, excavation of the north chamber revealed the body of an adult male with a hammerstone close to his left hand and a partially worked core in his right (fig. 18). Deliberate deposits in the ditches and forecourts of several tombs and at a number of enclosures add weight to the idea that the act of

working was sometimes accorded a measure of symbolic significance. For the most part, we have tended to explain these deposits away as no more than the knapping of stone encountered during the digging of ditches. However, this seems difficult to sustain in cases where the patterning of flintwork in ditches respects the patterning of other materials. Nor can we dismiss the possibility of deliberate deposition where clusters of debris occur in the forecourts of particular tombs. In certain cases this material suggests the working or breaking up of tools and in others it seems that materials used at these sites were buried with some formality.

In short, it seems that stoneworking may have held a metaphoric significance which was integral to the manner in which certain sites or rituals were understood. It is possible that tools and flakes were deposited as gifts or provisions for the ancestral community, and these acts may have provided a medium through which links

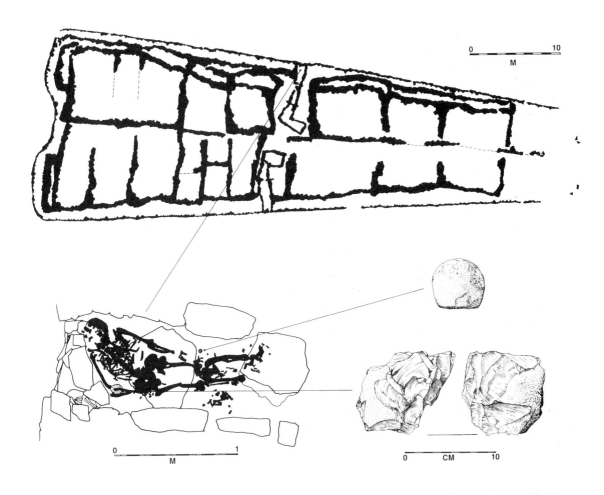

18 Towards the end of the Earlier Neolithic, the articulated body of a man was placed in the entrance to the north chamber of Hazelton long cairn in Gloucestershire. The chamber itself contained the disarticulated remains of several individuals who had been deposited some time before this final act of burial. Close to his hands were a flint core and a pebble hammerstone. These may have been placed as markers of the skills of the deceased and as tools for use in the afterlife.

between the ancestors and the living could be expressed. In other cases, the deposition of tools and waste may have been undertaken to celebrate the skills or roles of the deceased, to draw links between stoneworking and particular categories of person, or to mark the completion of specific ceremonies. A few assemblages may even reflect the production of tools that were subsequently removed. Carried and used among the living, these artefacts may have been endowed with a special significance derived from their association with the ancestral realm and with particular ceremonial events. As such, they may have served as particularly potent technologies for remembrance. It is with this idea in mind that we can turn to the more formal retouched artefacts of the Earlier Neolithic.

## Technologies of remembrance

Paradoxically, the general absence of stone tools from the interior of many tombs may indicate their broad associations. Where funerary ritual placed an emphasis upon the collective over the

39

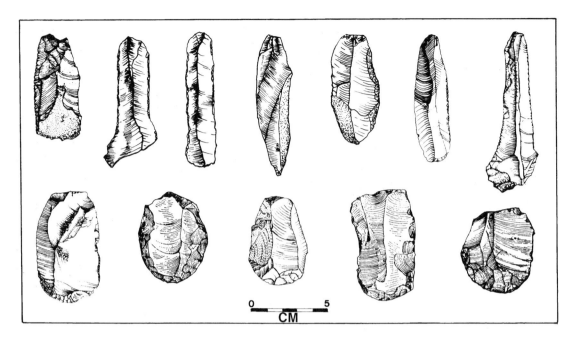

19 Serrated flakes, retouched flakes and scrapers from Earlier Neolithic contexts.

individual, it may often have been regarded as inappropriate or even dangerous to bury grave goods which carried ideas about the identity or persona of specific people. Here it is perhaps relevant that the one context in which associations are more common is in the round barrow tradition of north-east England, where the interment of small numbers of articulated bodies is found. These associations include forms that probably took anything from a few minutes to several days to make, and there is no reason to suppose that all stone tools were linked to people in the same way or to the same degree. However, variations in the conditions under which different classes of artefact were made, used and discarded, may provide clues as to the roles that they played.

Like cores, flakes and blades, various elements of the Earlier Neolithic 'tool-kit' were probably made in an almost casual and unconsidered manner. These acts may have been in keeping with an unspoken consensus regarding acceptable procedures and forms but more often than not practical expediency may have been all that was considered. Endscrapers and serrated flakes, a variety of other scraper forms and simple retouched flakes are common in many Early

Neolithic assemblages (fig. 19). Retouched points and borers are also relatively widespread. Beyond the constraints imposed by raw materials, these artefacts do not appear to vary a great deal from one region to another. Exceptions to this rule include serrated flakes, which are rather less common in Scotland, and distinctive 'hollow' scrapers. These are particularly common in Ireland, although examples have been recognized on the Cumbrian coast, in north Wales and at sites in the Western Isles.

Simple though many of these artefacts are – many the products of no more than a minute or two of activity – we should not assume that investment in production provided the sole index against which things were valued. This may have been important in certain cases, but for many artefacts significance may have arisen from the practical and social contexts in which they were engaged or the conditions under which they were acquired. For tools made and used in a variety of ways and by a wide range of people there may have been little or no scope for the drawing of specific associations. However, where an artefact was associated with particular practices or activities it might also have carried ideas concerning

20 Earlier Neolithic hammerstone, blades, scrapers, fabricators and single-piece sickles (Museum of Archaeology and Anthropology, Cambridge).

the cultural significance of those acts and the divisions of labour and authority they entailed.

These ideas are useful, but they are often difficult to explore in cases where distinctive associations are absent. This appears to be the case with Earlier Neolithic fabricators, rod-like tools which have parallels in Later Mesolithic contexts (fig. 20). Although three sub-types have been claimed, there is little formal variation in this class and no evidence to suggest that the production and use of these tools was either practically or socially restricted. Often abraded or worn on both ends, they may have served as strike-a-lights, but were probably also used in working other materials including leather and perhaps stone. Where these activities were the preserve of particular people these tools may have taken on a metaphorical significance, helping to characterize individuals in terms of their roles in day-to-day life. This became more important towards the close of the period, but during the Earlier Neolithic at least, fabricators do not appear to have been singled out as 'objects of thought'. They probably possessed a routine connection with the particular people who made and used them. But they do not seem to have been drawn upon in the making of explicit statements about the cultural significance of particular activities, nor in the definition of people as specific social categories.

The serrated flake provides a further example. Widespread in their distribution, these simple tools often retain a gloss or polish along their reworked edge. Functional analysis indicates that this distinctive gloss is created during the cutting of plant materials, and various studies have suggested an association with harvesting. The same function has also been suggested for the rarer single-piece sickles that have been recovered from Earlier Neolithic contexts. Often characterized by a crescentic outline, these artefacts display the extensive and invasive retouch which is common to many Neolithic tools (fig. 21). Although the gathering of plants other than domesticated crops would produce similar wear patterns, the connotations of these tools may have been drawn from the cultural milieu in which such activities were conducted. The creation of elaborate single-piece sickles is interesting because it suggests an explicit link

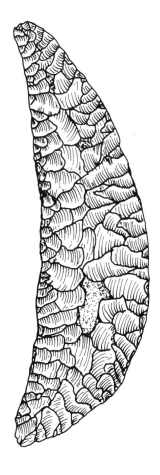

21 Invasively flaked single-piece flint sickle.

between an artefact category and a specific area of economic practice. Since serrated or unretouched flakes would have been eminently serviceable, the care and precision exercised in the making of these artefacts may be related to the symbolic importance that was attached to harvesting as a feature of Neolithic life. Here it is tempting to fall back upon comparative analysis and suggest that gathering or harvesting may have had a stronger association with certain sections of particular communities. However, in the absence of direct material associations or other corroborative evidence, this remains uncertain. In any case, it may be inappropriate to assume that age or gender distinctions were necessarily mapped out in such a rigid and simple manner.

The example of elaborate sickles is suggestive but it may not be typical. It is likely that fixed links between categories of artefact and categories of person may have been more the exception than the rule. The significance of particular artefacts may have often been more localized, immediate and mutable. This may well have been the case with the scrapers that dominate so many Earlier Neolithic assemblages. With the exception of endscrapers, many of these simple tools were made on the larger and broader flakes produced during the early stages of making narrow flake/blade cores. Others were produced on flakes from different forms of core, and their features reflect a different pattern of working. The large platforms on many flakes reflect the placement of blows further into the body of the core. This would have had important consequences for the form of flakes, encouraging the removal of pieces that were generally quite broad and thick – ideal 'blanks' for scrapers.

There is no reason to suppose that the production and use of most scrapers was anything other than a routine act. This moment of stoneworking was probably undertaken when needs arose or perhaps while people sat around the fire. Once made, scrapers would have been used in working a variety of materials and many show signs of considerable wear. Like retouched or otherwise utilized flakes, the widespread spatial distribution of scrapers on many sites suggests that they were, for the most part, unremarkable. People may have been able to differentiate between scrapers made by others on the basis of their raw material and form, and where examples were hafted the potential for recognition may have been further enhanced. However, like fabricators, there is little to indicate that these artefacts were drawn upon to any great extent in the making of statements about the identity of particular people. Having said that, these mundane tools were occasionally caught up in acts that made them objects worthy of comment, and here we can turn to the evidence of pits.

## Acts of interment

As already mentioned, large bowl-shaped pits are often the only substantial sub-surface features marking the presence of Earlier Neolithic activity. Up to 2m (6½ ft) in diameter and 1m (3¼ ft) in depth, they may occur in isolation, in small clusters or in profusion on open settlements and at ceremonial enclosures. Several characteristics of Earlier Neolithic pits indicate that their creation and use held an importance which extended beyond any practical concern with storage or waste disposal. As Julian Thomas has pointed out, the shape of these features would have rendered them unsuitable as storage facilities and it seems that many were rapidly dug and backfilled.

It is also difficult to explain the contents of many pits as simple accumulations of debris. While the majority do contain refuse, this 'rubbish' was often carefully chosen and sorted prior to deposition, and may have involved the selection of material from larger middens or from the residues of particular events. Many contain large and freshly broken sherds of pottery representing several vessels. These fragments occasionally formed a lining or base for the pit as a whole. It is also common to find the bones of both domesticated and wild animals together with burnt residues of other organic materials and fragments of human bone. Many pits also contain cores, waste flakes and retouched tools. These may include items such as axes, laurel leaves and arrowheads, but it is more common to find scrapers or flakes. In certain cases, tools show signs of deliberate breakage.

Nowhere are these characteristics more dramatically demonstrated than in the case of a large Earlier Neolithic pit on Coneybury Hill in

Wiltshire. Work by Julian Richards and others has demonstrated that this massive feature was rapidly packed with a variety of materials. Only its uppermost layers reflect a more gradual process of weathering and infilling. The faunal assemblage from this feature is dominated by evidence for the butchery of at least ten cattle and several roe deer. These deposits were augmented by the inclusion of smaller quantities of bone from other wild species, including red deer, beaver and trout. Careful excavation of the primary deposit also resulted in the recovery of about 15kg (33lb) of pottery sherds. Although complete pots are absent, this massive assemblage reflects the purposive deposition of sherds from a number of locally made, round-based vessels that were probably used for the preparation and consumption of food. In addition, the primary deposits yielded a lithic assemblage comprising some thirteen cores, flakes, blades and twenty-five scrapers, three of which were burnt. At least two scrapers may have been broken during production and several of the flakes were probably created during the making of axes (fig. 22).

While the Coneybury pit is somewhat anomalous, if only in terms of the sheer scale of deposits, it does at least demonstrate that our tendency to see these features in prosaic terms may be misplaced. Although they may be slightly smaller, many of the Earlier Neolithic pits found throughout Britain challenge our expectations in much the same way. At the very least, they require us to ask what purposes may have been served by the rapid digging of a hole in the ground and the purposive filling of that hole with food remains, artefacts and even fragments of the dead.

We can begin by recognizing that the creation of these features would have been a localized event, incorporating the traces of a particular episode of consumption or a relatively brief period of activity. Some may even have been created as the final act of a ceremonial feast. Under these circumstances, what may have been important was not the disposal of rubbish *per se*, but rather the bringing together of the symbolic properties carried by materials that had been transformed by cultural acts. Food had been prepared and consumed, other organic materials had been burnt, and stone had been worked and used by

people prior to deposition. In other words, these deposits may have been important in marking and celebrating the presence of culture and settlement in a landscape generally dominated by the wildwood. For that reason, episodes of pit digging may have been of signal importance at both the beginning and the end of a period over which a particular place was in use.

Given the presence of wild species in many pits, we are unlikely to be dealing with a rigid and simple dichotomy between nature and culture – between the wild and the tame. However, these distinctions may have been important in marking a human presence through localized rituals that harnessed many routine or familiar materials. Tools associated with certain tasks and perhaps with specific people may have been particularly important in guiding the interpretation of these events. This may have been just as important where waste from tools was incorporated, as it was where tools themselves were interred. These materials would have introduced tasks or people as a 'presence' within the pit itself, and within the ceremony that accompanied its creation.

Drawn from different spheres of day-to-day experience, and from different people, these deposits may have contributed to the process by which the identity of specific communities was sustained. As the ashes of a communal fire slowly cooled, people may have gathered around a pit as the final act of a local celebration before the community moved on to another seasonal camp. Together with the residues of the feast itself, they may have brought other tools and materials to be placed in the earth. Some of these tools may have spoken of the tasks that people had undertaken in the provision and preparation of different elements of the feast. Others may have been metaphors for the activities undertaken at a particular place or for the tasks performed by particular people. Passing almost unnoticed into the ground, a small clutch of flint scrapers may have carried the grease which had been built up in the long hours that certain people had spent cleaning the hides and pelts of different animals. Rapidly covered by broken pots and soil, the bones of some of these animals may have reminded spectators of successful hunting trips and of the prowess of certain individuals in the

43

Bone

Pottery

Flint

0          50

CM

22 Plan of the Earlier Neolithic pit at Coneybury, Wiltshire. The contents of this pit may be the debris from an episode of feasting gathered up and deposited with some formality in the ground. In addition to around forty pottery vessels represented in the assemblage, the large number of flint blades and bones of wild animals has been taken as evidence that those responsible for this feature were highly mobile. Julian Richards, the excavator of the site, has drawn a contrast between the locally made pots in this pit and the more exotic ceramics found nearby at Robin Hood's Ball, a causewayed enclosure. In his view, this contrast indicates the existence of different groups: those connected to broader exchange networks who partic-ipated in seasonal ceremonies at enclosures, and those who were excluded. This argument is tempting, but it is only one way of interpreting the evidence. Certain people may have been excluded from enclosures at particular times, but both sites may have been created by the same group. The distinction between the assemblages from the two sites may reflect differences of context and intention rather than the existence of distinct cultural groups. Perhaps some feasts were held to cement the bonds between communities before they dispersed to other seasonal camps.

   Pit deposition on Earlier Neolithic settlements may have also been undertaken to mark the connections between particular families and the land upon which they lived and worked. Occasionally, this may have been enhanced by the inclusion of fragments of human bone.

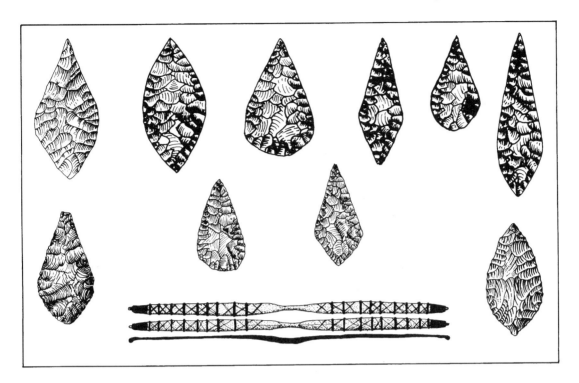

23 Leaf-shaped arrowheads from Earlier Neolithic contexts and reconstruction of an Earlier Neolithic bow from Somerset.

capturing of game. Like the planting of seed corn, these deposits may have been laid down to ensure the fertility and continuity of the community in later seasons and its right of access to particular places.

Similar themes can be considered where the fragmentary remains of people were included in pits. Presencing the dead in a direct and palpable way, these deposits may have reaffirmed the links that bound particular families to areas of land and to their ancestors. In other cases, an association with the dead may have had a rather more direct significance. Where pits were linked to the rites of passage that marked the death of an individual, their contents may have comprised those artefacts that were generally excluded from tombs. Tools and materials that carried ideas relating to the identity of a particular person may have been deposited in the midst of the living community, and here it is perhaps significant that many pits would have remained visible long after they had been backfilled. Knowledge concerning the precise contents of particular pits may have

been forgotten, confused or otherwise changed with the passage of time, but this is to miss part of their character. These features may have influenced the ways in which certain sites were subsequently used or understood, but it was at the time of their creation that the redolences and associations of their contents would have been most clearly appreciated.

## Points of reference

Like single-piece sickles, laurel leaves and leaf-shaped arrowheads demonstrate the emphasis upon invasive retouching and pressure flaking which is a characteristic of the Earlier Neolithic (fig. 23). It is again difficult to understand the emergence of these techniques of working as a simple product of the changing demands faced by farmers. Questions of practical utility were probably important, but it may be equally significant that pressure flaking and extensive retouching allow for a considerable degree of control over the form of artefacts. In other words, the appearance of at least some of these objects may have as much to do with how they were perceived as how they were used.

This dual concern with form and function can be seen in the case of the leaf-shaped arrowhead. While general parallels for this distinctive shape have been drawn with projectiles from Rössen and Michelsberg contexts on the Continent, few examples suggest direct importation. Like the first round-based pottery vessels, they may reflect a process of referencing and making objects which carried ideas about the significance of particular activities and the divisions of labour and authority that they entailed. It is therefore interesting that, alongside cattle and the axe, the bow and arrow is one of the more common representational motifs in the Megalithic art of western Europe. Although miniature bows have been recovered from the Somerset Levels, representational motifs are all but absent in Britain. However, continental cases may suggest something of the symbolic order in which these artefacts and resources were held. Like the cow and the axe, the bow and arrow may have been potent symbols for Neolithic communities, and, in the case of archery at least, it may be that we are dealing with an activity which was closely associated with men.

The suggestion that archery was a male activity does not rest solely upon its links with hunting and fighting. Where leaf- or lozenge-shaped arrowheads are associated with Earlier Neolithic burials, they are generally found with men. In a number of cases arrowheads were buried within people rather than as grave goods. This appears to have been the case at Tulloch of Assery B, Haddenham and at a number of Severn-Cotswold tombs. Elsewhere, evidence for violent injury or death is marked by the presence of the tips of arrows embedded in bone. Examples here include Ascott-under-Wychwood in Oxfordshire and the Fengate flat grave, where arrowhead tips were found in the vertebrae and ribs of adult males. Few though they may be, these examples remind us that authority over certain material and symbolic resources may occasionally have been challenged through direct conflict. Indeed, episodes of conflict are well attested towards the close of the Earlier Neolithic. At enclosures such as Crickley Hill (Gloucestershire), Maiden

Castle and Hambledon Hill (Dorset), numerous arrows appear to have been fired during attacks and many bear impact fractures indicative of use.

In other cases, the conditions under which arrows entered tombs is rather less clear. At Chute 1 for example, arrowheads appear to have been placed close to the disarticulated pelvis of a female, echoing a pattern also seen at Wayland's Smithy. Although it is difficult to take the idea very far, these examples may reflect the manipulation of the sexual symbolism of arrows. A similar measure of uncertainty surrounds the two leaf-shaped arrowheads located in the north chamber at Rodmarton, which is dominated by the bodies of older men. More formal deposition can be seen further to the north-east, where Ian Kinnes has documented the purposive burial of projectiles with men beneath round barrows. Such associations are rare in the south at this time, but here at least we may be seeing the provision of grave goods which made basic statements about the social persona of the individual (fig. 24).

The form of lozenge- or leaf-shaped arrowheads leaves little doubt that they would have been effective in both hunting and warfare, but their social importance should not be overestimated. Despite the existence of a measure of regionalization, manifest in the distribution of kite-shaped and ogival forms, there is no reason to infer the existence of several distinct classes of arrowhead. These regional patterns probably reflect the impact of different raw materials and localized traditions of production, and, like scrapers, it seems that arrowheads were made at many sites. The possibility that they were only made by men cannot be tested, but whatever the case it is useful to think of individuals making their own arrows in accordance with established practice.

With the addition of hafts and flights it may have been relatively easy to draw distinctions between the quivers of people belonging to different groups. This may have been important in contexts where different communities came together, but in general it seems that arrows were important as basic markers of male identity. Carried and used on a regular basis, the bow and the arrow may have provided a relatively simple metaphor for men. Placed in pits and in other formal deposits, these items may have carried associations with specific people and a more general

24 Leaf-shaped arrowheads and laurel leaves from eastern England (Museum of Archaeology and Anthropology, Cambridge).

concept of maleness into different areas of social experience. Exceptionally delicate or large examples interred with burials may reflect the elaboration of this distinctive male item to signal an aspect of the social identity of the deceased.

Similar connotations may have surrounded the laurel leaf, a rather larger retouched artefact that occurs in both Earlier and Later Neolithic contexts. Like many arrowheads, the vast majority of these distinctive tools were fashioned through the invasive bifacial working of larger flakes, and given the similarity of their form it is perhaps unsurprising that they have been interpreted as spearheads. This is by no means impossible, but since many laurel leaves are slightly asymmetrical (a characteristic which would have impeded their flight) they may also have served as retouched knives. Laurel leaves are again found in a variety of contexts, although their production may have been emphasised at mines and causewayed enclosures. Together with the flaked and polished axe, these contexts form the focus for the next chapter, and we shall return to laurel leaves there. Here, however, it can be suggested that, like arrowheads, these artefacts may have been items of personal gear carried and used by particular people on a regular basis (fig. 25).

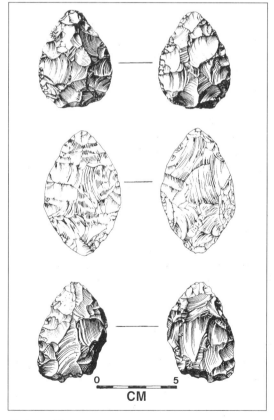

25 Laurel leaves.

47

Whether or not laurel leaves were specifically associated with men remains open to question, but at one site – Hurst Fen in Cambridgeshire – links between them and arrowheads can be suggested. Traditionally seen as an unenclosed settlement, it is possible that Hurst Fen was originally bounded by an enclosure ditch. What is important here is the character of the stone recovered from the numerous pits and other contexts on the site. This assemblage reflects the use of flint of varying colours, qualities and sources, a pattern which is by no means uncommon in areas where chalk and gravel provided alternative sources. However, it seems that a particularly distinctive orange flint was more regularly used for the production of arrows and laurel leaves. This seems difficult to understand in practical terms since the orange flint is similar in most respects to the other materials found on the site. It may be that the use of this particular raw material was guided by a perceived association between arrowheads and laurel leaves. We cannot tell if this association was with men, or with some other attribute of personal or communal identity. However, this example does suggest that raw materials themselves occasionally provided a dimension through which certain values and distinctions could be drawn. It is with this potential in mind that we can turn to the production and circulation of axes during the Earlier Neolithic.

# 3 Contexts for production and exchange in the Earlier Neolithic

At an early point in the Neolithic, a highly polished axe was placed by the side of what is now called the Sweet Track in Somerset, a wooden pathway built between areas of drier land during the Earlier Neolithic. Close by lay a small offering contained in a simple pottery bowl and elsewhere were scattered other offerings and chance losses. This beautiful axe commands our attention but its importance extends beyond the character of its depositional context. What is also remarkable is the material from which it is made, for this distinctive speckled green jadeite has its source on the Continent (fig. 26).

The Sweet Track axe provides a point of departure from the patterns discussed in the previous chapter. There it was shown how the simple possession and use of many Earlier Neolithic stone tools may have played an intimate part in shaping the social identities of people. Carried forward through the dull compulsion of everyday life, some may have quietly sustained the divisions of labour and authority

26 Jadeite axes from (*left to right*): Histon, Cambridgeshire; Sweet Track, Somerset; Bottisham, Cambridgeshire (Museum of Archaeology and Anthropology, Cambridge).

that animated particular communities. Hafted, carried and otherwise displayed, they may also have contributed to the process by which people came to recognize themselves and others as members of distinct yet interconnected communities. In the case of arrowheads, they occasionally provided a rather more direct medium for the resolution of conflicts between groups.

At certain junctures, a few of these artefacts became objects of thought. Associated with specific acts or with categories of person, they were drawn upon during ceremonies at tombs and other formal contexts in the formation of more explicit statements regarding the qualities and position of people. At other times, they may have helped to sustain more general propositions about the order of things in the social and natural world. These themes are just as important here, but the discussion remains limited unless we consider one of the most basic potentials of objects – their portability. They can be carried or moved from one context to another and, perhaps more importantly, they can be transferred between people.

## Stone and flint axes

In many respects, the axe or adze is one of the most informative of Earlier Neolithic tools. This may be partly a product of our analyses and preconceptions, but it does seem that the importance originally accorded to axes may have been profound. Flint axes were already being produced, circulated and used during the Later Mesolithic. Distinctive 'tranchet-blow' axes and adzes have been found widely, and in southern Britain Julie Gardiner has shown that these flaked core tools of varying sizes continued to be made and used during the Neolithic. However, the onset of the Neolithic also saw important changes in the character of axes and in the conditions under which many were produced. It is at this juncture that we see the first widespread appearance of ground and polished (as opposed to flaked) axes, and the emergence of a series of highly visible flint and stone sources.

One of the reasons for the interest in Neolithic flint and stone axes is the success with which their points of origin can be located. Some sixty years of petrological research have resulted in a

picture of the distribution of stone axes in relation to a number of known sources, and it is now a commonplace to talk of 'groups' of products (see fig. 4). In addition, excavations at flint mines and stone axe sources have shed valuable light on the character and chronology of production. Stone axe sources have a markedly western and northerly distribution, reflecting the exploitation of raw materials often found in upland locations. They include the porcellanite of Tievebulliagh and Rathlin Island; the volcanic tuff of Great Langdale; the augite granophyre of Graig Lwyd and the gabbros of Cornwall. These particular sources are perhaps the largest of their kind, but smaller examples, such as Killin in Perthshire, or Dinas in north Wales attest to the production of stone axes in several regions. In many cases these materials were flaked into shape before being ground or polished, and production sites can be characterized by many tons of waste flakes and other debris. In others, the form of axes could only be realized through pecking and grinding; all that might remain from this process is a hammer and a handful of dust.

With the exception of a number of Mesolithic examples found in Wales and Ireland, it seems that the production of ground stone axes began in Britain towards the end of the fourth millennium bc. This seems to have been followed by an increase in the scale of dispersal patterns during the first half of the third millennium, when certain groups of axes appear to be concentrated in areas remote from their sources. There is also evidence for the importation of ground and polished axes into Britain. Porcellanite axes and adzes from the Group IX sources at Tievebulliagh and Rathlin Island have been found in considerable numbers in Britain, and even occur quite close to other sources. Like the example found close to the Sweet Track, jadeite axes have also been recovered in a number of areas, and to these can be added a smaller number of 'Scandinavian' flint axes – distinguished by their square section and occasionally by their colour. These artefacts are common on the continental side of the North Sea, where many scatters contain the distinctive flakes generated during the later stages of production. Flakes of this character are almost unknown in this country, and this suggests that like the jadeite examples, the majority of these axes were also imported as finished forms.

By contrast, the major flint mines have a marked southern and easterly distribution on the chalklands of Britain. Earlier Neolithic mines have been found in Wessex and on the South Downs. The mining complex at Grimes Graves, Norfolk, dates to the later phase of the period. Other major flint sources have been located at the Den of Boddam in Scotland, and in north-eastern Ireland, although in both these cases, axe production was probably not a major concern. Major coastal deposits, such as those at Beer Head in Dorset and Flamborough Head in Yorkshire also appear to have seen long sequences of use for the production of a variety of artefacts. Problems with the characterization of flint have meant that we do not understand the distribution of flint mine products in anything like the same detail as we can for other types of stone. However, it does seem that flint axes also circulated over relatively broad areas from around the same time.

We are not dealing here with black and white patterns, but with trends and differences of emphasis. Axes of both flint and stone were produced away from the major sources throughout the Neolithic, reflecting the exploitation of surface exposures of flint, small coastal and riverine deposits and glacially distributed material. Some of these sources may have been repeatedly exploited, while others probably reflect the more sporadic or opportunistic use of material exposed in the roots of a fallen tree or in the bank of a river. Similar patterns of raw material procurement are indicated by the cores, debitage and other tools that characterize many Earlier Neolithic assemblages. Polished stone axes recovered from Mesolithic contexts in Wales and Ireland suggest that this pattern of surface exploitation had a history which extended far into the past. What is important here is that the majority of these earlier polished forms are made from mudstones, schists, shales and pebbles. They do not reflect the development and concerted use of the major axe sources prior to the Neolithic.

In keeping with the modern tendency to consider technology as hardware, the appearance of ground and polished axes has been seen as a function of the changing demands that accompanied a switch to farming. Grinding itself has generally been considered in functional terms, as a treatment which may influence the efficiency of the tool and reduce the chances of breakage. This was probably important, but it may be equally significant that this laborious process highlights the colour and qualities of the raw material to a far greater extent than flaking. It also offers considerable potential for controlling the form that an object may take. Similar ideas have informed our understanding of the distribution of axes, and the literature abounds with references to 'trade' and 'factories', and to 'middlemen' satisfying the needs of farmers across Britain. More recent studies have highlighted an association between axes and causewayed enclosures, and have cast these sites as nodal points within large-scale trading monopolies. Others have drawn upon mathematical models of exchange to argue that the broad dispersal patterns reflect the bulk movement of certain groups of axes to secondary redistribution centres.

Stimulating though these studies have been, we are still some way from capturing the character of axe production and circulation. For example, it is easy to be misled by the overall scale of axe dispersal. We often grant the patterns a measure of coherence which may bear little or no relation to the varied conditions under which they were formed, nor the partial knowledge of the wider exchange 'system' held by people in different local or regional traditions. Particular regions may be dominated by the products of specific sources (fig. 27), and the significance of axes may have varied from one area to another. In other words, it may be quite misleading to talk of a nationwide 'trade' in axes, when individual artefacts may have been circulated in different ways and for different reasons.

Equally, it is all too easy to take the scale of a number of the sources at face value, inferring the existence of factories and industrially organized labour. Here again we must be careful, for terms such as trade, factory and industry carry with them a series of sociological implications which need to be demonstrated rather than assumed. In fact, radiocarbon dates and simulation studies indicate that our distribution maps reflect patterns of hand-to-hand circulation that unfolded over generations. Similarly, the evidence from

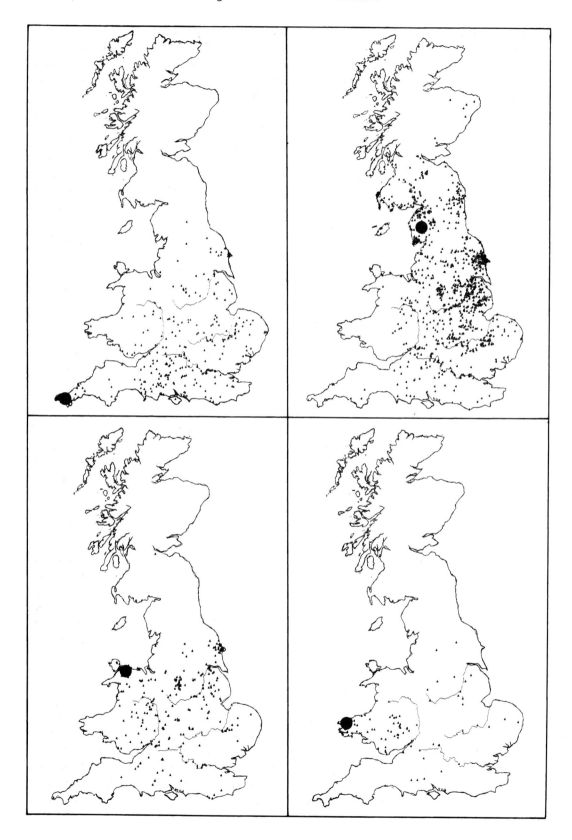

mines and quarries suggests that the massive field monuments visible today are the result of exploitation undertaken over several centuries. To this confusion of scale can be added the problem of motivation and demand. If we accept that the Earlier Neolithic did not witness a wholesale economic transformation, it becomes difficult to see the appearance of polished axes as a simple reflection of new practical concerns. In any case, this general model does not really account for all of the evidence.

Axes and adzes have mostly been recovered as stray finds, and many show signs that they were used and reused over long periods. These practical roles included tree-felling, carpentry and digging, and, where tapered blades were made, coppicing and woodland management may have been important concerns (fig. 28). Occasionally, however, the impression is given that subtle conventions may have guided the manner in which axes were treated or deposited. For example, flint and stone axes have been recovered from pits, where their deposition may have played roles similar to those discussed in the previous chapter. Concentrations of axes have also been found in causewayed enclosures, and a small number have been recovered from Earlier Neolithic funerary contexts. Axe fragments were recorded in the filling of the tomb at Lochill, while at Calf of Eday on Orkney, two stone axes were located on a shelf in the interior of the tomb. In addition, a distinctive Scandinavian axe forms the primary deposit at Juliberries' Grave in Kent.

Axes also appear to have been deliberately deposited in considerable numbers in rivers such as the Thames and many exotic examples are found in areas which are rich in raw materials. So-called 'Group VI' axes from Cumbria are particularly well represented in Yorkshire, while those from the Sussex flint mines occur in high frequencies in Wessex and East Anglia. Patterns of damage suggest that many of the axes recovered from these more formal deposits were used, and this calls into question the rigid distinction that we have tended to draw between the functional and symbolic properties of tools. This distinction was probably real enough where axes were so thin or highly polished that they would have shattered on impact, but it may be unwise to assume that we can infer the values assigned to all axes simply by characterizing their form or usefulness (fig. 29).

As with arrowheads, clues as to the significance accorded to axes can be gained from a variety of contexts. Once again, it is interesting that the axe is one of the commonest representational motifs to occur in the Megalithic art of western Europe. Depictions of hafted and unhafted axes have been recorded in a variety of contexts, and it is not uncommon to find spectacular deposits of axes within or close to tombs. It has even been suggested that large standing stones such as 'Le Grande Menhir Brise' may be monumental representations or skeuomorphs of axes – their heavily pecked surfaces echoing the methods used to produce axes from stones which could not be flaked into shape. A similar case might be made for the Rudston Monolith in Yorkshire.

This emphasis upon representation suggests that axes had the potential to be powerful symbols, and many have argued that they were closely associated with concepts of maleness and adulthood. We may lack these more dramatic representations in Britain, but it is likely that this same basic link would have been recognized. Given the evidence for the circulation of axes and adzes in the Later Mesolithic, it is quite possible that these associations had a long ancestry.

27 Distribution of stone axes from four western sources identified through petrological analysis (see opposite). Archaeologists have interpreted these 'dots on maps' in a number of ways. Traditionally seen as evidence for intensive nationwide trading networks, it is now recognized that these patterns may have taken as much as a millennium to develop. More recent studies have made use of mathematical models which explore the changing character and frequency of axe use with increasing distance from a source. These formal models are based on the idea that different types of exchange or trade will each create a distinct archaeological signature or 'fall-off' pattern. These modelling techniques remain useful, but it is now generally acknowledged that the link between pattern and process is not as clear as has often been assumed. The bulk of axe dispersal patterns are likely to reflect hand-to-hand exchange or the movement of axes across the country in a series of small 'steps'.

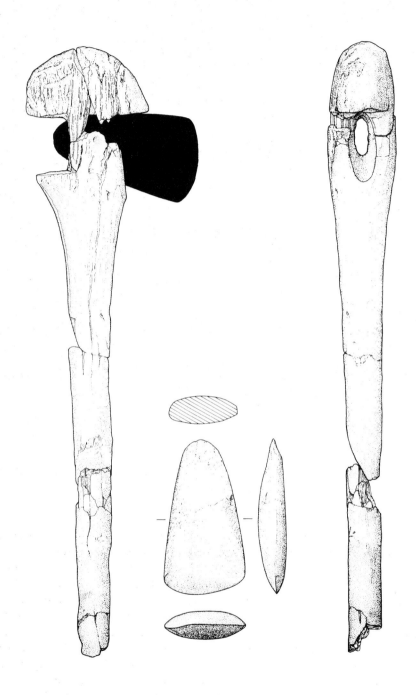

28 Hafted axe from Shulishader in Scotland (drawn by Helen Jackson).

29 Flaked and ground axes of flint and stone. Note the square-sectioned 'Scandinavian' axe to the left of the picture (Museum of Archaeology and Anthropology, Cambridge).

Perhaps because of this, changes in the character of axes, and in the conditions under which they were made, used and deposited, may have been one of the media through which the concept of 'being Neolithic' was carried forward. While the vast majority of axes were undoubtedly used, they may have possessed significance as markers of social identity. They provided metaphors for some of the qualities and roles that defined people in the Neolithic world.

## The gift of stones

These observations return us to the conditions under which axes and other artefacts were circulated during the Earlier Neolithic. Evidence from a number of areas indicates that both artefacts and raw materials were probably transferred between communities (fig. 30). In addition to axes, large flint nodules appear to have been moved from the south and east into western and northern parts of Britain. Artefacts of Arran pitchstone have been found throughout Scotland, and flint from County Antrim appears to have found its way into Britain, where it occurs as flakes, cores and other tools (fig. 31). These patterns are by no means confined to stone. Although most ceramics appear to have been locally produced, round-based pottery made from the distinctive gabbroic clays of the Lizard in Cornwall, has been found in enclosures and settlement contexts in Dorset and Wiltshire. These

30 Hoard of axes from Malone, Belfast (the Ulster Museum).

patterns are probably the only surviving traces of complex networks of communication that also saw the movement of livestock, and perhaps people, between different communities and regions.

Many of these dispersal patterns are likely to be the result of hand-to-hand movement rather than bulk trade, and some undoubtedly reflect the transfer of objects and materials to meet basic practical demands. However, as the evidence of axes and gabbroic pottery suggests, the circulation of objects may also have served rather different purposes and here their symbolic connotations were perhaps equally important. Because of their associations with particular practices and perhaps with categories of person, these objects may have provided media for exchanges which helped to renew the bonds that existed between different communities. For example, the movement of pottery may have had relatively little to do with its immediate role as a practical container. These vessels may also have carried ideas about the identity of the people who made and used them, and the significance of food preparation and consumption as a cultural act.

It is this potential for objects to carry a constellation of ideas and associations which is often drawn upon in exchange, and here it is useful to consider the role of the gift in non-capitalist societies. Where identities are closely tied to the possession and use of things, the transfer of an object may create bonds between people that persist after the moment of transaction is complete. Unlike many of the commodities that circulate today, gifts may remain inalienable. Moreover, through its use, and its passage from one context or person to another, the exchanged object acquires a history which refers not only to the past and present order of social relations, but also to future ties and obligations. Exchange is thus an important medium through which debts and obligations are built up, and social positions negotiated over time. In other words, we can think of the circulation of objects as a practice which is central to the classification of people. Although forms of gift exchange may differ in terms of the ways in which they reproduce social relations, the practice of 'keeping while giving' is often an important medium through which webs

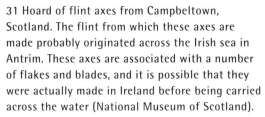

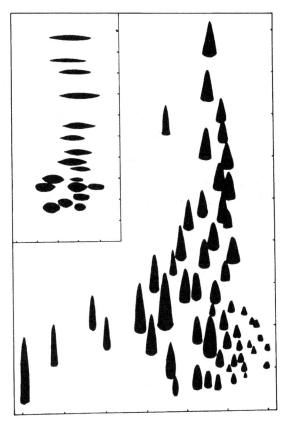

31 Hoard of flint axes from Campbeltown, Scotland. The flint from which these axes are made probably originated across the Irish sea in Antrim. These axes are associated with a number of flakes and blades, and it is possible that they were actually made in Ireland before being carried across the water (National Museum of Scotland).

of kinship and authority are reworked and sustained.

These ideas are important, but we should be wary of creating too rigid a distinction between gifts and commodities, using this to oppose non-capitalist and modern western societies. Even in our own culture, the creation, circulation and consumption of objects may be entangled in a disparate web of social and political concerns. Equally, there can be little justification for our tendency to romanticize non-capitalist societies, ignoring what Appadurai calls their calculative, impersonal and self-aggrandizing features. Many artefacts and resources probably did circulate as more or less alienated commodities during the Neolithic. But the concept of the gift goes some

32 Plot of variations in the dimensions of jadeite axes from Britain (after Wooley et al.,1979). Morphological studies have frequently been combined with distributional analyses and have been used to identify sub-groups or classes within particular categories of artefacts. In this case, analysis has identified a number of regional trends. Thin jadeite axes with a triangular plan are commonly found in northern Britain while smaller 'hachettes' and thicker examples are more common in the south. Some of these differences reflect the amount of use and reworking sustained by axes in different areas. The so-called 'torpedo' shaped axes placed to the far right of the diagram are typical of forms commonly found in Brittany.

way towards capturing the sense in which the circulation of some objects may also have played a rather more crucial social and political role.

One further issue needs to be considered here. While objects may possess cultural biographies, their significance is nevertheless dependent upon context. Their associations may be reworked through emulation, through changes in the conditions under which they are acquired and circulated, or through their deployment in different settings. This capacity for change may be even greater where the circulation of objects plays an important political role. For example, objects obtained as commodities may subsequently be deployed as gifts in different contexts. Equally, the significance accorded to gifts may be transformed as they move through different social spheres and from one region or 'regime of value' to another. This mutability even persists at the level of individual transactions. The exchanged object may be viewed differently according to whether one is the giver or the receiver. In archaeological terms then, we must acknowledge that the significance accorded to an object and the circumstances of its transfer may have changed through space and time.

Given these observations, there is little to be gained from maintaining a rigid distinction between the functional and symbolic properties of artefacts such as axes. Nor can we assume that the significance attached to the products of particular sources remained unchanged as they circulated in contexts away from their points of origin. Because of their associations, axes could also be drawn upon as media for exchange (fig. 32). These exchanges may have been undertaken in the context of marriage or initiation rites, in complex systems of bartering and in more ceremonial transactions between members of different communities. They would also have been undertaken with varying degrees of regularity at a lineage or corporate group level, and this may be why the products of specific axe sources are concentrated in particular regions. Although it may be simplistic to refer to these regional clusters as 'territories', they may reflect the persistence of

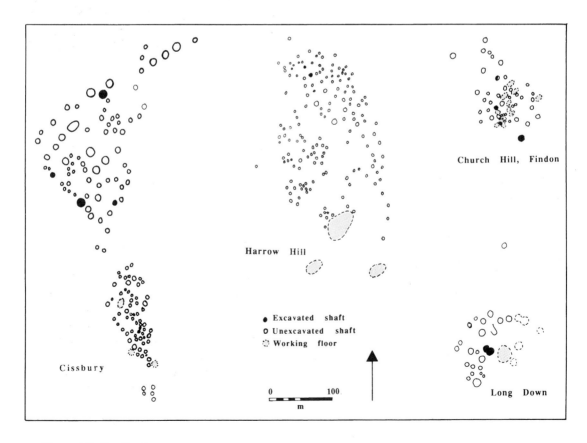

Church Hill, Findon

Harrow Hill

- Excavated shaft
o Unexcavated shaft
° Working floor

Cissbury

Long Down

0          100
m

33 Plans of Earlier Neolithic mines in southern Britain.

34 Great Langdale, Cumbria; an important source of Group VI stone axes.

particular networks of interaction over considerable periods of time. Whatever the case, the very use of the axe as an appropriate medium for exchange may have carried with it the consensus that particular transactions were an area of social life administered or controlled by particular members of the community.

## Digging for identity: flint mines and stone quarries

The roots of this consensus may have been established from the very moment that raw material was selected and here it should be recalled that the practice of exploiting mines and quarries for axe production was itself an innovation. Although they do appear rather earlier, it seems to have been the case in many parts of north-western Europe that large mines were rare prior to the Neolithic. Mundane though it may seem to us, this change in the character of production may have been no less dramatic and influential than the appearance of tombs and ceremonial enclosures.

Information regarding the character of this innovation can be gained from the sources themselves. Despite certain obvious differences, the upland stone quarries and chalkland flint mines of the Earlier Neolithic do share a number of characteristics (fig. 33). For example, it is clear that many were set apart from the main areas of contemporary settlement, even though adequate raw material could often be found 'closer to home'. In the case of the Sussex flint mines, the physical distances involved may have been relatively small. Equally, many of the upland sources such as Tievebulliagh, Graig Lwyd or Great Langdale (fig. 34) would have been visible from areas of settlement in the lowlands. This may also have applied to flint mines, where false cresting would have made these sites stand out as white scars above the treeline. Nevertheless, it does

35 Creag na Caillich or Killin, Perthshire; a source of Group XXIV stone axes.

36 A working floor on the margins of Creag na Caillich, Perthshire. The 'roughouts' produced at these camps were taken down to the lowlands for final grinding and polishing.

seem that these sites were physically marginal, a possibility supported by the lack of any evidence for settlement or domestic activity in their immediate environs (fig. 35).

Further links can be made in terms of the scheduling of source use. Evidence from a number of sources suggests that the earliest use of these sites was episodic or 'event-like'. For example, palaeoenvironmental data from Great Langdale indicates that the immediate area of the source witnessed the development of grassland rather earlier than in other parts of the Cumbrian uplands. Here the evidence accords with a model of episodic or even seasonal use by small groups which was embedded in broader cycles of movement associated with the husbandry of animals. In the case of the flint mine complexes, it is likely that only a small number of the shafts that are visible today would have been exploited at any one time. Here too, we see the residues of repeated episodes of activity by relatively small groups.

The inventories from a number of sites demonstrate that while axe making predominates, other tools are also found. These include the large and often crudely worked picks and hammers used in the process of extracting workable stone (fig. 36). Few of these are found on Earlier Neolithic sites away from a raw material source. Sickles, laurel leaves and arrowheads were also made at a number of flint mines, but at many of the western stone sources, axes were the only artefacts to be made in any numbers. Many sources also share similar characteristics in terms of the spatial organization of working. For example, it is clear that the flaked or roughed-out axes produced at these sites were taken elsewhere for grinding and polishing. These final stages of working generally took place within settlements in the lowland zone. However, the presence of 'axe polishing grooves' at West Kennet long barrow, and of polissoirs at enclosures such as The Trundle and Etton, indicates that the final form of axes may occasionally have been realized in rather more specialized contexts.

At a more detailed level, the character of a number of sources offers clues as to the choreography of activities on site. In the case of Great Langdale, recent research suggests that the earliest phases of exploitation saw small groups procuring stone along the outcrop of volcanic tuff

and undertaking initial reduction at the point of extraction. This seems to have been followed by the movement of angular blocks and large flakes of tuff to a series of temporary campsites which have been recognized on the major access routes away from the source (fig. 37). Similar patterns have been noted at Graig Lwyd. The majority of these camps lie within half an hour's walk from the outcrop itself and all are close to upland water sources. Here, the blocks were further reduced to create crude roughouts which often possessed symmetry in plan if not in section. The debitage found at these locations also suggests that the sequences of action followed during roughout production were varied and relatively unstructured. Little concern seems to have been given to the anticipation and avoidance of errors during flaking, or to the final form of the axes themselves. These roughouts were then taken down to the lowlands for grinding and polishing.

The chalkland flint mines offer a rather different understanding of the manner in which activities were organized. On the basis of evidence from sites such as Harrow Hill, it is possible that the digging of shafts may have taken place alongside the open-cast working of flint seams outcropping on or near the surface (fig. 38). Variation in extractive techniques is also attested at some of the upland stone axe quarries, and in one case at least, may be related to changes in the social context of production through time. We shall return to this point later, but first, we must move into the mineshafts themselves.

There can be little doubt that the practice of winning flint in this manner was one fraught with risks and uncertainties. On the basis of excavations at Cissbury, Blackpatch, Harrow Hill and Church Hill, it seems likely that the process of actually sinking the shafts may have been a group effort – requiring co-operation between a number of individuals. This would have also applied to the backfilling of shafts, which could take place after an interval of only a few days. However, once the shaft had been dug to the required level, often below higher seams of flint, it is possible to detect changes in the physical character of working. The radial galleries that run off from the majority of excavated shafts are generally quite narrow, although variations do exist in terms of the distance that they travel. As such, it would have been

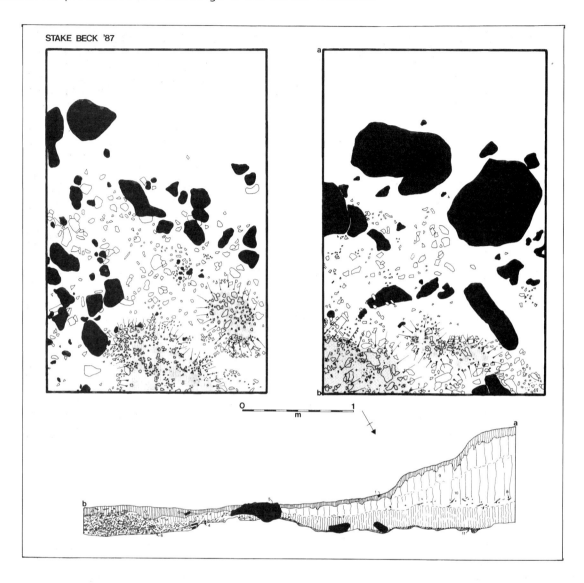

STAKE BECK '87

37 A working floor on the margins of the Group VI source at Great Langdale. Shaded areas denote distinct piles or dumps of waste flakes.

impractical for more than one person to work in a gallery at any one time. Indeed, abrasions and smoothing on the gallery walls at Harrow Hill give a vivid sense of the physical constraints within which individuals would have worked.

In certain cases, notably at Harrow Hill and Cissbury, links between different galleries and backfilled shafts may have been established during the course of working. However, the majority of excavations suggest that the entrances to individual galleries were maintained as discrete

features. This may be the case in one of the shafts at Blackpatch, where a wall of chalk blocks and debris was constructed to separate the entrances to galleries Four and Five. Small 'nests' of debitage and broken roughouts have been located in the shafts and gallery entrances at a number of sites. Some of these rejects may have been used as digging tools, but the waste flakes suggest that a limited amount of axe production was sometimes conducted at the point of extraction. However, the bulk of the flint located during the

38 Earlier Neolithic mine at Harrow Hill, Sussex, under excavation (courtesy of Worthing Museum).

sinking of the shaft and the working of the galleries was taken up to the surface in a relatively unmodified state. It was at working areas on the surface that the creation of roughout axes was generally undertaken.

In general, discussions of flint mines have tended to emphasise the practical constraints imposed by the local geology and topography. Shafts are seen as the only practicable method of reaching buried flint seams, and narrow, curving galleries represent the safest and most efficient strategy for maximizing returns and minimizing risks. Similarly, the fact that higher seams of flint have often been cut through in pursuit of lower deposits is usually taken to indicate that the miners were after flint of the highest quality. There is little point in challenging many of these arguments. What can be questioned is our tendency to take these characteristics, together with the

overall scale of mine complexes, as evidence that mining was an 'industry' in the hands of specialists. As we have already seen, working was probably not conducted on a grand scale, and while the high-quality stone in the lower seams may have been difficult to extract, it would also have been the easiest to work. It is also highly distinctive and thus easily recognizable.

Although it may not reflect the operation of specialists, the layout of these sites would have provided a 'frame' that structured the arrangement and movement of people. In other words, the practical organization of working would have provided a series of cues for people's understandings of their social as well as their physical relationship with others. Perhaps the most obvious point to be made concerns the shafts themselves. It remains to be seen how far flint might also have been obtained through more

63

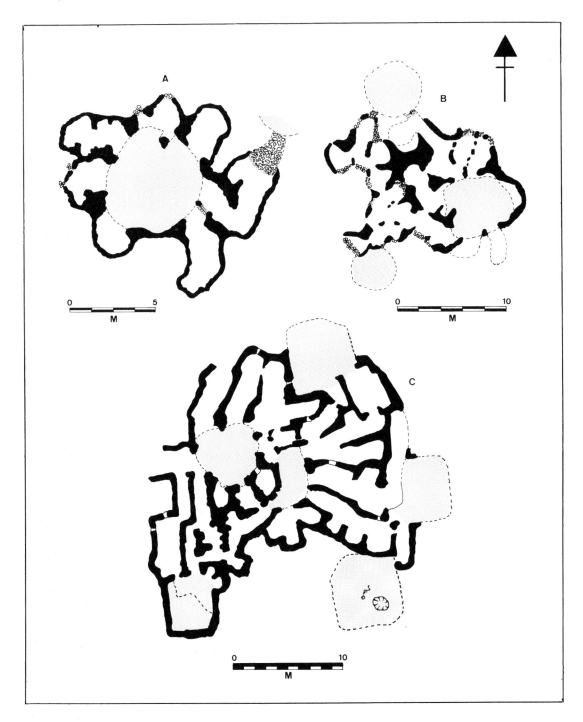

39 Shafts and galleries from three mining sites in southern England: A Blackpatch; B Harrow Hill; C Cissbury.

extensive open-cast working on certain sites. What is important here is that the shafts that characterize so many flint mines are distinct and bounded entities (fig. 39). They demarcate the areas within which work could be undertaken, and allow distinctions to be drawn between people in terms of who could participate. Once established, the sinking of shafts would have involved close physical contact and co-operation between a small number of individuals. In this sense, the demarcation and sinking of shafts would have been both a product of group endeavour, and a medium through which the identity of that group was reaffirmed.

Given their limited size, the galleries that spread from the base of many shafts may have provided the potential for distinctions to be drawn between individuals, and for links to be made between people and raw materials. This may also have been the case where axes were produced within the shaft itself, adjacent to the galleries from which the raw material had been obtained. However, the task of removing the bulk of the flint from the shaft, and the process of backfilling and restoring the ground would again have required close co-operation. With the move from the shaft to the surface working areas, further scope would have existed for the creation of links between individuals and the artefacts that they produced. This would also have applied at the camps established on the margins of several upland sources. Working in close proximity, peo-

40 Working stone at an Earlier Neolithic mine. The procurement and production of axes may have been undertaken from temporary camps established on the margins of mining areas. Despite their close associations with men, these events may have involved other sections of the community. However, it is possible that proscriptions surrounded people's actions. Perhaps only certain individuals were allowed into the shafts or onto working floors. Participating for the first time, a child may have learnt just as much about the historical and spiritual significance of their actions as they did about how to extract and work the dark flint that lay beneath their feet. Environmental evidence suggests that the landscape was probably more heavily wooded than it appears here (drawn by Judith Dobie; copyright English Heritage).

ple would have been able to observe the creation of axes by others, and would themselves have been observed. These more intensive episodes of axe production would have also provided a context in which the skills of bifacial knapping could be appreciated, learnt and developed. Proficiency or expertise in these routines may have helped to sustain very localized concepts of experience and authority, such as those that separated the young from the old.

The choreography of activities at axe sources may thus have helped to create and sustain a variety of social categories. Where the use of mines and upland quarries involved a measure of temporary separation from the wider community, this would have allowed distinctions to be made in terms of who was allowed to travel to the source. Participants in these events may even have come to be distinguished from other members of particular communities in terms of the stoneworking skills that they learnt at a source. The precise implications of these patterns of exploitation are difficult to determine. In some cases, sites may have been visited by groups drawn from different communities, in others, a source may have witnessed the arrival of people bound by closer kinship ties (fig. 40). As the skeleton of a woman at Blackpatch suggests, it is unlikely that access to these sites was entirely restricted to males. However, given the associations of axes, it is possible that mines and quarries provided contexts within which young males could undertake certain rites of passage associated with the arrival of adulthood. They may even have been places at which men from different communities met on a periodic basis. Once we accept that working may have been both small scale and episodic, there is no need to invoke notions of full-time specialists or factories. Rather, these sources served as distinct places at which it was appropriate to produce tools that marked aspects of a person's social identity. Embedded in routines of movement through the landscape, the character and tempo of activities at the sources may have been keyed into broader conceptual schemes concerning patterns in the lives of the individual, the community and the broader group. Perhaps these themes were highlighted in the stories that were recounted while people camped at these sites –

stories which spoke of the first breaking of the ground by the ancestors, or of the taboos that surrounded their use.

Carried away from sources and back to the world of everyday activity, flaked axes would have carried associations with specific people and with the circumstances in which they were produced. These associations would have been strengthened through the more time-consuming process of grinding and polishing which would have enhanced the appearance and recognizability of individual axes and may have added to their role as markers of identity. This process would not have ended there. With the passage of time, the day-to-day use of these and other tools would have added a patina of routine associations. Subsequent episodes of grinding and sharpening would have contributed to the gradual reworking of original forms and their links with particular people. These personal and categoric links would have been drawn upon when axes were exchanged and as they passed along the lines of affiliation and contact that linked different communities. Others may have been selected for deposition at certain times, and here it is interesting that out of the fourteen characterized flint axe 'hoards' in southern Britain, ten contain Sussex flint mine products. In these contexts at least, the ties those artefacts had to specific people may have been just as important as their utility.

In time, the sources themselves may have taken on some of the qualities of monuments. Alongside their place in an oral tradition, the depressions and scars that remained would have served as tangible reminders of the activities that had been undertaken at these periodic events. These traces would have been encountered on subsequent trips to the source, and in certain cases may have been visible as prominent landmarks. Rejects and flakes from the shaping and thinning of axes would have been easily identified, and piles of debris and backfilled shafts would have influenced patterns of working. For people returning to flint mines or stone quarries after an interval of time, and particularly for later generations, these traces would have played an important part in shaping their sense of place and the significance they attached to their labour and its fruits.

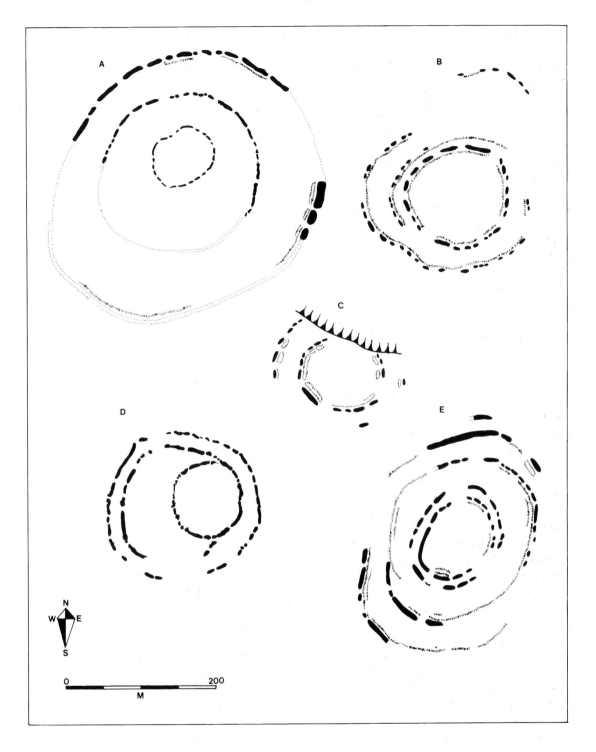

41 Causewayed enclosure plans: A Windmill Hill; B The Trundle; C Coombe Hill; D Briar Hill; E Whitehawk.

## Causewayed enclosures

Similar themes are important when we consider another context with which axes and other tools appear to have been associated during the Earlier Neolithic. Causewayed enclosures are large, circular or sub-circular monuments defined by one or more circuits of interrupted banks and ditches. These segmentary ditches echo the form of the trenches adjacent to many Earlier Neolithic tombs. Enclosures are effectively the first massive earthwork monuments to appear in the Neolithic, constructed, used, reused and abandoned between the end of the fourth and the middle of the third millennium bc (fig. 41). They enclose areas of up to 7ha (17 acres), and are likely to have been built through the co-operative effort of a number of groups. Roughly fifty examples are known, with a distribution that encompasses much of southern Britain. Isolated examples have also been identified further to the north and west, in Ireland, Yorkshire, Cumbria and perhaps Scotland.

Although it is probably stretching the point to talk of all enclosures being white, the contrast between these sites and their immediate surrounds would have been dramatic. As with mines and quarries, many enclosures were peripheral to the main areas of contemporary settlement, often situated in limited woodland clearings. A number are also located on or near to sources of raw

42 Animal bone in the ditch of Windmill Hill in Wiltshire. Formal deposits or dumps such as these may have been laid down to mark the conclusion of important feasts or ceremonies. Encountered at a later date, they may have provided tangible reminders of the events that had taken place in the past. At the same time, where certain animals or herds were linked to specific people, their bones may have provided metaphors for the ties that those people had with a particular site (Alasdair Whittle).

material, some of which may have been important during the Later Mesolithic. The vast majority were also used on an episodic basis, constructed, abandoned, reused and reconstructed over considerable periods of time. Botanical and faunal remains suggest that the use of many enclosures may have been seasonal, and embedded within broader cycles of movement associated with livestock – unlike their continental counterparts, very few contain evidence for permanent settlement. In those few cases where permanent occupation is apparent, it is generally associated with the final phases of their use. The one exception to this rule is the stone-built site of Carn Brea in Cornwall. One of the few examples of a settlement that witnessed violent attacks, the site is also associated with small clearance cairns and fields which have their closest parallels in Ireland. Other sites may only have witnessed one or two brief episodes of activity before permanent abandonment.

As these differences suggest, we should be wary of treating all enclosures as members of a distinct class, with common functions and histories. However, it does seem that in the context of seasonal routines of movement around the landscape, different communities may have come together to build and use these sites. This act of congregation may even have been celebrated in their physical form or layout. The act of building may have been a corporate endeavour, defining a common cultural focus for dispersed and fragmented groups on the margins of several territories. At the same time, the segmentary character of the ditches may reflect the labour of 'gangs' organized on kinship lines. Distinctions between different communities or lineages may have been maintained or expressed within the very fabric of these monuments.

In a number of cases, this dual emphasis appears to have been sustained over time. For example, at Briar Hill, Hambledon Hill and Staines, ditches witnessed distinct episodes of recutting in which this tradition of construction was maintained. This was also the case for part of the enclosure at Etton. In other words, it was the physical reconstitution of these sites at specific times which was crucial to the maintenance of ties between dispersed communities. Outside these events, many enclosures may have lain more or less 'dormant' in the landscape. Recent work by Alasdair Whittle at Windmill Hill has shown how a site that witnessed major ceremonial gatherings was also encountered and used in rather more mundane ways at other times.

This leads us to a consideration of the purposes served by these sites, and here we should acknowledge that the act of enclosure can be thought of in a number of ways. As Chris Evans has argued: 'It circumscribes that which is enclosed and demarcates that which is outside, and between the two it creates a boundary which can simultaneously be a physical or cognitive barrier and a transitional zone.' Passage across this threshold may have constituted a movement between arenas of value – from the everyday world of dispersed communities to the more socially charged atmosphere that attended encounters with others. Moreover, the scale of the causeways at many sites would have constrained this act of passage. People may have had to enter sites in a particular order or sequence, allowing distinctions to be drawn between groups or individuals. It is also possible that the ditch acted as a boundary to exclude particular people at certain times.

As Richard Bradley and others have pointed out, the assemblages recovered from many enclosures reflect an emphasis upon specific episodes of consumption. The presence of formal deposits in pits and in the fills and terminals of ditches at many sites (fig. 42), recalls the character of assemblages from the forecourts and ditches of a number of barrows. These intentional, often rapidly buried assemblages include concentrations of arrowheads, knapping clusters that can be refitted, pottery, and stone and flint axes. Deliberate deposits of animal bone are dominated by elements of cattle skeletons which may reflect feasting, and there is evidence that many enclosures witnessed activities associated with the defleshing and treatment of the dead. At Hambledon Hill, for example, Roger Mercer has suggested that the main enclosure witnessed the exposure of bodies, the awful silence of the site 'broken only by the din of crows'. At sites such as Abingdon, Staines and Etton, fragmentary human remains (notably skulls) have been found in a variety of contexts, and may reflect similar practices.

69

43 A small axe from the Lake District deposited in a pit at Etton causewayed enclosure near Peterborough (Francis Pryor).

Complete skeletons have also been recognized at a small number of sites, and in Wessex, at least, children may be over-represented.

This emphasis upon episodes of consumption is significant, because such activities often occur in the context of a variety of rites of passage – events which attend and animate important junctures in the life of the individual and the community. Such events are often divided into a series of stages – an initial phase of separation giving way to one of liminality, which is in turn followed by one of reincorporation. Moreover, the thresholds between these stages are generally subject to strict proscriptions. This is often vital, because such occasions involve the explicit expression of fundamental ideas about the identities of people and the order of things in the social and natural worlds.

It seems that one of the purposes that many enclosures served was the provision of a pro-scribed, liminal context, physically and conceptually distinct from the world of day-to-day practices. It was in these bounded conditions that important and potentially dangerous rites and activities could be undertaken. Enclosures may have provided a demarcated space (and time) at which the treatment and interpretation of the dead could take place. Indeed, if the dead could be left there until their flesh had decayed, this would have made it possible to synchronize the chance event of death itself within broader cycles or routines of movement and social practice. Under these conditions, the substantive identities of individuals could have been transformed prior to their inclusion in the community of the ancestors, or to their dispersal in other contexts. Funerals and other ancestral rites may also have been occasions at which it was necessary to renew or redefine broader lines of kinship and affiliation, and the importance of these bonds may have

44 A selection of exotic axes and axe fragments from the causewayed enclosure at Etton. The majority are from either the Lake District or Wales. Only a few of these fragments bear breakage patterns indicative of use and some may have been deliberately broken.

been strengthened by their celebration at enclosures.

These associations may also help us to understand why artefacts such as axes were consumed on these sites: reworked, smashed and placed in pits or other formal deposits. Examples include Maiden Castle, Etton (figs 43–4) and Hambledon Hill, where the pits from which axes have been recovered are those apparently associated with the exposure or treatment of the dead. If enclosures served as contexts in which dealings with the dead could be undertaken, then items which signified certain ideas about social identity may have been as important as the body itself. Rather than being a simple reflection of elite settlement or trade, the reworking, destruction and/or deposition of axes may have been closely tied to the transformation of the social individual on death.

Deposited with fragments of people, and with the debris from feasts, these artefacts may have served as mnemonics, helping to sustain the associations of a site and a sense of continuity for specific social groups.

This idea of rites of passage has further relevance, since death is just one of the thresholds at which social categories may be brought into sharp relief. Marriage involves the incorporation of outsiders into existing kinship structures and may provide access to labour, and proscriptions often surround the passage to adulthood. In each of these cases, the demarcation of specific places and times at which it is appropriate for particular rites to be undertaken is often crucial, and here the episodic use of many enclosures may also be significant. It is with these themes in mind that we should consider the production and exchange

45 A gathering at a large enclosure (drawn by Ivan Lapper).

of stone tools. Many enclosures are situated on or near to major sources of raw material, and the range of artefacts in assemblages found at these sites demonstrates the extent to which the domestic and the ceremonial were often intertwined. For example, core production and working is common, and the high frequency of scrapers and serrated flakes at sites such as Windmill Hill and Maiden Castle indicates that a range of processing tasks may have been undertaken. Querns and quern fragments have also been recovered, and at Etton these grinding stones may have been buried with some formality. Although serrated flakes and querns were probably used throughout the year, their presence in enclosures suggests that the harvesting and processing of crops may have been organized and celebrated as an important seasonal event, perhaps involving co-operation between different communities (fig. 45).

Evidence for the production of other tools can also be found in a number of assemblages, and in certain cases it may be that a particular emphasis was placed upon the production and/or finishing of artefacts such as axes and laurel leaves. Often these were made from materials outcropping on or near the site, but enclosures also saw the polishing of axes derived from more distant sources. Polissoirs have been recovered from Etton, Abingdon and The Trundle, while arrowheads, axes and laurel leaves appear to have been made at a number of sites. Evidence from Maiden Castle supports this suggestion: alongside the production of cores and the use of a variety of implements, the site also witnessed a significant volume of flint axe production. There is little evidence to suggest that these items were also produced in any numbers at contemporary sites in the vicinity, even though raw material would have been available.

It is unlikely that the contrast at Maiden Castle is quite as dramatic as it appears. Nevertheless, it does seem that some importance may have been attached to the production or finishing of objects such as axes in the context of other events at these sites. This may be why it is not uncommon to find deliberate deposits, not just of tools, but also of the waste flakes generated during their manufacture. The laying down of these assemblages may have been undertaken at the conclusion of particular episodes of production. But their presence in ditches and other contexts would have helped to sustain the idea that enclosures were an appropriate context in which to undertake certain forms of productive activity. This symbolic marking of a link between enclosures and production is suggested by the fact that formal ditch deposits were often respected in subsequent episodes of recutting.

This 'embedding' of procurement within other important events may also have involved exchange. The location of enclosures, their association with rites of passage and the episodic character of their use, may all have contributed to their suitability as contexts within which different groups might come together, and in which a variety of exchanges could be conducted. As already discussed, the capacity for exchanged objects to carry histories and project social relations into the future is often enhanced by conventions regarding the times and places at which appropriate responses can be made and obligations discharged or reworked. Furthermore, the circulation of objects within local regimes of value may require a transformation or reworking of their associations when they are introduced from outside. More often than not, these transitions are effected not only in demarcated places, but also at specific times, and in both these cases the episodic use of many enclosures may again have been crucial. Undertaken within a demarcated spatial and temporal context which was itself linked to broader routines of movement and economic activity, the circulation of artefacts, livestock and people would have defined relations of affiliation and authority within and between dispersed groups.

Such events would also have served to sustain the significance of objects such as the axe. Moving from one person and context to another, these tools carried people with them, symbolizing the lasting ties and obligations that bound individuals and communities. As such, they may themselves have come to be regarded as important tokens of value (fig. 46).

## Trajectories of change

So far we have seen how many enclosures provided a common cultural focus. Their seasonal

46 Axe polishing grooves at West Kennet long barrow. Although the grinding and polishing of many axes was undertaken within settlements, some were probably finished in more formal circumstances. In the case of West Kennet, the grinding slab that forms one of the tomb uprights was probably brought from another context and incorporated into the fabric of the monument. This act of incorporation may have been undertaken as part of the process by which the meanings and associations of the tomb were shaped. However, it is possible that the grinding slab continued to be used. Perhaps the axes that were finished under the gaze of the ancestors were accorded some additional significance which added to their roles as markers of identity and media for exchange (Stuart Piggott).

arising from relations of inequality within local lineage systems, and from unequal access to labour, land and important symbolic resources. This appears to have included access to objects whose circulation played an important role in the creation of social relations and the protection of political authority.

Changes in the character and content of tombs after *c.*2750 bc put some flesh on the bones of this argument. In contrast to the corporate emphasis of earlier generations, many later tombs reflect a greater stress upon individuals and perhaps particular lineages. This is indicated by the deposits at many sites, and by the fact that the overall frequency of long mounds decreases through time. The later (often more monumental) sites may contain articulated inhumations, occasionally accompanied by grave goods, and in general there is a decrease in the number of individuals represented at particular tombs (fig. 47). More often than not, these individuals tend to be adult males. This is also apparent in the smaller oval barrows which begin to appear in southern Britain at around the same time.

Taken together, these trends reflect the emergence of concerns similar to those which had guided the burial of individuals under round barrows in the north-east for several generations. Even where the outward appearance of long

construction, use and reconstruction was crucial for the reproduction of ties between dispersed communities. Yet the concepts embodied in these places were far from static. They could be manipulated to serve a variety of purposes, and it does seem that this manipulation was linked to broader changes in the nature of society through time. These changes probably arose from a series of contradictions or conflicts of interest within society itself. They may have included tensions mounds remained as a reference to the traditional associations of tombs, their contents placed a greater emphasis upon individuals drawn from dominant lineages (fig. 48). This may have been rather more than a simple reflection of the character of social and political relations. As places already invested with great symbolic importance, tombs and their contents may have been drawn upon in order to bring about or sanction changes in the social order. As such, these changes of emphasis may well have been an idealized representation which was wielded as a powerful weapon in arguments over the distribution of authority in society and the ties that bound particular people to places.

Other changes in the character of many tombs

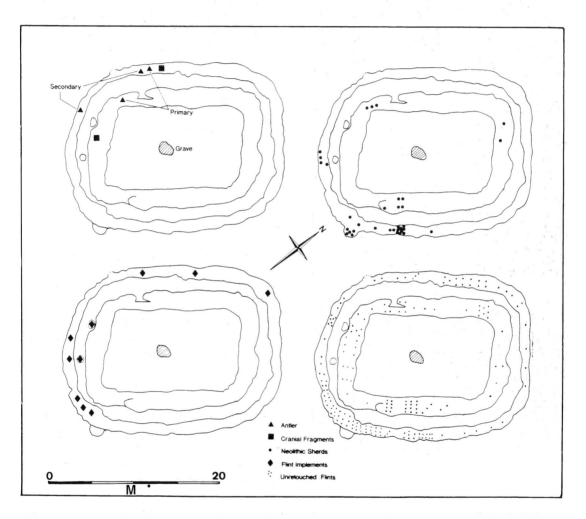

47 Plan of the double-ditched barrow at Barrow hills which was constructed on the margins of a causewayed enclosure near Abingdon. Originally a ditched enclosure, the site gradually developed into a barrow with additional ditch circuits. Recent excavation suggests that the south-western end of the site remained open at certain times: two large posts flank this 'approach' to the area of the grave, and it is possible that other posts in the ditches formed a façade at this end of the site. Spatial patterning on the site suggests that animal bone, stone tools and fragmentary human remains were deliberately placed in the ditches close to this entrance, their resting places marked by posts. Other details of the patterning reflect the continued importance of this area in front of the barrow as a focus for activities which may have included feasts (after Bradley 1992).

75

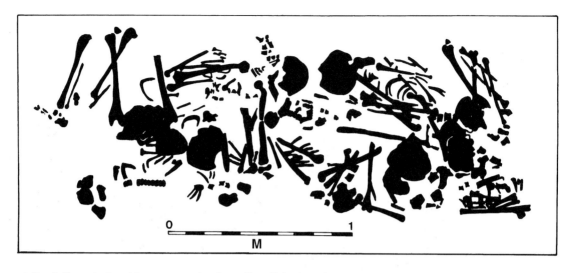

48 Partially articulated human remains from Skendleby long barrow, Lincolnshire.

add weight to this idea. Many appear to have been sealed up or closed at this time, and in some cases flanking ditches were extended to encompass the entire mound. Although activity continued in the forecourts, direct access to the ancestors was no longer possible (fig. 49). This may reflect the emergence of sections within society who acted as intermediaries between the living and the dead, exercising a measure of control over the manner in which these rites and monuments were to be understood. Where the ancestors linked people to places, and were seen as important influences upon productivity, this control may have allowed certain lineages to assert and legitimate a more authoritative position among the living.

Parallel changes in the character and context of enclosure use can also be detected. Additional circuits of ditches were added to a number of sites, including Abingdon, Briar Hill and Orsett, and in a few cases causeways were removed to create a continuous circuit. The provision of further circuits which respected an original design could be analogous to the recutting of ditches, in that it reaffirmed or reinscribed the traditional significance and associations of a particular site. On the other hand, concentric plans may also provide a frame for the hierarchical ordering of people and activities. This echoes the process evident in a number of tombs, where reference to the past and to an established tradition of mound form may have served to support changes in the

character and significance of ancestral worship. In certain cases the construction of outer ditches marked a change in the nature of enclosure use. At Abingdon the inner ditch enclosed a largely ceremonial area, while the outer circuit defined the perimeter of a relatively permanent settlement. Although a degree of uncertainty surrounds the phasing of the two ditch systems, the evidence from Abingdon reflects a trend apparent at a small number of sites, where settlement assumes a greater importance with the passage of time.

The establishment of settlement at particular enclosures may not have marked the termination of their 'ritual' significance. In fact, it may have involved a shift in the extent to which particular sections within society attempted to place themselves between those sites and the broader corporate group. Particular lineages may have come to occupy a dominant position with respect to specific sites and by extension, the activities that they witnessed. At times, this authoritative position appears to have been contested in a direct and dramatic fashion. At Hembury, Hambledon Hill, Carn Brea and Crickley Hill, changes in the nature of the boundaries fulfilled a practical as well as symbolic role. The defences at these sites are not only complex and substantial, they also retain evidence for episodes of conflict, for the violent death of individuals and the destruction of settlement.

There are further developments in the physical character and associations of enclosures that lend

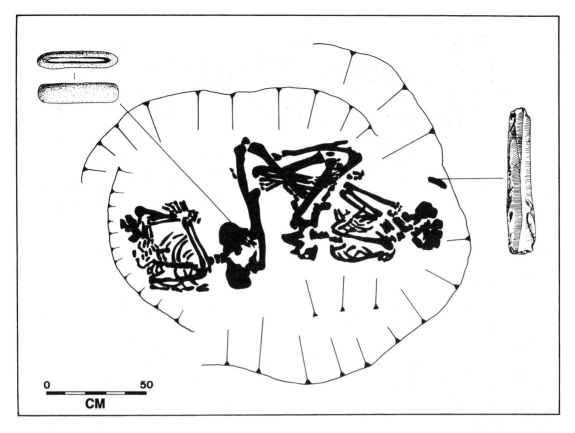

49 Detail of the burial at Barrow hills, a double inhumation of a man and a woman. Near the head of the woman lay a long flint blade with a smoothed edge. Close to the waist of the man was a jet belt-fitting and near his head a broken leaf-shaped arrowhead. Both of these grave accompaniments may have been items of personal gear carried and used by the people in life. They are typical of the grave goods found in Yorkshire, and, as such, reflect the movement of both objects and ideas between different parts of Britain at this time.

support to this argument. Oval or round barrows have been recognized at a number of sites, and at Hambledon Hill the association between the main enclosure and a barrow is strengthened by a series of parallels in the structure of their respective ditch deposits. In addition, cursus monuments have been recognized at Etton, Hastings Hill and Fornham-all-Saints, and both Maiden Castle and Crickley Hill witnessed the imposition of bank barrows. These massive linear monuments may represent a continuation of the long mound tradition, albeit in a somewhat different form. But their placement on enclosures would have constituted a fundamental reworking of the significance accorded to those sites and their place within the social landscape. Like permanent settlement, these changes may have

strengthened the association of specific sites with particular lineages, legitimating their control over a number of important practices. This may have had particularly important consequences for rites associated with the dead, but it may also have afforded a greater measure of control over the exchange of objects, livestock and people.

One last theme needs to be considered here. These changes appear to be broadly contemporaneous with an apparent expansion in the scale of stone axe dispersal in the second quarter of the third millennium bc and with the end of activity at many of the early flint mines. In addition, recent work at Great Langdale suggests that the character and perhaps the social context of stone axe production may have changed at around the same time (fig. 50). In this case, it is again important to

50 Roughout axe of volcanic tuff and associated waste material.

stress that we are dealing with changes of emphasis. Radiocarbon dates indicate that small groups may have continued to exploit the source and work the raw material along similar lines to those followed by earlier generations of producers. But it is at this juncture that we see the creation and maintenance of formal quarries, often placed in dramatic and highly inaccessible locations. The use of these locations had little to do with the physical quality of the stone itself, and may reflect the assignment of a special significance to stone retrieved from isolated and even dangerous places. Raw material with precisely the same properties was available at other locations which presented far fewer problems of access. In many cases this does not appear to have been exploited to anything like the same extent.

Changes can also be detected in the spatial organization of working, with a far greater emphasis placed upon the execution of all stages in roughout production at the point of extraction. In other words, the passage of time saw an increasing concern with the demarcation of areas in which it was appropriate for working to be undertaken, perhaps by different groups. In addition, technological analyses indicate radical changes in the actual process of working around a piece of raw material. The debitage from many of these later sites reflects a greater concern with the anticipation and avoidance of errors, and with the maintenance of recurrent routines during flaking. Put simply, the massive waste assemblages found on these sites reflect the careful realization of the final form of the axe during flaking. The roughouts carried away from these sites would have required relatively little grinding and polishing before that final form was achieved.

The changes in Cumbria may reflect a greater emphasis upon local production for exchange with groups outside the region. Following the pattern established further to the south, these exchanges may have been undertaken at junctures when different groups came together. Although they are relatively rare, sites such as the large enclosure recently discovered beneath the stone circle known as Long Meg and her Daughters, may have provided a context for these meetings. This site lies to the east of the Cumbrian massif, and is situated close to one of the principal routes through the Pennines to Yorkshire, where Cumbrian axes are found in considerable numbers (see also below). As before, there is no need to assume that these changes can be captured by industrial or mercantile metaphors. Nor should we see them simply as a reflection of increases in the scale of demand in areas at great distances from particular sources. In fact, it seems that the *character* of that demand may have been changing towards the close of the Earlier Neolithic. Although exchange had long been a medium for the reproduction of bonds between communities, it may have gradually become a practice through which relations of political authority were established and expressed.

Under these conditions, the exotic origins of stone axes may have provided a rather different set of potentials for the signification of broader ties between people, and perhaps a measure of control over patterns of circulation (fig. 51).

51 A stone axe quarry in the central Lakeland fells. Perched high on the face of the mountain, these quarries may have been the places to which people travelled in order to make important tokens of identity and value. The precarious and inaccessible location of these quarries may have helped to shape the meanings attached to the axes themselves and may also have been one of the ways in which particular groups demarcated the areas in which it was traditionally appropriate to work.

Rather than simply uniting people, the circulation of exotic axes may have become an important medium for the drawing of social and political distinctions which went beyond age and gender categories. This idea finds some support in one aspect of the data from Yorkshire, where Group VI axes from Cumbria are well represented. These were generally polished over their entire surfaces, while those made of locally occurring erratic stones were often ground only on their cutting edges. These differences in treatment suggest that distinctions may have been drawn between functionally identical tools according to the conditions under which they were acquired, and thus their cultural biographies.

In certain respects, the sequences of change identified at sources such as Great Langdale invite models which work at a relatively general level. Thus it is tempting to combine these sequences with evidence for the demise of flint mines, and to argue that some of the more distant western sources developed in the way that they did precisely because they were more distant. In other words, the scale of the deposits at these sites may reflect the considerable lengths of time over which their products circulated in different regions and in different social contexts. By the same token, the end of activity at Earlier Neolithic flint mines may be a reflection of the difficulties that were encountered in controlling access to the raw materials that were used to produce important tokens of value.

These arguments may have some utility, but while the discussion remains at this level it is difficult to understand the effects that these broader changes would have had within specific local contexts. No doubt the relationship was far from direct, but these broader changes in the spheres in which axes and other objects circulated, would have had important consequences in their areas of origin. In the case of certain upland sources, the long-established practice of axe production may have become a field within which specific groups exercised a greater degree of control and influence. The changes at Great Langdale may reflect the emergence of distinctions between local communities in terms of their relationship with the source and with the broader social networks which carried the products beyond the regional horizon. Although our understanding of the Neolithic sequence in Cumbria is rather limited, these distinctions may themselves have become an important source of authority among local groups. They may have also provided the conditions under which skill in stoneworking assumed a greater significance. However, like the passage of axes beyond the horizons of particular regional systems, the question of skill or specialization carries us towards the Later Neolithic.

79

# 4 Sermons in stone: the Later Neolithic

In chapter 3, we saw how the choreography of procurement and production may have helped to sustain the association of axes with people, and with specific fields of social and economic practice. Carried and used on a day-to-day basis, these markers of personal identity were also drawn upon in varied ways. As elements in formal deposits, the cultural biographies of axes would have shaped the ways in which certain rites or practices were understood. Similarly, as media for exchange, the movement of axes would have contributed to the reproduction of the bonds which linked communities in broader corporate structures.

We also saw how axes produced and circulated within specific regions gradually came to travel greater distances, so that they occur in considerable numbers as exotica in different parts of Britain. Some probably made this journey carried over people's shoulders, but many others passed along established exchange networks – their significance changing as they moved from one region or regime of value to another. This was not the case with the products of all sources, nor with all classes of artefact, but it does seem that axes were drawn upon in a rather different way towards the close of the Earlier Neolithic. Rather than simply marking identity and mediating local ties of affiliation and obligation, axes became important tokens of value, circulated in exchanges that helped to define political relations between members of different groups.

In certain cases, these changes in the spheres in which axes circulated may have contributed to a change in the social context of production itself. This need not have involved the emergence of specialists, but control over production, and over exchange pathways, may have assumed a greater importance with the passage of time. These themes are all the more crucial for our understanding of the Later Neolithic, where control over production, the circulation of artefacts and complex depositional practices appear to have been major concerns. However, we must begin by considering more basic attitudes towards the working of stone.

## Working stone

In locational terms, evidence from several regions suggests that this was a time of expansion (fig. 52). Surface scatters of stone with Later Neolithic affinities occur in many of the areas emphasised earlier, but new sites appear on soils that had previously seen little concerted exploitation. For example, the Upper Thames valley saw consistent settlement towards the mid third millennium bc, and a similarly late date can be assigned to settlement expansion in other areas, from parts of the Fens through to the eastern lowlands of Cumbria. This broad pattern is supported by the available environmental evidence. Although pollen cores in a number of areas reflect localized phases of woodland regeneration, the trend towards open grassland, scrub and cultivation accords with the lithic evidence.

Further changes in the character of lithic scatters can be added to this picture. In contrast to the Earlier Neolithic, the later phase of the period witnesses a marked increase in the size of scatters. Where these had taken the form of discrete clusters of material, now they appear as dense and continuous spreads of worked stone across much larger areas. This trend can be discerned in the west and in Scotland, where Later Neolithic settlement assemblages are often much larger than their Earlier Neolithic counterparts. However, this trend finds its clearest expression in the flint-rich regions of southern and eastern Britain. Extensive spreads of Later Neolithic tools and waste have been identified in eastern Yorkshire and in parts of the Peak District, echoing the patterns documented in areas such as Cranborne Chase in Dorset and in the environs of Stonehenge. These scatters often

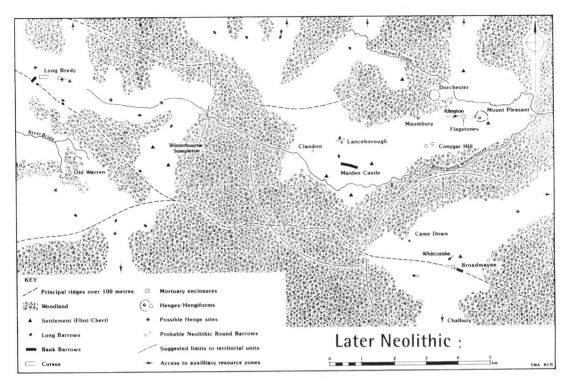

52 Changes in the landscape 2: model of the Later Neolithic landscape along the South Dorset Ridgeway (courtesy of Peter Woodward and the Trust for Wessex Archaeology).

reflect the location of settlement on or close to surface deposits of raw material, and in the south, a close correspondence with areas of clay with flints can be seen.

Although many upland sources remained marginal to the settlement zone, some of the places exploited as mines in the Earlier Neolithic saw later settlement involving the use of material occurring on the surface. Later Neolithic shafts have not been found at these locations, and in general the distinction between production sites and settlements was rather more blurred than it had been in the past. On the South Downs, Julie Gardiner has shown that many settlements witnessed the production and use of a wide variety of tools, including flint axes. This can also be seen in parts of Wessex, in areas such as Wilsford Down near Stonehenge and on the downlands around Avebury. It is also apparent at sites on the sand and gravel ridges and 'islands' of East Anglia.

Despite the considerable size of these scatters, there is no reason to envisage the rapid appearance of large villages; most settlements were probably no larger than several households practising garden-plot cultivation and managing livestock (fig. 53). What these patterns suggest is a change in the nature of settlement, in particular a turn away from the routine seasonal mobility patterns of the Earlier Neolithic and an emphasis upon the movement of settlement within smaller areas. This development was not taken up equally throughout Britain. On the one hand, nucleated settlements dating to this time are known in northern Scotland (fig. 54), and, on the other, the use of upland or 'wet' areas such as the fens or Breckland of East Anglia may have remained seasonal in character. But in many areas these patterns of movement, perhaps tied to stock movement, or to the 'budding-off' or division of communities, would have created the continuous spreads of material that we see today.

Subtle changes in the character of cores and core working provide clues as to the significance of these broader trends. By the mid third millennium bc, narrow flake or blade cores are

81

individual flakes also have a tendency to be larger, reflecting the lack of preparation and the placement of blows further into the body of the core. Material of this nature is almost ubiquitous on Later Neolithic sites in many parts of Britain. However, unlike earlier blade cores, this homogeneity may arise from the lack of a clear or consistent set of procedures, rather than the persistence of a particular way of working. Given the technology involved it is not easy to determine whether cores reflect a clear intention to produce broader and squatter flakes, or simply that people were content with these products. Cores were probably worked with varying degrees of concern for the form of flakes. Yet as we shall see below, this may have been determined by the uses to which particular flakes were to be put.

Together with the general characteristics of scatters, this material indicates that the Later Neolithic saw a general decrease in the scale of routine mobility patterns. A move away from portable and adaptable tools, and the more profligate use of stone, might be expected in circumstances where routine movement over considerable distances was no longer a paramount concern. However, this only accounts for a part of the picture. Alongside these patterns we find evidence for the working of cores of a rather different character. These range from large split nodules, some of which may have been related to bifacial tool production, through to more consistent forms such as discoidal or levallois-style cores (fig. 55). These latter forms reflect the controlled and extensive preparation of stone for the removal of distinctive broad flakes. These flakes often served as 'blanks' for the production of arrowheads, and in the case of larger cores, may also have been a point of departure in the production of elaborate knives.

This more formal pattern of core reduction was both intentional, and of a different order to the production of broad and irregular flakes on many multi-platform cores. It is not possible to explain these rather more specialized forms as simple products of a change in mobility patterns. What they may reflect is the attribution of some significance to certain arrowheads and elaborate knives. In order to capture something of the roles that these items played, we must first explore the broader milieu in which they developed.

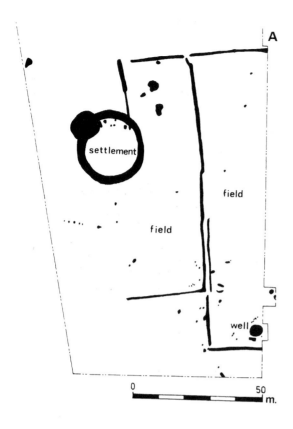

53 Plan of settlement features at Fengate, Cambridgeshire.

relatively uncommon in assemblages from many scatters and excavated sites. Long blades remain as a sporadic feature of Later Neolithic assemblages in many areas, but these generally appear to have been made as blanks for the production of retouched tools such as knives. In place of the emphasis upon blades and narrow flakes, we find a wider range of core forms, reflecting a variety of approaches to flake production, and a wider array of (often larger) tools.

This variety resists simple generalizations. In many cases, the form of cores reflects a decrease in the level of concern exercised in the preparation of platforms and in the controlled removal of more or less standardized flakes. Multi-platform cores – struck from all sides and occasionally reused as hammers, are often larger than Earlier Neolithic cores, and flakes tend to be broader and thicker than before. Platforms on

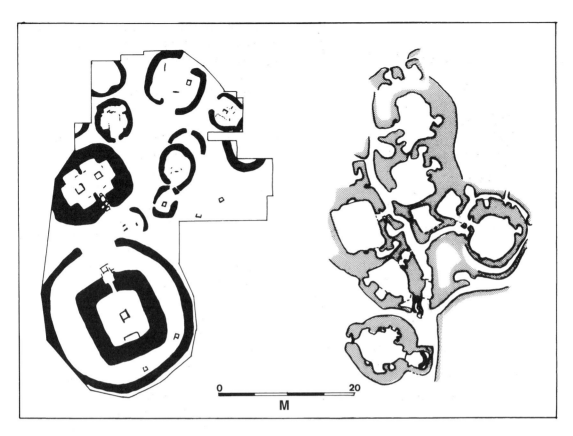

54 Outline plans of the settlements at Barnhouse (*left*) and Skara Brae (*right*) on Orkney. Evidence from Barnhouse suggests that the working of many materials was conducted at a household level and in the central area of the settlement. However, one house appears to have seen a greater degree of 'industrial' activity, marked by the presence of large quantities of pumice. Similar patterns can be seen at Skara Brae, where one structure appears to have been used as a context for the heat treatment of flint and chert. The heating of stone was sometimes undertaken to transform or otherwise enhance its flaking potential, and this has led to the interpretation of this house as a workshop. This can be contrasted with a house set apart from the main core of the settlement and the only other building retaining evidence for incised decoration on the walls. In this case, the interior of the house appears to have been left undisturbed; pottery, bone tools and other materials had been left *in situ* and the bodies of two women were found beneath the floor. Given these different material associations, it is possible that each building was accorded some broader symbolic significance. Perhaps each was conceptually linked to particular sections of the community. Such links are unlikely to have been static or monolithic. However, there may have been times when their use reaffirmed basic age or gender distinctions within the community.

## Regional traditions

In many areas, the final centuries of the Earlier Neolithic were marked by developments in a number of different fields of social practice. These included changes in funerary rites, and in some areas a greater concern with the individual in death. Developments can also be detected in the level of control exercised by certain groups over the activities conducted at enclosures and tombs.

In some cases this may have been tied to struggles for position within broader corporate systems, and to the use of the ancestors, exchange and other forms of ceremonial practice

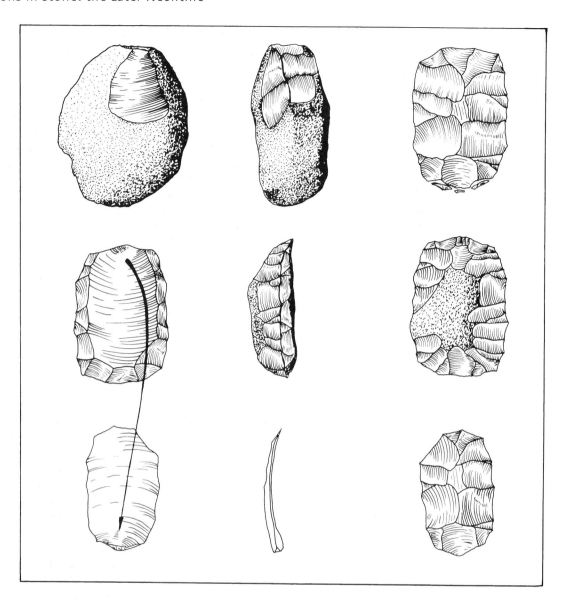

55 Principal stages in the preparation and working of a levallois core. The products of this way of working were often reworked to produce arrowheads and knives. Many of these tools may have served as markers of identity, and it is possible that this way of working stone was itself invested with a particular social significance.

as political resources. Competition for dominance or authority often involved the modification or elaboration of existing sites, but new monuments were also constructed. Occasionally these two strategies could even be combined, as was the case with massive bank barrows, such as those built over earlier enclosures at Maiden Castle, Dorset and Crickley Hill, Gloucestershire. The sheer scale of these

sites suggests that they were constructed to address an audience which extended beyond the immediate community.

A connection with the dead can be detected in another contemporary class of monument although here the links with funerary traditions took a rather different form. Cursus monuments are paired ditches with internal banks and closed ends which are found in many parts of Britain

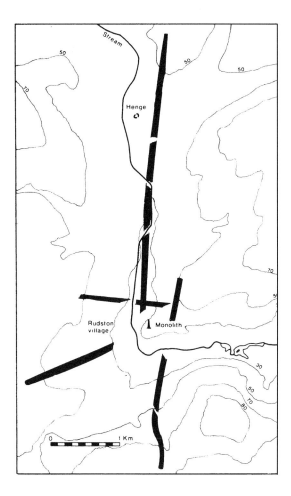

56 Concentration of cursus monuments at Rudston, Yorkshire.

others reflect several episodes of construction and extension. Although their particular roles are unclear, an association with ancestral rites and perhaps with seasonal gatherings and processions seems likely. This is particularly evident at the Dorset Cursus, which incorporates two long barrows and is aligned so as to highlight the setting of the midwinter sun (fig. 57). This massive earthwork separates two broad landscape zones, one dominated by evidence for settlement and the other by ceremonial sites. It appears to have remained a focus for various forms of activity for many later generations (fig. 58).

Ceramic assemblages bear witness to developments in the character and perhaps the role of pottery, with the emergence of decorated Peterborough Wares in southern and central Britain, and other regional variants. These new vessels appeared alongside undecorated forms, the shouldered Peterborough Wares with their unbounded decoration reflecting the gradual reworking and elaboration of elements within the Earlier Neolithic ceramic repertoire (fig. 59). This process continues during the third millennium, and variants within the Peterborough tradition, such as Mortlake, Ebbsfleet and Fengate Wares indicate changes in the character and distribution of decorative traits through time. As their names suggest, different ceramics may occur in different parts of Britain, and a series of 'style zones' have been postulated. However, these zones are by no means as distinct or discrete as we have often supposed, and are unlikely to reflect the territories of distinct ethnic groups. They probably reflect the localized reworking of a variety of themes and associations which crossed the boundaries of kinship, rather than an adherence to rigid regional templates. It has been suggested that pottery production may have been predominantly associated with women; under these circumstances, the blurring in the distribution patterns may be related to the movement of people (and thus ideas about form and decoration) through practices such as marriage outside the immediate community.

This process of recombining and elaborating morphological and decorative elements may have also had its source in the circumstances in which pots were often used. As Julian Thomas and others have pointed out, pottery may have

(fig. 56). They vary in size from several hundred metres, such as the Springfield Cursus in Essex, to the Dorset Cursus, which crosses nearly 10km (6 miles) of chalk downland. Although they may occur in isolation, it is also common to find small clusters of these sites incorporated in monumental complexes. This can be seen at Dorchester-on-Thames, at Llandegai in Gwynedd, and in eastern Yorkshire, where several cursus monuments converge on the imposing Rudston monolith.

Like causewayed enclosures, some cursus monuments were built relatively rapidly, while

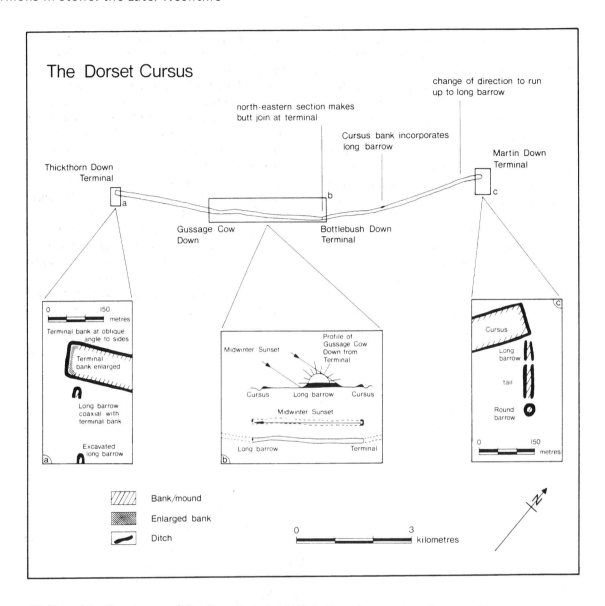

57 Plan of the Dorset cursus (after Barrett *et al.*, 1991). Laid out in a number of stages, this cursus appears to have served as a boundary between areas devoted to the dead and those parts of the landscape in which we find more evidence for settlement. Incorporating earlier tombs into its fabric, and aligned on the midwinter sunset, the monument remained a focus for funerary rites and periodic gatherings for many generations.

been employed not just as a household container, but also as a vessel of consumption in specialized rites and transactions from the earliest times. These roles may have varied from one time and from one region to another, but by the close of the Earlier Neolithic, decorated ceramics were an essential element in a number of important social practices. Secondary associations with long mounds, enclosures and cursus monuments, and links with round barrows, suggest that part of the significance of these vessels arose from their use in feasts and as offerings, particularly those connected to ancestral and other funerary rites.

As these examples indicate, many of the changes that mark the close of the Earlier Neolithic involved the drawing of connections with earlier times, places and practices. Where they were explicitly drawn, these references to the past may have masked novel claims to authority and may even have granted them a degree of legitimacy. However, the mid third millennium sees the emergence of new categories of site and artefact, and new forms of social practice, where this evocation of direct links with the past is rather less apparent. Taken together, these developments suggest that the Later Neolithic not only witnessed important changes in the social and political geography of Britain, but also a reworking of some of the basic categories or landmarks of the social world.

The character and timing of these developments varies markedly from one part of Britain to another, so much so that it is useful to divide the country into a series of regional systems. Distinctions can be drawn between these 'core areas' according to the varying degrees of emphasis placed on ancestral rites, the control of ritual and the supernatural, or the celebration of particular individuals as sources of power and authority. Just as these emphases are by no means clear-cut, so it may be inappropriate to attempt to define strict boundaries for these regional systems. However, useful distinctions can be drawn between areas such as Yorkshire, where personal prestige and authority appear to have been emphasised from an early stage, and Wessex, where a more explicit concern with the ancestors and the monuments of the past gives way to other forms of ceremonial activity.

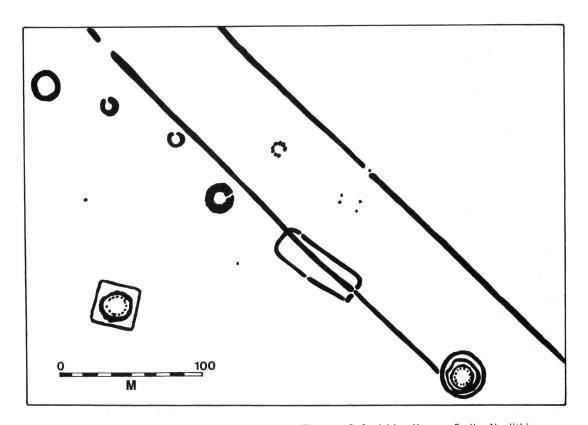

58 Detail of the monument complex at Dorchester-on-Thames, Oxfordshire. Here an Earlier Neolithic mortuary enclosure was cut/augmented by a larger cursus monument. The passage of time saw the addition of ring-ditches and henges to this complex and the use of the area for gatherings, processions and funerary rites. While the earliest components of the complex are aligned on important lunar events, the sun appears to have been the main point of reference for the builders and users of the later sites.

59 Peterborough Ware vessels (drawn by Chris Jones).

The development of regional differentiation can also be detected in tomb architecture and mortuary practices. With the gradual erosion of the long mound tradition comes the appearance of round barrow or ring ditch burials outside the north-east. Initially rare in Wessex, where activities around older tombs continued for some time, examples occur as far afield as the Thames valley and southern Scotland. The character and contents of these sites reflect a development of the concern with specific people – often adult men – that was suggested for some later long barrows and oval mounds. Part of this concern is manifest in the provision of a variety of grave goods, deposited with or on the bodies or cremated remains of individuals. These sites could be revisited, as at Duggleby Howe (Yorkshire), where a barrow inside a small causewayed enclosure was the focus for several later burials. In other cases, the evidence reflects a single event – the digging of a flat grave or the construction of a small cist – quite different from the repetitive use of ancestral tombs.

Rather different developments can be seen elsewhere. In parts of western and northern Britain, earlier tombs give way to developed passage graves, many of which incorporate important celestial events such as the midwinter sunrise or sunset into their main axis. It is only towards the end of the third millennium that a tradition of individual burial makes a firm imprint in these regions. On Anglesey for example, areas defined by the presence of several chambered tombs saw the construction of large round mounds such as Bryn Celli Ddu and Barclodiad y Gawres, characterized by a central chamber reached via a long passage. This sequence may reflect a shift of emphasis, away from household or family tombs towards sites which placed the ancestral realm in the hands of specific groups. Similar sites are found further to the north, reflecting the existence of extensive networks of contact and communication along the Atlantic seaboard of Britain. They include Quanterness and Maes Howe on Orkney, which may have been broadly contemporary with the settlements at Skara Brae and Barnhouse (fig. 60). Variations on a similar theme can be seen in the Clava cairns of north-east Scotland, and in the entrance graves of the south-west, but the best-known examples are found in the Boyne valley in Ireland, many of which are decorated with elaborate and abstract carvings.

Although the burial of single individuals is not the dominant theme in these areas for some time, access to these tombs was probably restricted. Moreover, the physical arrangement of the interior of many sites, the use of areas of light and darkness, and the placement of different designs, may all have provided cues or frames for the classification of different deposits and different people. This may have been particularly important in the case of sites like Quanterness, where the substantial deposits reflect the bringing together of human remains collected from other tombs. Working from the details of their form and contents, Colin

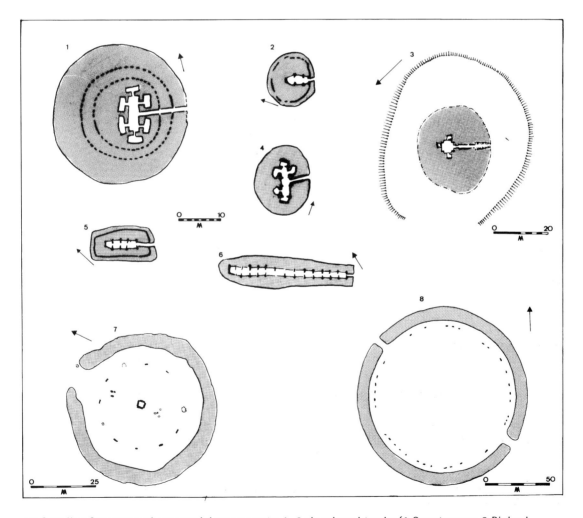

60 Orcadian funerary and ceremonial monuments: 1–6 chambered tombs (1 Quanterness; 2 Bigland Round; 3 Maes Howe; 4 Isbister; 5 Knowe of Yarso; 6 Knowe of Ramsay). 7–8 henge monuments (7 Stones of Stenness; 8 Ring of Brodgar).

89

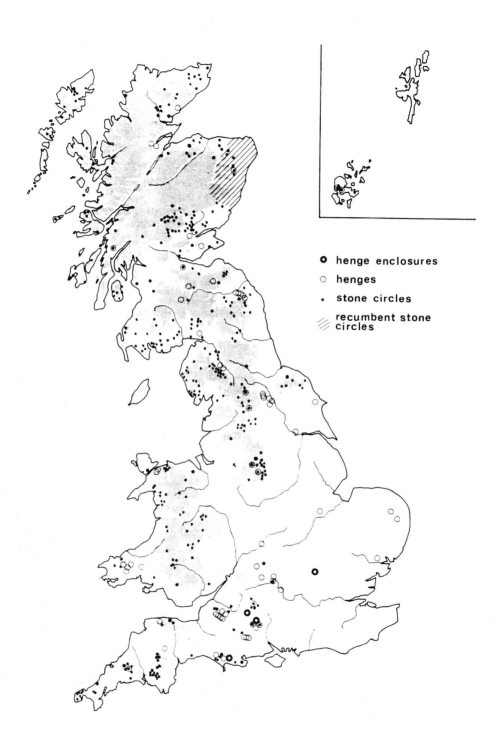

○ **henge enclosures**

○ **henges**

• **stone circles**

⁄⁄ **recumbent stone circles**

61 Distribution of henges and stone circles in Britain (after Darvill 1987).

Richards has suggested that sites such as Quanterness provided a medium through which a small section of the living community were able to monopolize the ancestors and their powers. He also argues that the principles of order and orientation underlying the layout of these sites can be found in the spatial arrangements that typify contemporary domestic contexts such as Barnhouse. For example, the largest house at this site shares a number of structural features with Maes Howe. Equally, many of the hearths on settlement sites appear to have been aligned on the position of the rising and setting sun at both midsummer and midwinter. This suggests that in life, as in death, the spatial and social organization of people's activities may have been informed by general cosmological principles.

The Later Neolithic also sees the appearance of henges and large stone circles (fig. 61). Henges are large public monuments defined by a circular ditch and an external bank, with between one and four entrances. They vary in size from small 'hengiform' sites, through to the massive henge enclosures of Wessex such as Marden. Here again, marked regional differentiation is apparent. For example, henges first appear in northern Scotland, and perhaps in Ireland. Some of the earliest dated sites, such as Stenness and the Ring of Brodgar, are found on Orkney, where their construction may mark a decline in the importance of passage tombs. Several centuries appear to have elapsed before similar sites occur further south, and it is again possible to differentiate between areas such as the Thames valley or north Yorkshire, where clusters of small henges create a ceremonial focus, and parts of Wessex, where massive sites like Durrington Walls and Mount Pleasant were constructed.

These variations reveal important regional differences in the extent to which large amounts of labour were mobilized for the construction of ceremonial monuments. This in turn may indicate differences in the level of political centralization from one area to another, but it is also clear that some of the monument complexes that are visible today are the result of many generations of activity. This may even apply to individual sites, where later monuments may have drawn upon or altered the significance already ascribed to a particular place. In the case of henges, earthworks may have been added to existing sites, defined by arrangements of timber posts and other structures. This appears to have happened at Balfarg in Scotland, while at Dorchester-on-Thames in Oxfordshire, and Thornborough in Yorkshire, henges were built upon or adjacent to existing monuments. Earthworks themselves could also be augmented over time. At Avebury, successive phases of activity saw the erection of the stone circle within the area defined by the bank and ditch, and the addition of avenues which linked the site to other points in the landscape. Equally long and complex sequences of development can be traced at Mount Pleasant and Stonehenge.

Like some of the earlier tombs and cursus monuments, the form and orientation of some Later Neolithic ceremonial sites demonstrates a concern with movements in the heavens. Basic celestial alignments have been identified at a number of sites, including the large stone circles of Cumbria. This need not mean that astronomical observation was their sole purpose. Rather, they probably reflect a concern with scheduling important gatherings and social events in tempo with celestial and seasonal rhythms. They also indicate that the realm of the supernatural was of some importance to the living. Links with the heavens and the supernatural may have helped to sustain an air of mystery and perhaps a sacred dimension to these events, embedding the actions of people within broader conceptual schemes. Indeed, ritual knowledge, including details of celestial alignments, may have been the preserve of certain people or groups within society, and, as such, a source of authority and an object of competition.

It is difficult and probably inappropriate to try to specify single functions for henges and stone circles. Some of the smaller sites were used or reused as cremation cemeteries, as at Stonehenge and Dorchester-on-Thames, and fragmentary human remains are by no means uncommon at many henges. However, like the earlier enclosures, dealings with the dead may have comprised only one aspect of their use. Many of these arenas saw the periodic congregation of large numbers of people; indeed, their construction and subsequent elaboration would itself have required vast quantities of labour. Feasting, or the large-scale consumption of

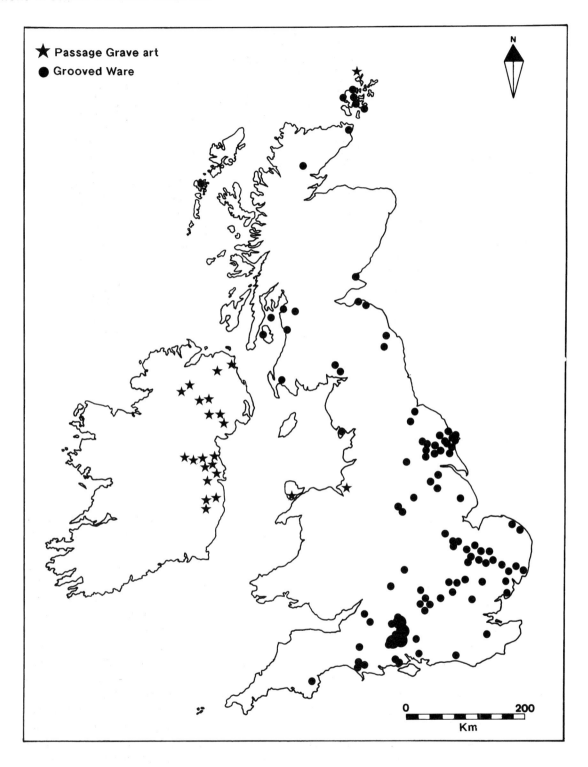

62 Distribution of passage grave art and Grooved Ware in Britain.

63 Grooved Ware vessels (drawn by Chris Jones).

pork, appears to have been an integral part of these events, and many henges seem to have provided a focus for the purposive deposition of a variety of artefacts.

We shall return to these practices later on, but one category of artefact serves to highlight what at first sight appears to be a paradox. While certain lines of evidence point to a measure of regionalization in Later Neolithic Britain, others suggest the existence of complex lines of contact between different areas. In a number of regions, henges show a close association with Grooved Ware, a distinctive class of flat-based pottery which also occurs in Later Neolithic pits. Like the monuments themselves, Grooved Ware seems to have been in use in northern Scotland several centuries before it occurs in the south, and its appearance marks a break with established ceramic traditions, even though these continued to be used. Grooved Ware pots are generally much larger than other contemporary

vessels, and are often characterized by applied cordons and bounded decorative motifs, many of which have their source in the art of Irish passage graves (fig. 62).

The particular meanings of these symbols lie beyond our grasp, but what is important is that Grooved Ware, like many of the monuments described above, reflects the existence of complex networks of interaction that stretched across large areas of Britain (fig. 63). Given its size and composition, Grooved Ware was probably made locally in most areas, and this suggests that it was ideas as much as objects and people, which travelled along these lines. These not only included ideas relating to the form, decoration and use of pottery and other artefacts, but also concerning the form of monuments and the character of their use. Like the motifs found in passage graves and on Grooved Ware, the ways in which these concepts were understood and drawn upon probably varied from one regional

93

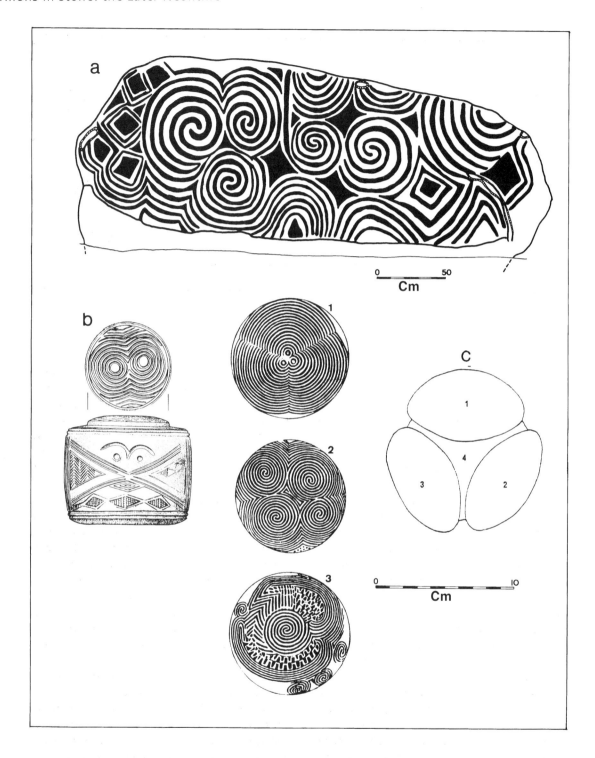

64 In addition to Grooved Ware, motifs derived from passage grave art are found on a variety of portable items. Here the entrance stone from the tomb at Newgrange in Ireland is shown above a decorated chalk drum from Folkton, Yorkshire, and the three faces of a carved stone ball from Towie in Aberdeenshire.

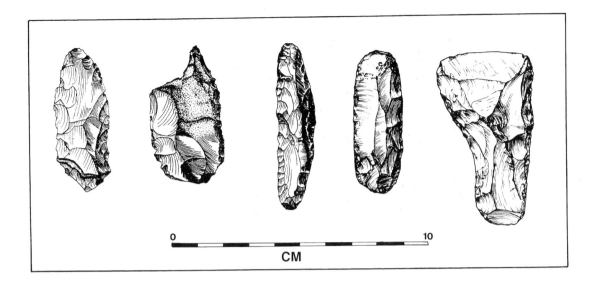

65 Later Neolithic flint fabricators, borer and flaked axe.

tradition to another. However, it does seem that exotica – objects, motifs and ideas derived from distant sources – played an increasingly important role in moulding the social and political contours of the Later Neolithic (fig. 64).

## Assemblage variability

These broad sequences of change find echoes in stone tool assemblages. As noted above, the mid third millennium bc marks a broad threshold across which changes in the character of core working can be detected; some of these reflect a general impoverishment or lack of control in stoneworking, but others indicate a measure of specialization or formality in the steps taken to produce flakes. At the very least, this suggests that no single model or explanation can account for the characteristics and roles of all stone tools at this time.

A similar degree of complexity can be detected in the retouched tools that were made and used during the period. While far from standardized, Earlier Neolithic assemblages were characterized by a relatively restricted range of artefact types. Moreover, when axes are taken out of the equation, variation between assemblages is generally continuous and not particularly marked. Although a few artefacts occasionally became

'objects of thought' to be drawn upon in social discourse, the ideas that they carried were largely unconsidered, and the degree of conscious strategy behind their use was probably low. This situation changes towards the middle of the third millennium with the appearance of a significantly wider variety of artefacts. Not only that, several lines of evidence suggest the operation of a series of subtle conventions regarding the conditions under which a number of these artefacts could be made and the circumstances in which their use and deposition was possible. This protocol even extended to encompass rules of combination with other artefacts and materials. These conventions were by no means rigid, but by the Later Neolithic, the social dimensions of some artefacts appear to have played an active part in determining the manner in which they were treated.

These changes in the character of stone tool assemblages stem from a variety of sources. On the one hand, the period sees an increase in the range of crude core and flake tools, including picks, rod-like implements and smaller bifacially flaked pieces, particularly in areas where raw material was in plentiful supply (fig. 65). Many lack any clear or consistent definition of form and reflect a high degree of expediency and variability in production and use. Moreover, few show signs

95

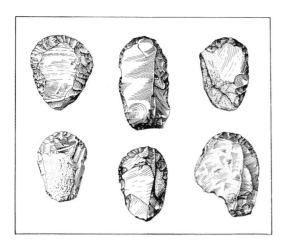

66 Later Neolithic flint scrapers.

of any attempt to follow consistent flaking routines, and there seems to have been little concern with the avoidance of errors and mis-hits during production. Earlier Neolithic parallels for some of these artefacts are generally restricted to mines and quarries, but by the latter part of the period, their distribution is far more widespread.

In keeping with the trend away from narrow flakes and blades, this increase in the frequency and distribution of large, crude artefacts accords with the idea that routine mobility was no longer as important as it had been. Like the bulk of the flakes made on multi-platform cores, these implements were probably produced and used in the context of a variety of activities, then discarded with little formality. Some would have been particularly well suited to tasks such as digging, either in the context of exploiting surface deposits of stone or during cultivation. However, a strong association with these or other specific tasks has yet to be demonstrated, and it seems more likely that the production and use of these tools was unrestricted, both in practical and in social terms.

Similar arguments can probably be applied to many scrapers. Scrapers remain one of the most common forms found on Later Neolithic sites (fig. 66), but subtle changes can be identified. These take the form of a gradual decrease in the frequency of endscrapers made on blades or narrow flakes, and are in keeping with broader technological trends. In their place there is an emphasis upon scrapers with retouch extending along one or both sides, as well as at the distal end of flakes. Although irregular forms are by no means uncommon, many scrapers display a measure of symmetry along their long axis. In the case of large, invasively flaked 'horseshoe' or disc-like scrapers, this form may have been maintained through reflaking once an edge had become worn.

The vast majority of scrapers were probably made and used under much the same conditions as they had been for many generations, and if they carried any specific significance at all, this was probably derived from their immediate association with the individuals who made and used them. As in the Earlier Neolithic, this may have made them appropriate elements for deposition in localized rites, but the vast majority were probably discarded with little comment or acknowledgement. However, one relatively rare class can be distinguished in terms of the manner in which it was made and the conditions under which it was occasionally deposited. Flint scrapers with ground and polished edges have been noted in a number of areas, particularly Yorkshire, where one was recovered from a pit associated with Grooved Ware at Rudston Wold East.

Edge-ground scrapers are one of a range of artefacts found in Later Neolithic contexts which depart from the patterns associated with larger, crudely flaked tools and retouched flakes. While a number of elements in contemporary assemblages point to a general downturn in the level of control or precision exercised in stoneworking, a few artefacts display characteristics which suggest just the opposite. These include elaborate flint and stone axes and adzes, plano-convex, discoidal and polished knives, specialized arrowheads, carved stone balls, polished or finely flaked chisels, laurel leaves and maceheads. Together with jet items, bone pins, boars' tusks and carved chalk objects, some of these artefacts occur as exotica in areas remote from their sources, and many appear to have been accorded a measure of special treatment. Occasionally this is manifest in the character and context of their production, their pristine condition or their patent lack of utility. For the majority, however, a special status can be inferred from the circumstances attending their deposition.

Varied combinations of these artefacts have been recovered from burials, hoards and other formal deposits, and a series of structuring principles seem to have guided their association with Peterborough and Grooved Wares in different contexts. The character of associations with different ceramic styles varies from one region to another, but in general, it is more common to find a closer association between Grooved Ware and exotic items such as stone axes. Given the distribution of both Peterborough and Grooved Ware, this is unlikely to reflect the existence of distinct cultural groups. It may in fact relate to the drawing of distinctions within groups regarding the conditions under which certain artefacts could be used and deposited by specific sections of the community, particularly in the context of important rites or celebrations. Distinctions can even be detected at a broader level. Regional survey has shown that many of these elaborate or exotic items cluster in or close to monuments – a pattern found in areas as far apart as Wessex, the Peak District, Yorkshire and mainland Orkney.

## The social dimensions of stone

How are we to understand these patterns? Together with their physical character, the restricted distribution and contexts of these artefacts has long been taken as evidence that some were accorded significance as valuables. However, this means very little until we ask how their production, circulation and deposition were organized, and explore the roles that they may have played in contemporary society.

Attempts to make sense of these patterns have taken a wide variety of forms, but one of the more persistent arguments is that the Later Neolithic witnessed the development of prestige-goods systems. Drawn from a number of anthropological studies, prestige-goods models start from the idea that dominant or elite groups within a society may create and maintain their position by controlling the production, circulation or consumption of status items and other symbolic resources in ranked or restricted spheres. Much the same ideas underlie the concept of peer-polity interaction. In this case, it is

argued that dominant groups in different regional settings engage in socially restricted exchanges with each other in order to obtain objects that they may subsequently deploy as status items. These objects mark wider connections and alliances, and are at the same time restricted enough to serve as important media in local networks of gift exchange.

It is easy to understand why these general models have enjoyed a measure of popularity. They appear to make sense of some of the data, in particular, the movement of objects and even ideas from one part of Britain to another. More importantly, they recognize that the political relations that are built on such a basis are often fluid, competitive and inherently unstable. The significance or exclusive character of particular status items can be easily undermined through emulation and through changes in the conditions under which they are acquired and used by different sections within society. Control over production may be difficult to maintain, and new networks of alliance and exchange may create different conditions for the acquisition of important wealth items.

This perspective finds its clearest expression in Richard Bradley's discussion of the changing character of Neolithic ceramics (fig. 67). Following the sequence from undecorated vessels through to Peterborough and Grooved Wares and beyond, he suggests that each category was initially highly specialized, and associated with a restricted range of practices and people. With the passage of time these status items became objects of competition and emulation by others: their special status or significance was gradually undermined, creating the need for innovation and for the definition of new and exclusive categories of decorated vessel.

These ideas are useful, but they may not provide a sufficient basis for understanding the varied conditions under which objects may have circulated during the Later Neolithic, nor perhaps the trend towards regionalization itself. In the first place, the increased emphasis upon exotica does not have to be seen as the product of direct, long-distance transactions between different regional elites. Rather, it probably reflects the passage of objects through a series of overlapping exchange networks established

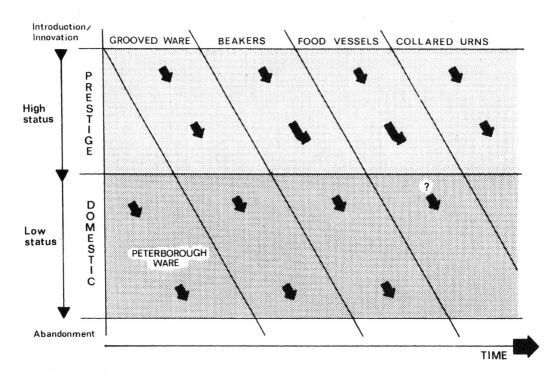

67 The changing significance of ceramic traditions during the Neolithic and Early Bronze Age as proposed by Richard Bradley (after Darvill 1987).

between different communities. In other words, it may be simplistic to think of these core areas or regional systems as largely discrete or distinct entities. We may be dealing with a series of different local traditions which lacked clear boundaries, and which were, in fact, connected at a variety of different levels.

Equally, it is probably simplistic to assume that a prestige-goods model really accounts for more than a fraction of the patterns that we can recognize. As we shall see in chapter 5, competition for certain status items or symbolic resources was probably important, as was the creation of extensive networks of contact and alliance. Moreover, the manipulation of objects and ideas derived from distant sources would have provided a variety of potentials for both creating and protecting local structures of authority and dominance. However, the production, circulation and deposition of stone tools was probably harnessed to a much broader range of social imperatives. Some of these may have been far more prosaic and localized.

This may also have been the case with pottery. Although they may have played specialized roles, the Later Neolithic sequence may reflect the emergence of different classes of ceramics for different social practices, rather than the simple succession of categories of elite paraphernalia. Perhaps some vessels were more appropriate for use in rites which spoke of the local order of things, while others were more commonly associated with the celebration of the exotic and the supernatural. These possibilities are difficult to explore, and this may be one of the reasons why prestige-goods models feature so strongly in the literature. However, the evidence from several regions provides clues as to the ways in which stone tools were caught up in the reproduction of more localized categories and relations.

## Points of contention

We can begin by considering the changing character and context of arrowheads. As long ago as 1935, Graham Clark drew attention to an apparent

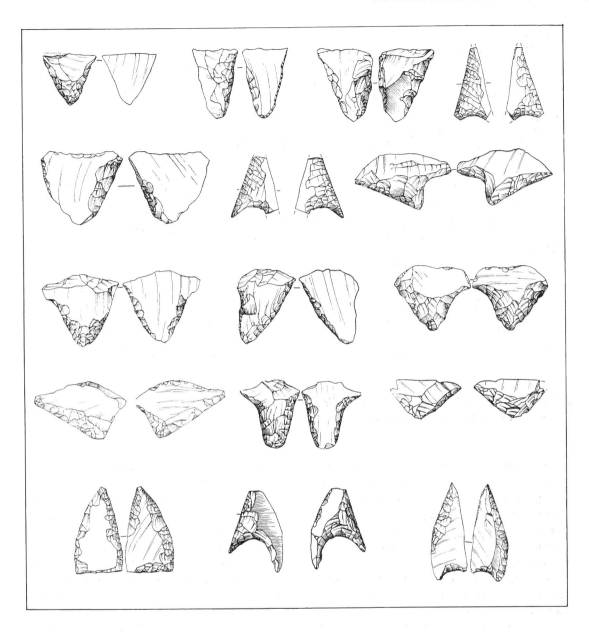

68 Later Neolithic arrowhead forms (after Clark 1935).

increase in the diversity of arrowhead forms in the Later Neolithic. Although leaf- or kite-shaped points persisted for some time, they now appear as elements within a wider array of distinctive projectiles, including 'petit-tranchet derivative' transverse, chisel and oblique forms (fig. 68). While it may be unnecessary to adhere to all nine of Clark's original 'types', this increase in variability is nonetheless clear. Equally clear is the lack of any strong regional dimension to these patterns beyond a concentration of ripple-flaked oblique arrowheads in Yorkshire. In other words, it is difficult to see this proliferation of forms as a simple reflection of cultural preferences or shared ways of working in different regions of Britain. Nor is it easy to explain these patterns entirely in functional terms. The implication to be drawn from this is that the form of arrowheads was a

99

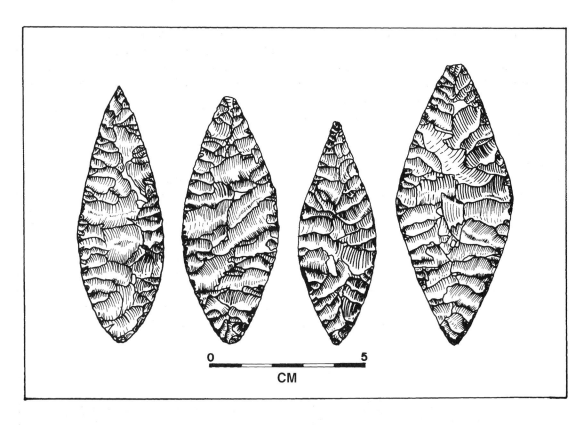

69 Elaborately flaked leaf-points from a burial at Winterborne Stoke, Wiltshire.

more active issue in social discourse than it had been during the Earlier Neolithic.

This is also suggested by the contexts in which different examples have been recovered. Transverse or chisel arrowheads have a widespread distribution in many parts of Britain. However, a small number have been found in association with burials, and in Yorkshire at least, chisel forms are often found in assemblages containing Peterborough Ware. By contrast, oblique forms display a pronounced clustering which is difficult to understand as a product of chance loss. They have also been recovered from mortuary contexts, and in the case of burial 7 at Duggleby Howe, they occur together with transverse forms. Significant densities are found close to monuments, or to monument complexes such as Rudston in Yorkshire. They also occur in henges such as Durrington Walls, and display a close association with Grooved Ware, not only in these contexts but also in formal pit deposits.

A further dimension can be added to these patterns. The vast majority of arrowheads were made widely, many requiring no more than a few minutes from the creation of a flake to the finishing of the tool. However, some were also the products of distinctive cores, while others, such as ripple-flaked forms with their striking parallel scars, display a concern with form and elaboration which probably had little to do with questions of utility. Distinctive 'tortoise' or levallois cores cluster within larger scatters of lithic material in a number of areas, including coastal Yorkshire, parts of Wessex and the Thames valley. Although larger examples may have been used to produce blanks for knives, many were also closely associated with the production of arrowheads.

These spatial distinctions may be significant. They suggest that while many tools were made widely, perhaps even communally, the production of certain artefacts may have been restricted to specific working areas within a settlement. As in the case of Barnhouse and Skara Brae, certain zones within settlements may have been closely associated with particular activities and with those sections of the community who traditionally performed those tasks. As a result, the physical layout of settlements may also have served as a basic 'map' of some of the distinctions and divisions which animated those communities. Similar practical and social distinctions may have been sustained where the production of particular tools was more or less confined to workshops in settlements further to the south. This has been suggested for ripple-flaked forms in Yorkshire. These have their highest densities close to the Bridlington coast and in the vicinity of Rudston, and some have argued that they may be the products of a specific workshop or even a single craftsman. Although this last possibility seems unlikely, the pattern does suggest that production itself was structured and perhaps restricted in some way.

Taken together, these patterns suggest that what had long been a simple but distinctive item of male gear became a vehicle for making more explicit and complex statements about the identity of a person (fig. 69). These statements may have made some reference to the tasks with which archery was associated, but it is difficult to separate each type on functional grounds. However, the decline of the leaf shape – an excellent piercing design – in favour of forms less likely to kill may indicate a change in the nature of hunting, and perhaps in the nature of conflict.

Unlike earlier leaf-shaped forms, there is less evidence that later arrowheads brought about the death of people, nor do we find concentrations associated with assaults on major sites. In other words, the development of the Later Neolithic may have seen a shift away from open conflict, where the killing of opponents was the primary aim, towards a series of more graded

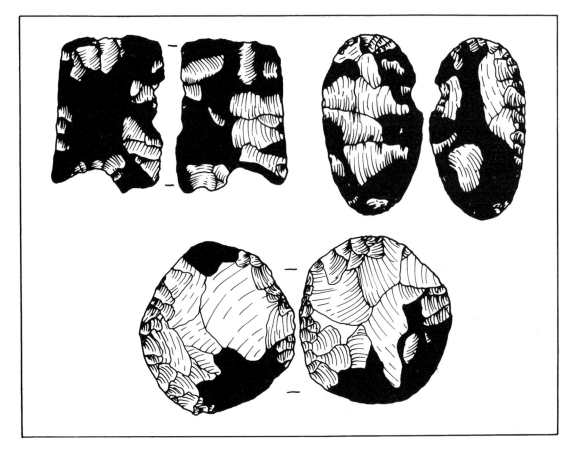

70 Flaked and partially polished flint knives.

encounters. Restrictions on the character and scale of violence are by no means unknown in our own society, where tensions at both a national and international level may be dealt with in different ways according to broader economic and political conditions. In the case of the Neolithic, however, boundaries and sanctions may have separated skirmishes and cattle raids from more ritualized forms of combat. Under these circumstances, participation, display and performance may often have been more important than actually killing an opponent. For that reason, arrowheads capable of producing shallow, but wide and profusely bleeding wounds may have been more appropriate.

In effect, while archery remained as a distinctively male activity, the form of the arrowhead itself (perhaps along with hafts, bows and quivers) came into focus as an object of thought in the Later Neolithic. Sometimes made under specialized conditions, these artefacts may reflect a tendency towards controlling the production or circulation of personal items as was suggested

for certain axes. In this case, however, it may have been accomplished through the demarcation of areas and/or people within settlements, rather than through the physical separation of a source from the world of day-to-day activity. This local aspect to production may mean that the significance of these forms also lay close to home. Arrowheads may have taken on a more active role in defining the status and identity of a person, not only in terms of their gender, but also their position within particular age classes, or within broader networks of affiliation.

## Elaboration and display

The tendency towards proliferation and elaboration can also be seen in other classes of artefact. Flaked and ground or polished chisels occur more widely and in greater numbers than before, as do a variety of knives, from laurel leaves through to discoidal and plano-convex forms (fig. 70). Some of these knives display traces of grinding and polishing, either on their edges, or

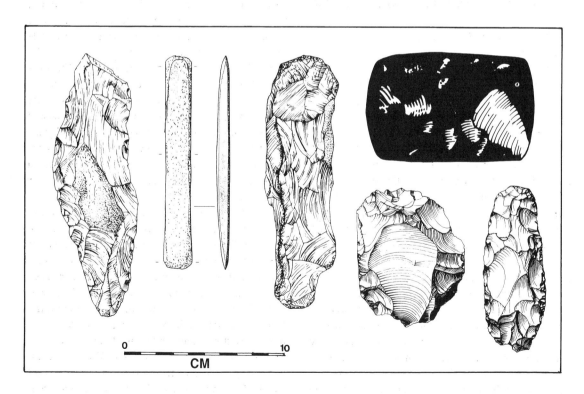

71 Later Neolithic stone tools: crude picks; ground stone chisel, polished flint knife and discoidal or levallois core.

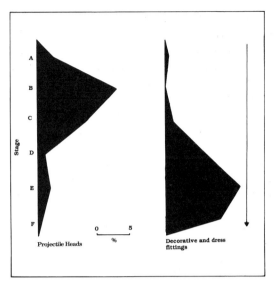

73 Model of the changing character of grave associations during the third millennium (after Kinnes 1979).

72 The York hoard. This dramatic array demonstrates the emphasis that was placed upon the selection of distinctive raw materials as well as a concern with the elaboration of artefact forms (National Museum of Scotland and Yorkshire Museum).

over their entire surfaces – a practice taken to its logical conclusion with the spectacular rectangular knife found with a burial at Duggleby Howe. Some of these knives may have been made on flakes from specialized cores, and the possibility exists that their production may also have been socially restricted. Examples have also been recovered in association with other materials in pits, and as elements within stone hoards.

These artefacts illustrate an increasing concern with important themes in stone tool production. The elaboration of tools, or the creation of distinctive patterns through flaking and/or grinding is manifest in many areas and on a variety of classes of artefact. Like the polishing of axes, this concern with form and appearance may have been one of the means by which artefacts were made more recognizable. It may thus signal a concern

with the closer definition of artefact categories which in some sense 'stood for' people. Indeed, the simple proliferation of tools in the Later Neolithic reflects a greater concern with the differentiation of people through the medium of the tools that they carried and used (fig. 71). This may also account for a trend in funerary associations identified by Ian Kinnes, who suggests that the passage of the third millennium saw a marked increase in the range of artefacts buried with people (fig. 72). Although projectile points dominate at an early stage, this gives way to an emphasis on a much wider range of artefacts, including other tools and decorative items (fig. 73).

In other cases, this process of definition was initiated at an earlier point in the production process. This can be seen in Yorkshire, where the circulation and formal treatment of stone was important from an early stage. Imported stone axes, particularly those from Cumbria, were already circulating in this region during the Earlier Neolithic. By the later phase, the roles played by these items may have been augmented by a range of highly distinctive flint artefacts, including elaborate flint axes, maceheads, and some of the knives, chisels and arrowheads discussed above. Many are made from raw material obtained within the region.

103

74 Flaked and polished scrapers, chisels, knives and axes (Museum of Archaeology and Anthropology, Cambridge).

The sources for many of these artefacts were the substantial coastal deposits of flint that can still be seen in the vicinity of Flamborough Head, where massive surface scatters suggest a concentration of productive activity. At Beacon Hill, small excavations within a large scatter resulted in the recovery of production debris, together with unpolished flint axes, tortoise cores and discoidal knives. Stone axes, including two from Cumbria, were also recovered. Although most of these materials were not exotic in the strict sense of the term, aspects of their character suggest a similar concern with recognition and thus with the maintenance of specific categories (fig. 74). For example, many axes appear to have been made of flint selected because of its distinctive colour. Axes of orange, red and banded or mottled flint have been recognized in a variety of contexts in eastern Britain, from East Anglia up to southern Scotland. Their

distribution is similar to that identified for stone maceheads by Fiona Roe, and attests to the importance of lines of contact and communication running along the eastern coast. The use of distinctive pieces of flint for axe production has also been noted in southern England.

Given the characteristics of flint, particularly when derived from coastal deposits, it is often impossible to determine precise locations within a general source area. However, this emphasis upon distinctive raw materials does suggest that some importance was attached to the ability to recognize the context from which certain items were derived. Whether these contexts took the form of specialized workshops remains unclear, but the production of at least some artefacts may have come under close local supervision. This may have facilitated the association of classes of artefact with specific people. Carried and displayed on an everyday basis or in the context of

75 Polished flint axes from Smerrick, Banffshire. The distinctive form and mottling of these axes suggests that they may have been made in southern Scandinavia (National Museum of Scotland).

important ceremonies, the distinctive characteristics of these artefacts may have made them valuable as markers of a person's standing in the community. In other cases, the special character of production may have been more directly geared towards the roles that certain artefacts played in exchange.

These themes find their clearest expression in the case of axes (fig. 75). While stone axes continued to circulate, the Later Neolithic sees important changes in the character of distribution patterns. For example, Cumbrian axes persist in Yorkshire throughout the period, but by the later third millennium, they rarely occur further to the south, where axes from Cornwall are found in increasing numbers. These shifting distribution patterns are by no means clear-cut, but they may signal changes in the orientation of networks of alliance and exchange through time,

reflecting some of the difficulties encountered in maintaining the pathways along which important status items circulated.

Other characteristics of axes may reflect similar themes. Although a clear sequence of changing types is not apparent, there seems little doubt that the Later Neolithic saw an increased concern with the form of axes (fig. 76). As the evidence from Great Langdale suggests, this concern may have increased prior to the close of the Earlier Neolithic, but by the mid third millennium bc, it is taken a stage further. Carefully ground side facets on large Cumbrian axes are also found on examples made of flint and Irish porcellanite, and may reflect a deliberate attempt to emulate exotic or important forms in other materials. A similar pattern has been noted in south-east England, where Andrew Herne has suggested that the wide blades of some Later

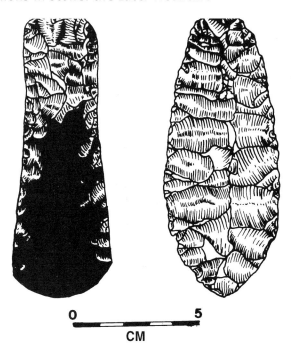

76 Edge polished axe and elaborate flint knife from Biggar Common, Lanarkshire.

Neolithic flint axes evoke the characteristic form of imports from Cornwall.

Once again, the most dramatic examples are to be found in Yorkshire (fig. 77). At Whitegrounds, the body of an adult male dated to 2570 bc + 90 was placed in the centre of an existing cairn. Associated with the body was a belt fitting made of jet and an elaborate waisted axe with a finely polished cutting edge (fig. 78). Similar forms have been identified elsewhere, leading Terry Manby to suggest the existence of distinct classes. These 'Duggleby' and 'Seamer' types take their names from the circumstances in which they have been recovered (fig. 79). Closely associated with funerary contexts and hoards, they were probably never intended for use, and the high quality and precision of their production has been taken as evidence for the existence of craft specialists. This remains open to debate, but whatever the case, it does seem that the period saw an increased concern with the definition of forms which could stand for people (fig. 80).

Although the picture of axe production and consumption is comparatively rich, these were

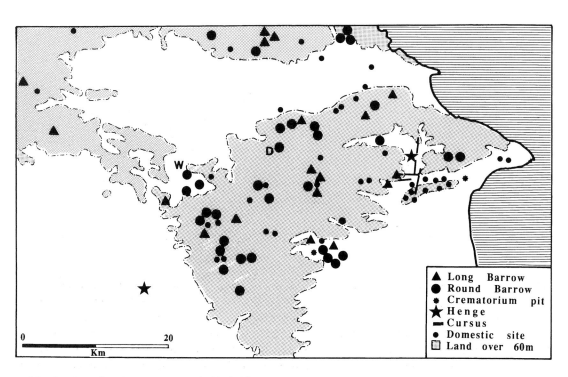

77 Distribution of major monuments in Yorkshire.

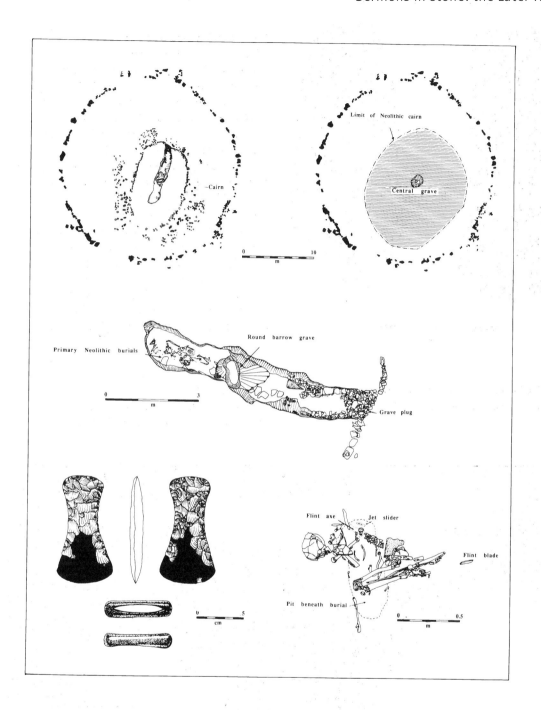

78 Burial patterns at Whitegrounds, Yorkshire. The first phase at this site saw disarticulated human remains placed in a grave beneath a low cairn. After an interval of time the site was reused, becoming the focus for the articulated burial of a man with a polished jet belt-slider and a distinctive 'Seamer' axe. Whether or not there was any continuity of observance between these two events will never be known, but it is likely that the reuse of the site represented an attempt to draw upon its historical associations as a way of giving meaning and importance to the secondary burial. The objects buried in this secondary grave may have spoken of the identity of the deceased and his standing in the community.

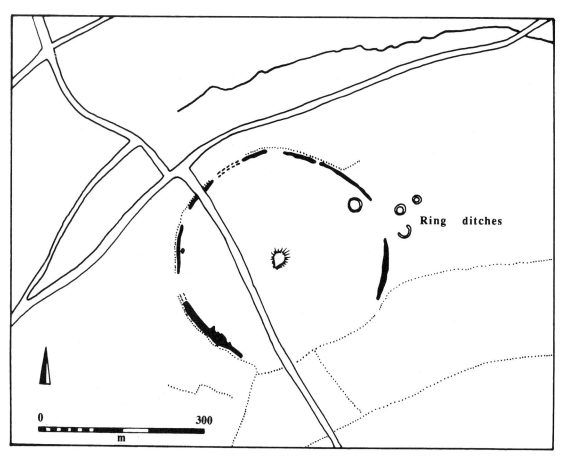

Ring    ditches

79 Outline plan of the monument at Duggleby Howe, Yorkshire (after Kinnes *et al.*, 1983).

by no means the only artefacts to carry social and perhaps political weight. Alongside axes, adzes and elaborate knives, the Later Neolithic also saw the production of perforated maceheads and carved stone balls. It is possible that many of these distinctive and occasionally enigmatic artefacts played similar roles in defining categories of person. Indeed, with the passage of time, some may even have come to usurp or replace artefacts such as axes as important tokens of value and identity. This is particularly intriguing in the case of stone maceheads (fig. 81), which may have been developed to emulate or refer to earlier examples made in antler. These earlier forms are relatively rare, but examples have been found in funerary contexts such as Duggleby Howe in Yorkshire and Liff's Low in Derbyshire (fig. 82).

The vast majority of maceheads were pecked and ground into shape, and for that reason there is very little evidence for the conditions under which they were produced. Like axes, it is probable that many were made where time and raw materials allowed, while others were created at more specialized sources. Work by Fiona Roe and others has shown that many ovoid, pestle and cushion maceheads were made on pebbles and other erratic material, particularly in north-eastern England and Scotland. However, many reflect the same concern with the selection of distinctive and easily recognizable raw materials. Some were made of stone from sources that had previously witnessed axe production including those in Cumbria, north Wales and along Whin Sill in the north-east. A small number of maceheads even reflect the reworking of polished axes into new forms. Maceheads have their closest associations

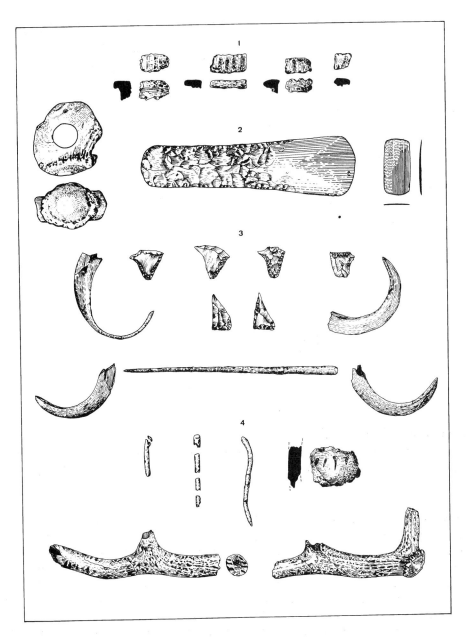

80 Selected artefacts from a sequence of burials in the mound at Duggleby Howe. The body of a man was laid in a central shaft grave accompanied by a shallow bowl, two flint cores and a series of flakes. The bodies of an adult and child and fragments of a third human skull were incorporated in the filling of this grave. Following these interments came the burial of a man with a series of objects which lay close to his chest. These included the 'Duggleby-style' adze and antler macehead shown. Close at hand lay another burial of an adult with a polished flint knife placed next to his face. There may have been an interval of time before further burials were added to the site. These included adult inhumations accompanied by arrowheads, bone pins and tools made from boar's tusks and beaver incisors, and further bodies of adults and children with no material associations. Later still came a series of cremation deposits arranged concentrically around the centre of the mound. These were finally sealed when the mound was enlarged with chalk rubble (after Kinnes et al., 1983).

109

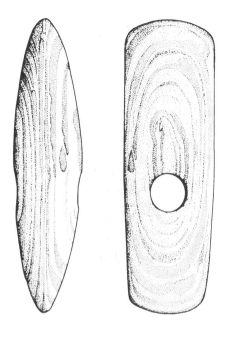

81 Perforated macehead/reworked axe made from Group XXIV hornfels (drawn by Marion O'Neil).

with Grooved Ware, and are thus a relatively late development in the Neolithic sequence. Occasionally faceted or decorated, they continued in use during the Early Bronze Age.

The function of maceheads is difficult to determine. A few were clearly never intended for anything other than display, but others may have served an immediate practical purpose. Some perhaps saw service as hammers, but it is also possible that many were used as weapons. As such, they may reflect something of the qualities that defined people's standing in the community. As martial symbols or metaphors for fighting, they suggest that the final stages of the Neolithic saw an increased concern with the role played by particular individuals in the resolution of local conflicts between different communities or kin groups. The use of maceheads as weapons, and as reminders of the role that certain people were bound to play in protecting communal interests, was probably important. It may have been these roles that were referred to where they were used as grave goods, as at Site 2 at Dorchester-on-

82 Selected grave goods from Liff's Low, Derbyshire (National Museum of Scotland).

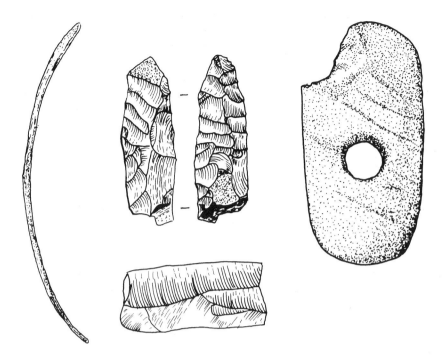

83 Grave goods from Site 2 at Dorchester-on-Thames, Oxfordshire.

Thames and Ormiegill in Caithness (fig. 83). Distribution patterns suggest that they were also drawn upon in exchanges which wove communities into broader webs of contact and alliance (fig. 84). In other words, they too possessed the capacity to stand for people and the potential to carry those people into other contexts. Concentrations of maceheads in north-eastern Scotland echo the distribution of carved stone balls and axes from Killin in Perthshire. High densities have also been noted in Orkney, where they have been found in close proximity to settlements such as Skara Brae, Rinyo and Barnhouse, and ceremonial sites such as the Stones of Stenness and Maes Howe. It is possible that these regional clusters correspond to broad regimes of value – areas within which particular categories of artefact were regularly used as status items for several generations (fig. 85).

Similar ideas may help us to understand the appearance of enigmatic carved stone balls. Found almost exclusively in Scotland, these curious and often beautiful artefacts are contemporary with a series of irregular spiked stone objects, such as those found at Skara Brae and

Quoyness in Orkney. Just as they possess no clear function, so there is little contextual information beyond a vague association with funerary sites. Moreover, there is little evidence to suggest that many balls were exchanged over considerable distances. With the exception of examples from Kirkton, Roxburghshire and Hillhead, Orkney, the majority were probably made in locally available stone (fig. 86). In the absence of a clear link with exchange, it has been suggested that they were hereditary items, held by particular kin groups and passed down from one generation to another.

Although it lacks a clear spatial order, variation in the character of carved stone balls can be detected. Out of a known total of 411, about 65 per cent possess six projections. A far smaller number have over a hundred projections, and others display incised decoration which recalls the designs found on Grooved Ware and in passage graves (fig. 87). In practical terms, these distinctions are interesting, as they hint at different degrees of expertise in working. Multiple projections or complex designs, such as those seen on the ball from Towie, would have

111

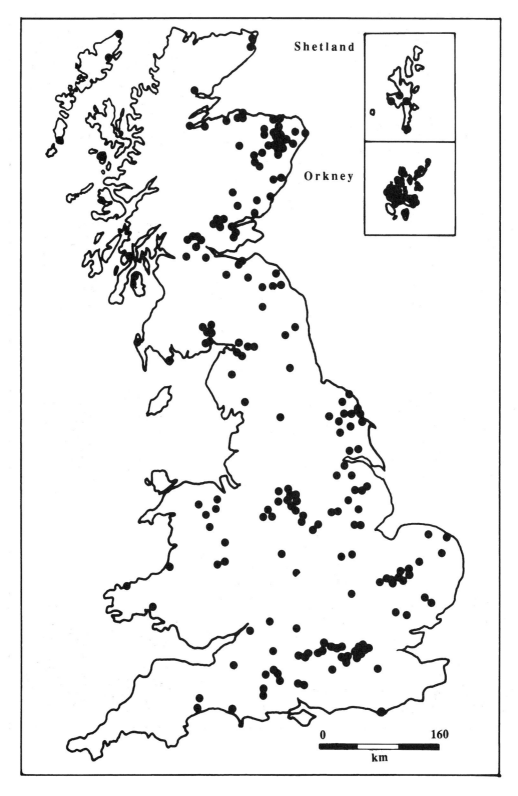

84 Distribution of stone maceheads (after Roe 1979).

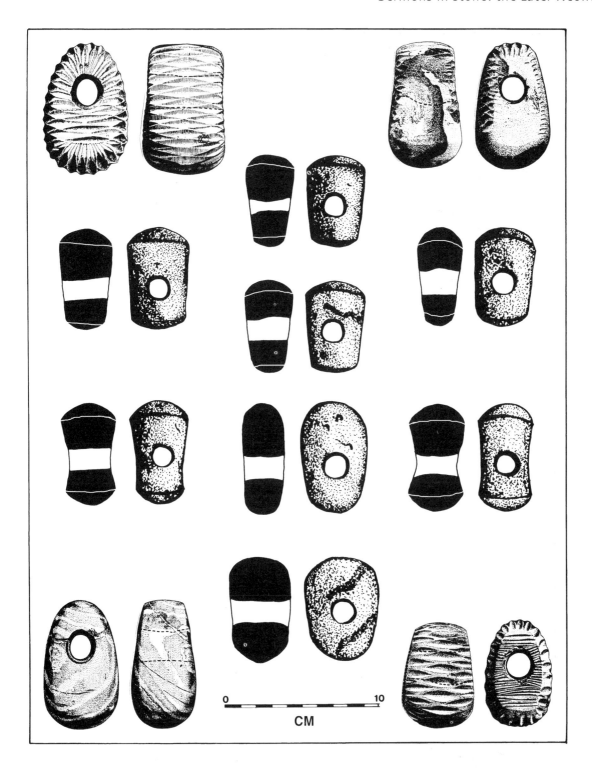

85 Perforated maceheads of flint and stone.

86 Distribution of (A) carved stone balls and (B) Group XXIV axes in Scotland

required careful mapping and a high degree of control and anticipation in working around a three-dimensional surface. By contrast, the creation of six projections is rather more straightforward, requiring only that the maker maintain a sense of opposing faces.

Whether these distinctions reflect a measure of control over production remains to be seen. However, the links with passage grave art suggest that certain motifs may have been used to shape the significance attached to particular objects and the contexts in which they circulated. As with Grooved Ware, these designs may have taken on very different meanings as they circulated on portable objects away from tombs. However, the presence of these exotic motifs may have contributed to the roles that these items played in signalling the place of a person within the social world, their connections with others and their right to participate in (or even preside over) important social practices or ceremonies.

## A plethora of purposes

Given the diversity of the artefacts discussed in this chapter, the limitations of prestige-goods models should be apparent. They may be valuable in certain cases, but they do not allow us to capture some of the more local concerns that were satisfied through the provision of stone tools. What these trends suggest is that artefacts were increasingly drawn upon in order to communicate and sustain a variety of ideas concerning the identities of people. An emphasis appears to have been placed heavily (but not exclusively) on adult men, but the sheer diversity of these personal items suggests that gender distinctions were by no means the only issue addressed through this medium. Membership of particular age classes and bonds of affiliation have already been mentioned, but broad trends in funerary practice suggest additional themes. Like the emergence of individual burial, the production and use of many of these artefacts may have been tied to an increasing concern with the

87 Carved stone balls (National Museum of Scotland)

genealogies of the living. In other words, this proliferation of tools and ornaments may also have been geared towards the marking of an individual's place within particular lines of descent and inheritance.

The associations of these artefacts could be drawn on in many ways. Worn or carried by particular people, they may have helped to reaffirm their position within communities as well as in broader groups. This capacity may even have been reinforced through the existence of constraints upon where (and perhaps when) these artefacts could be made or obtained and the circumstances in which they could be used or worn. Once created, their presence may have helped to define the manner in which a number of aspects of social life were understood. When passed down from one generation to another, their acquisition and display may have helped to define the position of individuals within networks of descent, and may even have sanctioned the inheritance of authority. In this case at least, the patina of handling and service that they carried

may have added to their appreciation by others. Apart from their role in exchange, the use or deposition of these 'dominant symbols' in ritual or ceremonial activity would have introduced various qualities or aspects of a person to that event. Brought into combination with each other, they may have allowed more complex interpretations.

In the case of pits, the deposition of different artefacts with Grooved Ware or Peterborough Ware may have been undertaken for a variety of reasons. As in the Earlier Neolithic, these formal acts of deposition would have been singular events at which concepts of place and person may have been brought into sharp relief. Many of these pits again appear to be associated with episodes of consumption or feasting, and with fragmentary human remains. Many also contain concentrations of exotica as well as local material, and as a class of site, pits with these characteristics tend to occur near ceremonial foci.

At monuments such as the Dorset cursus or later henges, the clustering of exotica may reflect

115

periodic gatherings in their environs, perhaps in the context of building or using the sites themselves. Other pits may have been dug within settlements, but in both cases, the cutting and filling of these features may have served to reaffirm the links between particular people, their descendants, and specific places in the landscape. As we shall see in chapter 5, they may also have provided a context in which to celebrate important meetings, when feasting and the ostentatious burial of valued items were used to negotiate ties and obligations among participants.

Similar purposes may have been served through the deposition of artefacts with individual burials. Under these circumstances the array of artefacts placed on or with the corpse perhaps addressed a number of issues. These tools may

have signalled or even celebrated ideas about the particular identity of the deceased, providing material metaphors for their place within a web of different social relations. This may have had important consequences among the living, where the inheritance of position or authority may not have been beyond question. At the same time, the choice of artefacts may have been tied to more idealized or general links between categories of person and specific areas of social and economic life. Although some of these tools were never actually used, they nonetheless referred to similar forms and thus perhaps to specific tasks or practical activities. At the moment of burial, the spoken word and the choreography of people no doubt played an important part in determining the manner in which events were

88 The flint mines at Grimes Graves as seen from the air (Derek Edwards, Norfolk Museums Service).

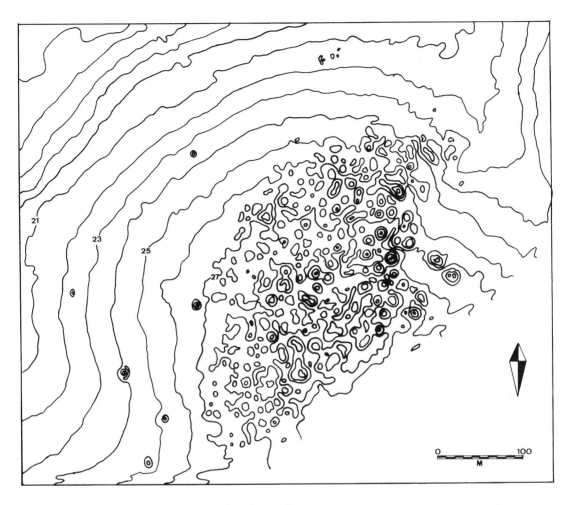

89 Plan of the shafts and surface features at Grimes Graves.

understood. However, the tableau of the body with its associated objects would have provided a vivid evocation of the persona of the deceased, and perhaps the order of things among the living.

## A mine of information?

One final context needs to be considered here, although in this case, there are rather more questions than answers. At Grimes Graves in Norfolk, several excavations have been conducted on what is the largest flint mine complex in Britain (fig. 88). Unlike other mines or quarries, there is little or no evidence for consistent Earlier Neolithic activity on this site. The practice of digging shafts for a high-quality black flint was a Later Neolithic phenomenon which con-

tinued through into the Early Bronze Age.

The sheer scale of Grimes Graves is best appreciated from the air although there can be little doubt that it would have constituted an impressive field monument when approached on the ground. Alongside areas of open-cast working, as many as four to five hundred deep and galleried shafts were sunk, creating mounds of upcast and floors of working debris that can still be seen today. As with Earlier Neolithic mines, this scale is deceptive (fig. 89). Work by Roger Mercer confirms that here too, working was organized on an episodic or seasonal basis, and may have spanned three to four hundred years. In other words, mining was still an event rather than a full-time activity. A similar pattern of seasonal exploitation has been suggested for a

117

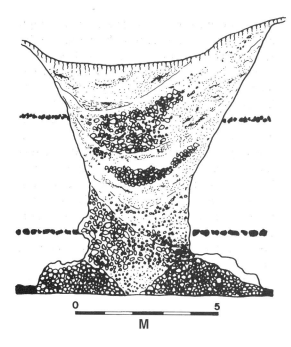

0                 5

**M**

90 Section through pit 1 at Grimes Graves. Note the layers of topstone and wallstone above the more substantial floorstone deposits.

number of smaller sources in East Anglia.

Like earlier mines, the character of shafts and galleries and the close working conditions maintained on the surface may again have provided a frame for ordering people. Here, however, some shafts may reflect the labour of larger numbers of people for considerable periods of time (fig. 90). The implications of this scale of working have been noted by Frances Healy. As she puts it:

> It is easy to see the excavation of a small open-cast pit by two or three people in one or two days as geared to the winning of good-quality flint for everyday use. It is less easy to see the excavation of a deep, galleried shaft by 20 people in two to four months in the same terms, bearing in mind that the immediate area abounds in more readily accessible flint of reasonable quality.

These estimates of time and labour may be a little generous for many shafts, but they do remind us that, as with other monuments, episodes of construction and use may have lasted for several weeks or months at a time. At Grimes Graves, and perhaps at other monuments, these episodes may have been embedded in seasonal routines of movement tied to the agricultural cycle and the husbandry of animals.

Given the patterns outlined in this chapter, the inventories from excavated shafts at Grimes Graves are particularly revealing. Here again, the evidence suggests that many items were 'roughed out' or flaked into shape before being taken elsewhere for final flaking and/or grinding. Axes again form a component of these assemblages, including examples made on distinctive tranchet flakes, but these are nowhere near as dominant as they were at earlier mines. In this case, the production of discoidal and plano-convex knives, arrowheads and perhaps daggers appears to have been emphasised, although few have been found on settlements in the general area. Levallois and large-blade cores are also more frequent than they are on other contemporary local sites, although they also occur at smaller sources. Moreover, the bulk of the pottery recovered from the site is Grooved Ware, which is generally associated with pits and ceremonial monuments in the region. Some of the Grooved Ware appears to have been placed in shafts with some formality, and two Cornish (Group I) axes were also found on the site, where they appear to have been used as digging tools.

Under what circumstances was this site exploited? The emphasis upon these distinctive items suggests that for some groups at least, the procurement or production of important artefacts was again an event which was demarcated in both space and time (fig. 91). Moreover, the dominance of Grooved Ware and the existence of a series of votive deposits in individual shafts suggests that the use of the mines may have been as much ceremonial and bound by convention as it was practical. Whether this involved people undertaking various rites of passage, or members of different communities congregating to extract stone is unclear. Nor is it easy to identify the hand of full-time specialists. If communities specializing in the production of artefacts for others were living around this source, their presence should be manifest in the occurrence of large quantities of Grimes Graves flint. Such material is present, and small concentrations of oblique arrowheads and elaborate knives have been identified. Yet the quantities involved are far too small to account for the output of a source where an individual shaft may have produced several tons of workable stone.

These patterns suggest that different people may have travelled over some distance to reach the site, and it is likely that this process of movement structured a number of different dimensions of its use. As with earlier mines, restrictions may have been placed upon who was allowed to travel to the site, as well as when such trips could be undertaken. This would have created the potential for restrictions to be placed on who was permitted to produce certain categories of artefact. Moreover, if the use of the

mines involved the coming together of people from different communities, the act of winning stone from the earth may have provided a context in which a variety of broader ties and relations could be negotiated or celebrated. Like the gatherings at henges, the environs of Grimes Graves may have witnessed the periodic congregation of members of different communities who engaged in a variety of social and economic transactions as an adjunct to the extraction of flint. Although individual shafts and working areas may have been closely identified with particular groups, it is possible that the entire complex may have provided a material metaphor for ties that bound those groups into a broader corporate entity.

There is no reason to assume that all the prod-

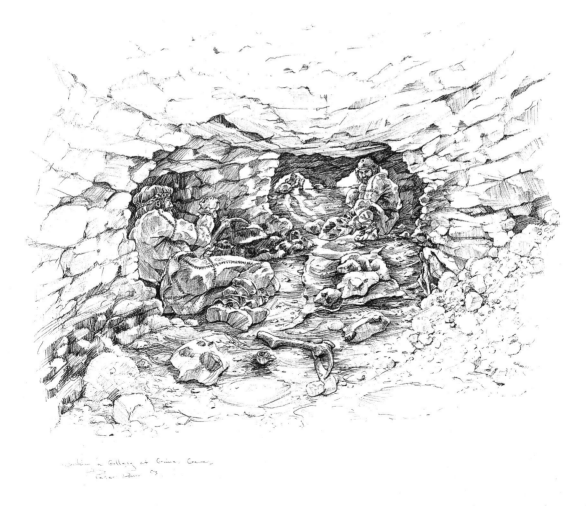

91 Extracting stone from the galleries of a flint mine (drawn by Peter Dunn; copyright English Heritage).　　119

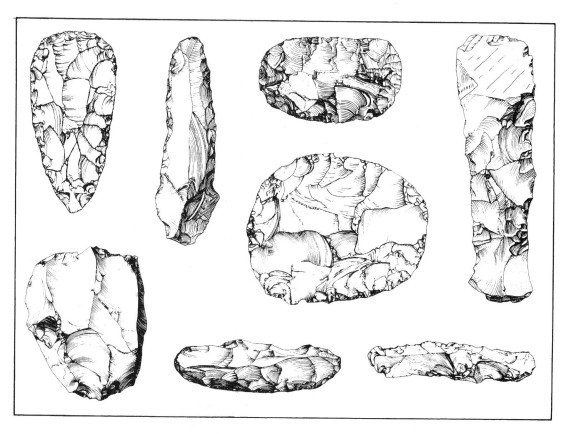

92 Flaked implements recovered during excavations at Grimes Graves.

ucts of this source served as prestige goods in the strict sense of the term, and it may be better to think of them as tokens of identity (fig. 92). Many of the tools carried away from Grimes Graves were probably drawn upon at a relatively localized level – their use and display contributing to the definition of people within their immediate social context. The possession of some of these items may have been a prerogative of men at certain times, while others could also be used by women. Some may have been restricted to adults, and in particular to the elders of different communities. Indeed the right to possess some of these artefacts, and to participate in their circulation, may have been restricted to these more senior individuals.

Some of these artefacts were also circulated between members of different communities, moving from hand to hand in a variety of transactions. Many may have passed into networks of trade and exchange extending to the west, while others travelled north into areas where the production or acquisition of distinctive flint artefacts played an important part in marking the position and status of people (fig. 93). It is again unlikely that all made this journey as prestige goods. However, the circulation of at least some of these objects may have been keyed into exchanges that had more direct consequences for the distribution of power and authority within particular regions. We shall return to this theme in chapter 5, following the passage of stone across the threshold which separates the Neolithic from the Early Bronze Age.

93 Closing ceremony in a shaft at Grimes Graves. As in earlier times, the winning of flint from the earth may have been as much a ceremonial activity as it was a technical exercise. Offerings were sometimes placed in shafts to mark the end of an episode of working. These included antler picks, some of which may have been deliberately broken, together with Grooved Ware and carved chalk objects. Perhaps the stone itself was invested with particular spiritual qualities, such that success or failure in mining was seen as a measure of the standing or fortune of particular people (drawn by Peter Dunn; copyright English Heritage).

121

# 5 Stone in the age of metal

In the previous chapter, we saw how the later third millennium witnessed a number of profound changes in the character of social life. The course of these developments varied from one part of Britain to another, but patterns of production and consumption indicate that many stone tools were caught up in these broader processes. The simple proliferation of tool forms suggests that many served to define boundaries between different aspects of day-to-day activity: at least some tools may also have provided material expressions of the divisions of labour and influence that existed within communities. Items of personal gear provided media through which aspects of the self were presented, from membership of particular age or gender classes through to position within local lines of descent and inheritance.

Many tools served these purposes simply through their routine use and their habitual association with particular tasks and people. Some were probably worn and displayed at important ceremonies, and a few may have been made specifically for interment with the dead. There is tantalizing evidence that the production of some of these tokens of identity was occasionally restricted, and that a series of conventions surrounded their use with either Peterborough or Grooved Ware. It is also clear that some were circulated over considerable distances.

These transactions probably took a variety of forms, and there is no reason to assume that every moment of exchange had dramatic consequences for the order of social and political relations. Nevertheless, the circulation or deposition of elaborate or exotic objects occasionally served a more direct political purpose. Rather than simply marking the standing of members of particular communities, their passage may have played a more active role in the negotiation of obligations, debts and authority. As discussed in chapter 3, the products of certain stone axe sources were circulating as important tokens of value towards the end of the Earlier Neolithic. By the Later Neolithic, these may have been joined by a series of more elaborate artefacts. Indeed, the proliferation of distinctive objects may reflect the difficulties that were encountered in maintaining the exclusive character of artefacts that mediated political authority.

This more strategic use of stone forms one of the central themes of this chapter, which encompasses the final stages of the Neolithic and the beginning of the Early Bronze Age. Traditionally seen as a threshold of technical innovation, the boundary between these two periods is far from clear. Many sites and artefacts remained in use across the transition, and this continuity is no less important than the material changes which have long been the focus of our attention. When looked at more closely, it seems that this transition was not so much a technical revolution, as a time of development in the media through which social and political relations were negotiated and reproduced.

## Arenas of value: henges and stone circles

These more overt political qualities of objects return us to the henges and earliest stone circles found across Britain. Built some time after most causewayed enclosures had fallen out of use, henges occur in a number of regions, while circles dominate western and northern parts of the country. Several excavations have failed to recover any substantial features within these sites. Others have revealed elaborate timber settings, circles, coves and other structures (fig. 94). Variability can also be seen in their locations, and the sense of marginality evoked by earlier enclosures is nowhere near as pronounced. Some occur in close proximity to large surface scatters while others are more remote from traces of settlement. Equally, some henges appear to have been constructed in comparative isolation, whereas others represent a stage in the more gradual development of monument complexes. Constructed in landscapes that were often dominated by earlier tombs, a few were even built on top of long-abandoned enclosures (fig. 95).

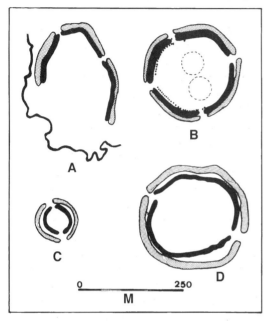

94 Henges and henge enclosures: A Marden; B Durrington Walls; C Thornborough; D Avebury.

Although this reminds us that the purposes served by these sites may have varied from one place and time to another, it does seem that a number were situated on important lines of communication. Many lie close to major rivers or natural access routes: Durrington Walls is situated on a prominent bend in the river Avon and the henges and large stone circles of eastern Cumbria cluster around the routes which cross the Pennines. Many sites would have required thousands of hours of labour for their construction, and as with the link with access routes this suggests a concern with lines of contact which extended beyond the immediate social horizon.

What significance did these sites hold for contemporary communities? For some archaeologists, the sheer scale of many henges has been taken as evidence for the emergence of chiefs – hereditary leaders who were able to mobilize large quantities of labour for the construction of monuments to their power and authority. This idea has its attractions, particularly when we consider the extraordinary scale of some of the henges in Wessex. Yet even here, it is quite conceivable that the building of many henges involved labour under the direction of members of different communities rather than a single individual or group (fig. 96). In other words, the evidence may reflect a social order which had much in common with what anthropologists term 'Big Man'

95 Knowlton henge, Wessex. The location of a Christian church within the boundaries of this site serves as a reminder that the traces of the past can be recruited to lend a sense of authority and permenance to new beliefs and new social orders. Constructed on or near to sites that were already 'ancient', many henges may themselves have drawn upon and reworked the traditional associations of particular places.

96 Building a timber circle at Durrington Walls. The henge enclosure at Durrington Walls contained a number of these circles, each requiring up to c. 8 ha (20 acres) of woodland for its construction. It is not known whether all of the circles stood at the same time, or whether they were built in sequence. Each may have been raised as an arena for a gathering and as a context within which members of different communities could meet to undertake important rites and ceremonies. The area may have witnessed some form of specialized settlement late in its history, but by the Early Bronze Age the banks of this massive enclosure were lost beneath regenerated vegetation. These banks can be seen in the background (drawn by Peter Dunn; copyright English Heritage).

systems. What is clear is that the construction and use of many sites would have involved the coming together of people drawn from different communities. These episodes would have provided a context in which distant kin were encountered, and in which relative strangers may have camped and worked in close proximity.

Although the evidence is fragmentary, the nature of these events can be inferred from the character of individual sites. Many monuments embody connections with movements in the heavens, and it is possible that their construction marks a pronounced concern with supernatural forces. Like the ancestors of Earlier Neolithic communities, these forces may have been called upon to ensure productivity and success in economic life. Linking seasonal routines to patterns in the cosmos, these sites would have imbued daily routines and labour with a sense of timelessness, making them appear natural and eternal. This may have been further enhanced where the location of henges 'referred' to or redefined the archaic associations of earlier tombs and long-abandoned enclosures. At the same time, henges may have been constructed or recruited to sanction the authority of particular people, providing a highly charged ceremonial context in which that authority could be both expressed and reaffirmed. In this regard, it is interesting that many henges are initially found in areas where there is little evidence for a strong tradition of ostentatious individual burial. In these regions at least, dealings with the supernatural may have provided an important medium for the maintenance of authority.

Other characteristics of henges can be added to this picture. They are sites where access and visibility were often highly constrained, and at which the right to enter at certain times may have been restricted. The imposing external banks and concentric internal divisions seen at many henges indicate that movement in their environs and their interior was often highly formal. Some sites, such as Mayburgh in Cumbria, have pronounced and imposing façades. Others made use of natural contours to enhance their monumentality when approached from a particular direction. The plans of a number of monuments suggest that processions and other choreographed patterns of movement were practised, and it seems likely that spatial divisions would have allowed distinctions to be drawn between people. The outer bank may have marked a boundary beyond which certain people were not allowed to pass, and internal arrangements may have made it possible to differentiate between participants (fig. 97). Those consigned to the margins would have been able to observe some of the proceedings, but certain activities may have been hidden behind screens and timber or stone settings.

Further information comes from the assemblages recovered during excavations. Many henges display a connection with feasting and with the dead. Fragmentary remains such as

97 A gathering at a smaller henge. Although the henge enclosures of Wessex have dominated our attention, it is likely that many of the smaller henges were equally important foci for periodic ceremonies. Like their more massive counterparts, these sites probably served as contexts in which important meetings and transactions took place alongside various rites of passage and dedications to supernatural forces (after J. Brayne).

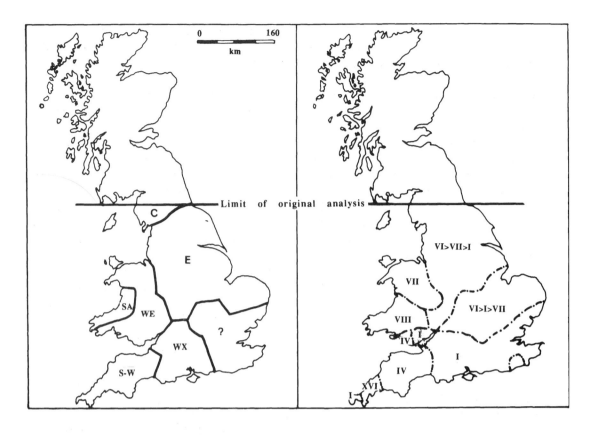

98 Relationship between Aubrey Burl's monument zones and stone axe distributions (after Bradley 1984).

skulls have been recognized in several areas, and cremations and inhumations also occur, often towards the margins of individual sites. In addition, the deliberate deposition of artefacts and other materials seems to have been a common feature of ceremonies conducted within their bounds. At Durrington Walls, a series of conventions surrounded the treatment of both artefacts and animal remains. Wild species, such as red deer, beavers and foxes, cluster around the southern timber circle, as do the bones of domesticated pigs. By contrast, cattle are more closely associated with the northern circle, and wild pigs and oxen seem to be confined to the outer ditch of the site. A rather different expression of this same process can be seen at Maumbury Rings in Dorset, a site defined by a circle of shafts up to 11m (36ft) in depth. Domesticated species dominate the lower levels of these shafts, but wild animals account for over 70 per cent of the assemblages recovered from the top 5m (16½ft). Fragmentary human remains – most notably skulls – are only found in these upper levels.

These patterns are difficult to understand, but they suggest that the classification of animals as wild or domesticated species played a part in determining how and where they could be deposited on ceremonial sites. As the products of hunting or of husbandry, these different animals may have carried associations with different categories of person, and their routine or formal deposition may have provided an expression of those distinctions. This may have been reinforced by associations with the bones of selected people. It is also possible that different areas or features on these sites carried different practical and spiritual connotations. These may have been harnessed during acts of deposition. Entrances, boundaries and focal points within henges may have provided a frame on which a variety of values and associations could be mapped.

Again at Durrington Walls, Grooved Ware is common on the site, but the designs on individual vessels seem to vary according to the contexts in which they were deposited; some vessels appear to have been broken or laid in isolation against the uprights of the timber circles. Similar patterns can be seen in the stone tools found on the site. These include heavy-duty woodworking tools which were probably used in the construction of the timber circles. However, arrowheads, flakes and other tools were also placed with some formality, echoing patterns of structured deposition on other contemporary sites. Some of these patterns recall the formal deposits found in earlier causewayed enclosures, but there are also important differences. Few sites have yielded comparable evidence for the production of artefacts within their bounds, nor for the interweaving of settlement and ceremonial activity. Ratios of tools to waste are generally high, reflecting use and selective deposition rather than manufacturing *per se*.

There are also grounds for inferring a relationship between henges and the circulation of artefacts. Concentrations of exotica tend to cluster in their environs, often reflecting purposive deposition in pits. Moreover, Aubrey Burl has noted that the distribution of different stone axe groups bears some correspondence to regional traditions of Later Neolithic monuments (fig. 98). A few direct associations with stone axes have also been noted. At Llandegai, for example, a Cumbrian axe was buried blade downwards on the perimeter of the site, and at Mayburgh in Cumbria a broken axe was recovered from the entrance. A rather different link can be seen at Woodhenge, where a chalk axe accompanied the burial of a child.

Sites such as Arminghall in Norfolk or Knowlton in Wessex are also situated close to outcrops of raw material, and three small mine shafts were sunk within a few hundred metres of Durrington Walls. In this last case, the presence of a transverse arrowhead in one shaft indicates that this activity may have been broadly contemporary with the monument. These patterns indicate that episodes of procurement and production may have been embedded in the periodic gatherings that many sites witnessed.

This does not in itself provide sufficient grounds for inferring restricted or specialized production, particularly since there is no evidence that the making of tools was focused within the sites themselves. Access to these raw materials may have been quite open, and it is conceivable that the collection of stone provided a context in which members of different communities worked in close proximity to one another. Unfortunately, we know little about the character of working in these areas.

This problem aside, the patterns do suggest that many henges and stone circles served roles that were similar to some earlier enclosures. They defined a space set apart from the world of day-to-day values, within which members of different communities could meet to undertake important rites and ceremonies (fig. 99). Here again, communal building projects would have provided a medium through which the existence of links between communities would have been

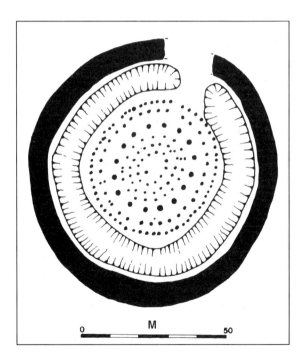

99 Woodhenge, constructed adjacent to the enclosure at Durrington Walls. As with the timber and stone circles found on other contemporary sites, the plan of this monument suggests that processions and other formal patterns of movement may have been a common feature of ceremonies.

127

100 Chalk axes from Woodhenge (National Museum of Scotland).

brought into focus. Moreover, the structured deposition of human remains in relation to different classes of animal and artefact may have reaffirmed some of the basic divisions of labour and influence that existed among the living. The very fact that people participated in these episodes of construction and observance suggests an acknowledgement of the principles of hierarchy and distinction which underlay contemporary political relations.

Despite some points of similarity, the form and contents of these sites suggest a rather different emphasis from that of many earlier enclosures. Henges may have had a more overt significance as arenas in which relations of power and authority could be both renewed and challenged. Control over ceremonies may have been a privilege and a source of status, as may have been the right to enter and participate. Perhaps these rights were restricted to certain people while others could only stand and watch.

Associations with Grooved Ware and with exotica also suggest that many henges provided a focus for celebrating and controlling the connections that spread beyond the local horizon. The very form of these sites signals the importance that was attached to concepts derived from places beyond the margins of everyday life. As Mary Helms has shown, exotic objects, motifs and

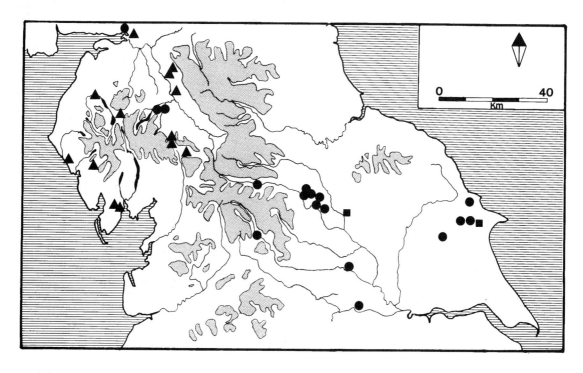

101 Distribution of Later Neolithic monuments in northern England. Henges are shown by circles, large monoliths by squares, and large stone circles by triangles.

ideas may serve a variety of purposes. They derive some of their significance from the simple fact that they mark connections: they provide tangible expressions of links with distant places and people, or with exotic forces and supernatural powers. At the same time, exotica have the capacity to be transformed as they move into new social contexts. Their associations can be manipulated or reworked so that they become important media for the creation and protection of political authority. In other words, they may be well suited to play the role of prestige goods. Given these characteristics, it is possible that henges provided a context within which to direct and contain the flow of important tokens of value (fig. 100). As markers of people's positions with-

in broader networks of affiliation, and as media for more local exchanges, tokens of value may have been channelled and transformed through these sites and ceremonies. In this way, it would have been possible to control access to such items, and to protect the political and economic relations that their circulation helped to create.

These ideas may help us to understand the location of many henges and the pronounced clustering of Later Neolithic monuments on the margins between Cumbria and Yorkshire (fig. 101). One of the purposes that these sites may have served was the demarcation of places and times at which people from different areas could meet to engage in important transactions. Sites such as Mayburgh or Long Meg and her

102 Aerial photograph of Long Meg and her Daughters, Cumbria, showing the outline of a larger (and earlier) enclosure which underlies one side of the later stone circle (Bob Bewley; Crown copyright reserved).

103 Attending a ceremony at the Sanctuary near Avebury (drawn by Peter Dunn; copyright English Heritage).

Daughters may have seen the coming together of people from either side of the Pennines. Long Meg is actually built on top of an earlier enclosure, and although direct continuity cannot be assumed, these periodic gatherings may have been a part of established practice for some time (fig. 102). No doubt some of the ceremonies undertaken at these sites involved the marking of celestial events, but this may not have exhausted their purpose. Marriages may have been solemnized alongside seasonal rites and other more mundane transactions, and the passage of Cumbrian axes to the east may have been mirrored by the flow of people, materials and obligations into the Lake District. Such transactions were probably undertaken at other times and in other places; but the special and perhaps sacred conditions established at these sites may have lent a particular significance to the

exchanges that they witnessed.

In short, the contexts in which status items were obtained may have been just as important as the objects themselves. Exchange may have been bound up with seasonal rites and the celebration of the supernatural to such an extent that the biographies of these objects took on added qualities. Where certain communities were able to exercise control over these meetings, they may have been able to sustain a measure of political authority. However, competitions for status and prestige may have been a regular feature of gatherings at henges and circles, as members of different lineages attempted to rework or renew their position within the local system, and within broader networks of alliance and affiliation.

Moving from camps established in their environs, members of different communities may have processed towards these monuments wearing regalia and carrying tools which marked aspects of their identity (fig. 103). Passing the banks and ditches, they entered an arena set apart from the mundane world, where their words and actions took on a more formal character. Here they may have participated in ceremonies dedicated to the renewal of the earth's fertility, harnessing ancestral and supernatural forces to ensure the continuity of the social and natural worlds. They may have undertaken rites to mark the passing of the dead and the handing on of authority to their descendants, at the same time engaging in competitive acts of feasting and exchange. Occasionally these rites included burials, which strengthened the ties between specific groups and the monuments themselves. The remains of these events were gathered up in middens or placed in pits, and

items of personal gear may have been set down as tokens to mark their completion. Observed from outside, and no doubt an important topic for discussion around the fire, these ceremonies may have been imbued with mystery and with sacred values which were enhanced by restrictions on access and vision.

Returning to their camps and to their close kin, participants may have carried with them objects and stories which told of bonds that had been forged or renewed. How much bridewealth had been paid? Who would trade with whom? Whose initiation had gone well and who had given the greatest feasts? It is difficult to speculate on what would have been heard around those fires, but it is probable that these 'tournaments of value' would have had implications that persisted long after people had returned to their fields and herds. Stories would have made the

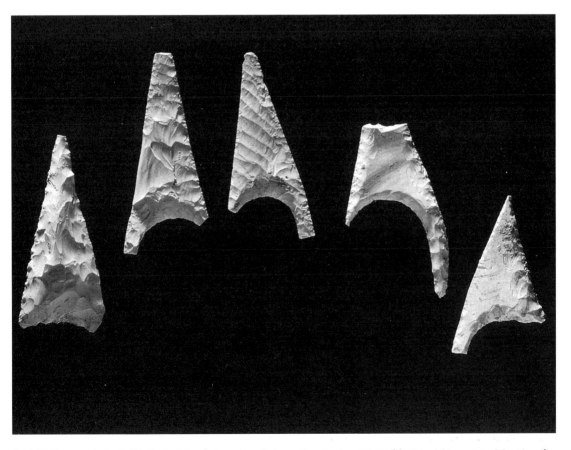

104 Oblique and ripple-flaked oblique arrowheads from Durrington Walls (National Museum of Scotland).

journey home, to be recounted and embellished, and tools and materials would have carried associations which signalled the standing of particular people and their obligations to others.

## Deposition and destruction

Many of these tools and materials were used or consumed in the course of day-to-day tasks, while others passed on as goods or gifts. A few were also drawn upon in more formal circumstances, where the themes and relations highlighted at henges were again brought into focus. Even in pits dug in settlements, Grooved Ware is often found together with similar deposits of animal bone, fragmentary human remains and exotic artefacts (fig. 104). A similar order can also be seen in Grooved Ware pits dug on or close to other categories of site.

Although they are probably not an expression of distinct cultural groups, we cannot tell what distinctions these objects and practices sustained. Perhaps Grooved Ware could only be handled by certain families or sections of the community. Perhaps its use was restricted to certain times and to specific rites. On this issue at least, much remains unclear. However, the inclusion of items of personal gear in many assemblages suggests a continued concern with themes and traditions that stretched back into the Earlier Neolithic. The bringing together of tools and materials drawn from different people, and from different aspects of social life, would have drawn attention to the proper order of relations within the community. Placed in the earth to harness local spirits and to ensure the continued fertility of crops and herds, these local acts of observance would have helped to renew the

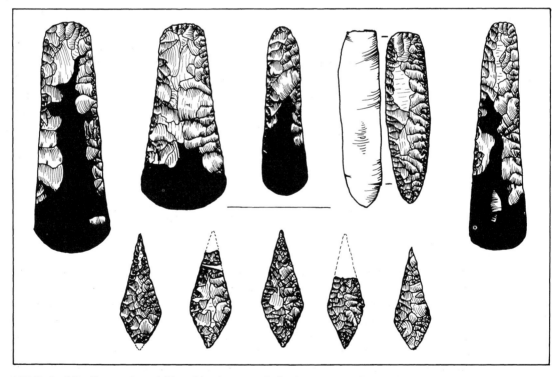

105 Part of the Seamer hoard. Placed in the mound of a barrow together with animal bone and human cranial fragments, this act of deposition may have been part of a later funerary ritual. Alternatively, it may have been an act of conspicuous consumption which demonstrated the wealth and prestige of the giver. We cannot tell whether this act was undertaken by the descendants of those who lay below, or by people who used the site to create a sense of ancestry and gravity to their actions.

historical and economic connections that bound people to particular places.

It is possible that these localized rites could only be performed by certain people within particular communities, but it is also likely that the burial of artefacts and materials often had a wider impact. This is suggested by the fact that Grooved Ware pits often show a close association with stone axes and other exotica – objects which may have stood for the ties and obligations which spread beyond the more immediate boundaries of kinship. Deliberate deposition during gatherings or meetings may have helped to cement ties between members of different communities, or to signal the eminence and standing of particular individuals. Episodes of burial or destruction may even have been undertaken when a particular bond or relationship was brought to an end. The stories and associations those artefacts carried would have been crucial to the proper course and interpretation of these events.

In other cases, the significance of these acts of deposition may have been derived from their immediate context. For example, hoards of single or multiple artefacts were occasionally placed in existing barrows. This appears to have been the case with the Seamer hoard in Yorkshire, which was interred in an existing mound together with small fragments of bone (fig. 105). Beyond the associations of the objects themselves, the performance of these acts on the stage provided by a burial mound may have lent a measure of gravity or importance to the proceedings. Perhaps these acts were undertaken by the descendants of those who lay below, or by others wishing to create and assert a more fictive sense of genealogical proximity.

Other hoards were probably created in the face of more prosaic concerns – the earth providing no more than a temporary resting place for artefacts that were meant to be reclaimed. Yet in certain cases it is clear that reclamation would never have been an option. Alongside hoards, significant numbers of axes have been recovered from rivers and other wet places. Indeed, stone axes have a strong connection with votive deposits and it is likely that this tradition of disposal may have had a long ancestry. Clusters of axes in the Thames include Scandinavian and

other exotic forms, and although many retain evidence for use, the majority recovered from watery contexts are slightly larger than those found on dry land. These clusters also include maceheads, at least one of which was made from Cumbrian (Group VI) stone.

These concentrations make little sense as the results of chance loss or shipwrecks, and probably reflect the purposive disposal of artefacts in contexts from which they could not be recovered. As with burial on dry land, the disposal of these important tokens of value may have provided an ostentatious demonstration of the pre-eminence of particular people. The simple capacity to give or dispose of wealth may have been just as important as its accumulation.

It is also possible that these offerings took the form of 'gifts to the gods', to honour local spirits, to harness certain forces or even to mark the passing of particular individuals. In that sense, the status of rivers as lines of communication may have contributed to their suitability as contexts into which personal items could be thrown. Yet where the giving of a gift creates obligations, the establishment of exchange relations with supernatural entities may have had important consequences for the perceived status of the giver. The apparently simple and – to us – irrational act of throwing axes, maceheads and pottery into rivers may have served as a dramatic and potent context in which people could enhance or protect their standing in the corporeal world.

## Social competition and the end of the Neolithic

Many of the henges constructed during the Later Neolithic continued to be used and elaborated in the Early Bronze Age. Although relatively rare in the earlier period, many more stone circles were also constructed at this time. Revisited and modified over the generations, the changing character and use of these sites was probably keyed into contradictions arising from tensions between dominant and subordinate lineages. These probably took the form of competitive struggles between 'Big Men', but may sometimes have involved the assertion of claims to more perma-

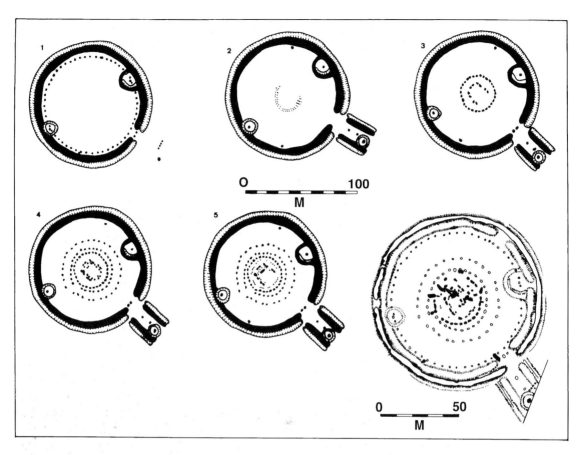

106 Simplified plan of the development of Stonehenge. Initiated during the Later Neolithic in a landscape inscribed with long barrows and cursus monuments, the first phase at the site bears a number of similarities with the site of Flagstones in Dorset. With the passage of time, Stonehenge became the focus for a series of cremations and other burials, eventually becoming a point of reference for extensive barrow cemeteries during the Early Bronze Age. There is no reason to assume that the meaning or significance of this site remained constant from the moment that the first ditch was dug until the time when the last lintel was raised. At certain times it may have stood as a symbol of corporate or communal identity – as a place where people could gather to honour the dead, call upon ancestral or supernatural forces and engage in important transactions. At others, it may have been more immediately understood as a monument to the power and authority of particular groups, a power that was both rooted and expressed in the right to officiate at important ceremonies. While it may be unnecessary to think in terms of astronomer priests, these ceremonies perhaps involved the manipulation of ideas concerning movements in the heavens. The passing on of this knowledge may have been one of the ways in which local and regional authority was maintained across generations.

nent hereditary authority. As dominant locales – places invested with potent social and historical significance – these monuments were continually drawn upon or 'rediscovered' to maintain or even challenge the order of political relations between different groups. Modern arguments over access to sites such as Stonehenge provide a

vivid example of how the monuments of the past may still be interpreted and drawn upon in different ways according to one's social and political position (fig. 106).

Some sites continued to serve as arenas of value as they had done for many generations, while others saw a closer identification with

107 The henge monument at Avebury (English Heritage).

funerary rites or even with specialized settlement. It was towards the close of the Neolithic that Stonehenge itself saw extensive modification, with the erection of the bluestones within the area defined by the earlier bank, ditch and timber settings. This new site built into the fabric of an earlier monument became an important focus for Early Bronze Age burial mounds. Although rather different in character, a similar shift of emphasis may have taken place at sites such as Knappers in Dumbartonshire. Within several generations, the henge at Mount Pleasant in Dorset was also transformed. Here the evidence suggests phases of neglect or abandonment followed by the raising of stones in place of earlier timber settings, and the eventual construction of a massive palisade.

135

An increasing emphasis upon defence or demarcation can also be seen at Forteviot in Tayside, and at Meldon Bridge in the Borders, where a timber palisade stretching 500m (1640ft) was built to enclose an area containing ceremonial sites and settlement. At Avebury (fig. 107), the passage of time saw the construction of the Silbury mound, enclosures defined by massive timber posts, and the use of avenues which linked the henge to other monuments. In this case, the connotations of the henge may have been extended to encompass other places in the immediate area. Alongside gatherings, feasts and other transactions, the pattern of monuments in this area suggests the exsistence of conventions regarding the 'proper' manner in which sites such as the henge should be approached. Following these conventions, people's movements and understandings would have been shaped by the encounters that they had on these well-trodden paths. Ancient tombs, sites such as the Sanctuary, and even burials placed next to stones in the avenues would all have helped to shape the significance that participants attached to their actions.

Other ceremonial sites may have been abandoned altogether. At Arbor Low in Derbyshire, a circle of stones was laid out within a henge but never raised, and the boundaries of Durrington Walls appear to have been lost in regenerated woodland at an early point in the Bronze Age.

These long sequences of elaboration, abandonment and reuse suggest that ceremonial monuments played a variety of roles in shaping the social geography of late third millennium Britain. People who were able to co-ordinate new episodes of construction, or control different forms of ceremonial activity would have had the potential to create and protect their claims to authority over land, labour and other resources. This may have been masked to a greater or lesser extent behind a rhetoric which stressed their role in working for common interests and the broader group. But their position as arbiters of how these sites were to be used and understood would have been both an expression of their authority, and a medium through which that authority was renewed.

The local and regional contours of social life were also continually being renewed or redefined by the circulation and consumption of material culture. The close demarcation of contexts for production and exchange, the elaboration of artefacts and acts of conspicuous consumption all suggest that the latter part of the Neolithic saw people fighting – both literally and metaphorically – with goods. Some of these struggles were localized and open-ended in the extreme – a constant feature of social reproduction. Caught up in the presentation of the self within extended families, portable artefacts may have been drawn upon in the definition of relations between family heads and between younger and older adults. Others were directed towards the place that people occupied in the broader social landscape, where the continual negotiation of political authority may have stimulated the emergence of specialists, the elaboration or emulation of artefacts and the 'demand' for exotica.

As far as we can tell, these developments took place against a relatively stable backdrop of subsistence practice. Research in many areas suggests a slow continuation of the trend towards clearance, but major swathes of woodland would have remained within a patchwork of open grass and cultivated plots. Cattle, pigs and sheep also appear to have retained their importance within regimes which set cultivation and pastoral activity alongside the use of a variety of resources. In the case of coastal settlements, extensive shell middens indicate that marine resources were also exploited where (and when) they were available.

Further aspects of the Late Neolithic/Early Bronze Age transition are manifest on the surfaces of many ploughed fields. Distinctive settlement scatters dating to the beginning of the second millennium are difficult to locate, and it has often been said that the dead must have buried themselves! Where they have been recognized, houses dating to this period are often diminutive, dispersed and occasionally associated with small field boundaries and droveways, the best-known examples being those identified at Fengate, near Peterborough. Only in northern Scotland do we find evidence for the persistence of larger nucleated settlements, and over much of Britain, domestic contexts seem to have remained relatively small and unelaborate.

Broader shifts in land-use patterns do appear to have taken place during the course of the Early Bronze Age. In areas such as Cranborne Chase in Dorset, the paucity of Early Bronze Age settlement evidence may reflect a gradual shift of emphasis towards the lowlands and the southern coast. What is important is that these trends develop over a considerable period of time. They do not represent a sudden departure from established traditions of movement and activity. For that reason, the 'gaps' in our evidence suggest a high degree of continuity in the pattern and purpose of landscape use across the threshold which sets apart our 'Age of Stone' from its metal counterpart. Many Early Bronze Age scatters probably make up part of the large spreads of Later Neolithic material that have been identified in many areas. Nowhere is this clearer than in eastern England, where a dense spread of Late Neolithic/Early Bronze Age surface scatters runs along the margins of the fenlands.

Other routine patterns of activity also remained relatively unchanged. The transition between the two periods is not marked by any major transformation in the basic character of stoneworking. Patterns of procurement, core preparation and reduction remained in keeping with those that had persisted for several centuries. Other tools also continued to be made. Scrapers, fabricators, chisels, knives and retouched flakes occur on many sites together with larger crude core tools. This lack of a sudden transformation in assemblages suggests that the first introduction of metal may have had little significant impact on the immediate character of many day-to-day tasks.

Given these general trends, it is perhaps surprising that the Early Bronze Age has sometimes been referred to as 'the renaissance of flintworking' in Britain. Such claims hardly seem justified on the basis of the vast majority of assemblages, but they may have some merit when they are set against the evidence for a restricted range of artefacts. The final Neolithic and the early stages of the Bronze Age see the appearance of new or developed categories of stone tool which appear to have been made and treated in a rather more formal manner than many of their contemporaries. These developments occur in conjunction with the appearance of a new category of pottery – the Beaker – and the introduction of metalwork to Britain. They may also be broadly contemporary with the decline of stone axe production at many of the larger western sources. It is this horizon that concerns us here.

108 Beakers from Cambridgeshire (Museum of Archaeology and Anthropology, Cambridge).

# A clash of symbols: Beakers, metal and stone

The appearance of Beakers alongside Grooved and Peterborough Wares has long been recognized as an important juncture in the British prehistoric sequence (fig. 108). Beakers have some of the earliest associations with metalwork in Britain and are often found in burials which develop or depart from established funerary traditions in many areas. There is rather less of a consensus concerning the significance that these distinctive S-profiled pots may have held for contemporary communities. Beakers were used alongside other vessels, but their form, character and context suggest something of a break with tradition. Technologically distinct from their contemporaries, these generally thin-walled vessels with their incised and zoned decoration represent a decisive innovation.

The source or inspiration for this innovation has long been traced to the Continent, and in particular to the Low Countries, where similar vessels had been in use for some time. For many years, this material link was taken as evidence that the end of the Neolithic saw a major influx of people – the Beaker Folk – into Britain. Many accounts envisaged the wholesale migration of continental communities, bringing with them new burial customs, knowledge of metalworking and even horses. This proposal no longer looks so attractive. It is now generally acknowledged that these changes probably result from the flow of ideas rather than the flow of people, and the associations with metalwork and horses no longer seem to be so exclusive. Some Beakers do appear to have been deliberate imports, but a great many more reflect the adoption of this new way of making, decorating and using pottery by indigenous communities.

Why did this happen? One suggestion is that Beakers and their associations represent an extension of the trend towards a prestige-goods economy and the celebration of individual status. In other words, the creation of ties and alliances across the Channel provided a medium through which particular kin-group heads were able to enhance or maintain their status, acquiring objects (or even the idea of objects) that could

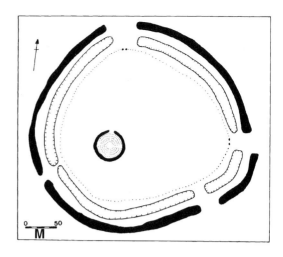

109 Simplified plan of Mount Pleasant in Dorset. Like Stonehenge, this site underwent a series of important changes in its physical character during the Later Neolithic and Early Bronze Age. Originally defined by a bank and ditch, the site saw the construction of internal timber and stone arrangements, and the eventual construction of a massive palisade. As with many other monuments, it may be simplistic to look for a single role or purpose to the site. It seems to have been a place where people gathered, and in which various ceremonies were undertaken. Smashed vessels in a number of internal features and close to entrances suggest that some of these ceremonies may have included feasts and other episodes of large-scale consumption.

serve as tokens of value. It has even been suggested that the 'Beaker package' of goods and ideas may have been deployed to disrupt or challenge an existing social order based upon communal rites and related forms of ceremonial activity.

This suggestion that Beakers may have played a specialized role is rooted in their close links with burials and other ceremonial sites. Settlement finds are also known, however, and the general character of associations appears to have changed over several centuries and from one part of the country to another. For example, Beakers appear to have been disseminated quite rapidly in Yorkshire, but in Wessex the earliest links are with long-abandoned enclosures such as Windmill Hill and with burials set apart from major ceremonial foci. There may have been an interval of time before they were also used and deposited at henges in the area, and this may have taken place during periods of elaboration or reuse. This finds its most striking expression at Mount Pleasant, where Beaker sherds occur in contexts associated with the later use of the site (fig. 109).

These patterns have led some archaeologists to infer the existence of two distinct political and ideological regimes: one – associated with the use of Grooved Ware – grounded in the use of large ceremonial monuments and control over arcane ritual; the other – associated with Beakers – emphasized personal prestige, exchange and genealogy as key political themes. Whether these two 'regimes' were actually in competition with each other remains to be seen. The varied regional traditions of the later third millennium certainly suggest differences in the emphasis placed upon individual burial, ancestral rites, exchange and other rituals as important political practices. Yet it may be unhelpful to oppose these themes or to see their varied use as expressions of distinct cultural groups. Each practice may have been drawn upon in different ways to address a range of overlapping issues, from the definition of immediate kin and categories of person, through to broader networks of political authority and alliance.

This point aside, it does seem that the beginning of the second millennium saw an increased emphasis upon the display of status through portable wealth and the negotiation of political authority through the circulation of various stone and metal sumptuary items. Caught up in different practices, artefacts such as Beakers were probably used and understood in a variety of ways. As the presence of direct imports suggests, it is possible that the ideas carried by a few of these vessels included references to particular networks of contact and alliance. However, the majority of Beakers were produced and used on a more local scale. References to distant customs and forces perhaps attended their use, and may have contributed to their significance; but this may have been of secondary importance compared to their role in defining more localized expressions of identity and social position.

Several aspects of the character and context of Beakers do suggest that their use marks something of a break with the past. In the first place, the simple size of these pots suggests a change of emphasis. Unlike many other contemporary containers, Beakers could be picked up with relative ease, and would have been well suited to use for personal consumption. Residue analyses from vessels such as the example from Ashgrove in Fife suggest that Beakers may have been associated with the consumption of alcohol and certain narcotics. This does not discredit the argument for their role as status items; if anything, it strengthens the idea that they were used in important ceremonies. But it does suggest a concern with individuals which was not articulated through earlier ceramics. In other words, pots may have been more closely identified with particular people than had hitherto been the case. Cutting across the categoric boundaries defined by the use of Peterborough and Grooved Ware, these vessels may have carried notions of personal status and position into many aspects of social life (fig. 110).

It is also possible that some Beakers were treated as hereditary items. Work on the 'grammar' of the designs found on many vessels has

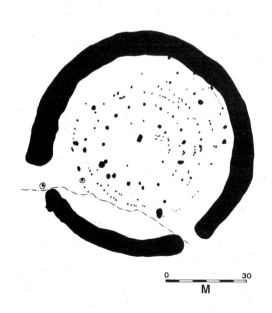

0    30
**M**

110 Simplified plan of Balfarg, a henge which became the context for a central cist burial during the Early Bronze Age.

shown that the character of decoration may have undergone subtle changes through time. Yet Beakers were being made and used for more than five hundred years, and against this backdrop, it is surprising that we do not find much greater variations in their form and character. This remarkable conservatism or stability suggests that some Beakers may have remained 'in view' if not in use for many generations, providing a model which was referred to when new vessels were made. It may be that these 'models' were handed down from one generation to another.

This increasing identification with individuals can also be seen in the contexts with which Beakers are closely associated. As on the Continent, these pots are often found as accompaniments to burials, where they may occur together with a number of distinctive artefacts – the so-called 'Beaker package'. This package was by no means uniform or unchanging, but it often included small items of goldwork, the first copper and bronze ornaments and weapons such as daggers. Metal axes are relatively rare in these contexts (fig. 111). Like the pots themselves,

these new materials may have derived some of their significance from their exotic qualities and their potential to stand as markers of connections. Indeed, the knowledge required in transforming ores into artefacts may itself have been closely guarded and surrounded by proscriptions. As Childe pointed out over fifty years ago, it is not unknown for smiths to be set apart from society because of the forces that are associated with their work.

It is perhaps unnecessary to follow Childe's model of itinerant metalworkers, but it is possible that metalworking was socially restricted. The earliest copper, bronze and gold objects seem to have been introduced from Ireland and the Continent, and it may be that local production also came under close supervision. Alongside control over exchange itself, limited access to technical skills and the uneven distribution of ores may have played an initial part in maintaining the exclusive character of these items. This would have been important where they were circulated in politically motivated exchanges, but would have also helped to sustain their use as media for displaying status and authority.

Stone artefacts associated with Beakers include nearly all of the forms which depart from the more general character of stoneworking seen on many sites. As before, these include tools that would have taken anything between a few minutes and a few days to make, and some were truly exotic while many others were made of locally available stone. One of the most widespread of these forms is the thumbnail scraper, a small circular tool with invasive retouch scars extending across most of its dorsal surface (fig. 112). In every area where they occur, it is possible to detect a measure of variability in the degree of precision and finish achieved in the creation of these tools, but the finest examples reflect a concern with the creation and maintenance of a new and clearly defined category.

These scrapers depart from the patterns of working found on many contemporary flakes, even though the skills they required would almost certainly have been within the grasp of many people (fig. 113). For that reason, it is possible that, while they may have been made widely, subtle conventions may have surrounded their use. Perhaps they were closely associated

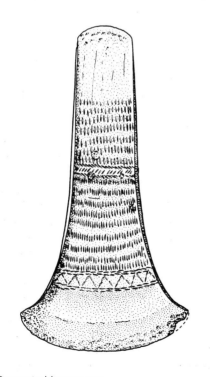

111 Decorated bronze axe.

112 Distinctive 'thumbnail' and other sub-circular flint scrapers – a common feature of many Beaker-associated assemblages (Museum of Archaeology and Anthropology, Cambridge.)

113 Flint core reused as hammerstone.

with certain forms of processing task, or with particular people? They may even have been regarded as an item for use on the human body, and this may be part of the reason why they occasionally appear as grave goods.

Alongside the thumbnail scraper, the barbed-and-tanged arrowhead is a common element in Beaker and Early Bronze Age contexts (fig. 114). Like Beakers, these arrowheads have close parallels on the Continent, notably in areas such as Brittany. Although many Later Neolithic arrowheads continued to be made and used, variations on the theme of the barbed-and-tanged arrowhead come to dominate many assemblages. As Stephen Green has shown, this variation has a regional aspect and may reflect subtle distinctions in traditions of percussion and pressure flaking from one part of the country to another. However, this is cross-cut by major differences in the degree of precision, control or attention to form realized in any one region. Examples such as those from Breach Farm, Glamorgan (fig.

141

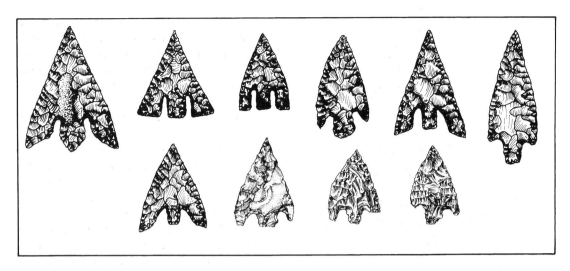

114 Barbed-and-tanged arrowheads.

115 Grave goods from Breach Farm, Glamorgan. Associated with the cremated remains of three individuals were a variety of grave goods. These included an accessory cup, a bronze axe and thirteen elaborate 'Breton'-style arrowheads. Also laid to rest were a series of blanks or roughouts for arrowheads, a flint knife and two stone arrowshaft smoothers (National Museum of Scotland).

116 'Conygar Hill'-style barbed-and-tanged arrowhead from Irthlingborough. These elegant and highly symmetrical forms have close parallels with barbed-and-tanged arrowheads in Brittany (courtesy of John Humble).

115), from Culduthel in Inverness or from the environs of Avebury may reflect the labour of people who were accorded a measure of status as specialists. Often found in funerary contexts, many of these wafer-thin points may have been made for display or for the occasion.

These exceptions aside, the vast majority of barbed-and-tanged arrowheads are likely to have been made under rather less restricted conditions (fig. 116). Working was probably on a small scale for personal use, as at Dalmore in Scotland, where a small Beaker-phase structure witnessed the use of quartz for arrowhead production. This distinction is also brought home by the presence of more mundane examples in graves, which often appear to have been the cause of death. The only hint of chronological change comes with Green's 'Kilmarnock' type, which occurs in greater numbers during the course of the Early Bronze Age.

Together with an increase in the number of burials where death or injury seems to have been caused by archers, this rise to dominance of a sturdy piercing arrowhead may be of some significance. Like maceheads, metaphors for conflict or for hunting seem to form a major component of the gear that was buried with men. This may also apply to a series of 'archers' wrist-guards'. These perforated stone plates may have

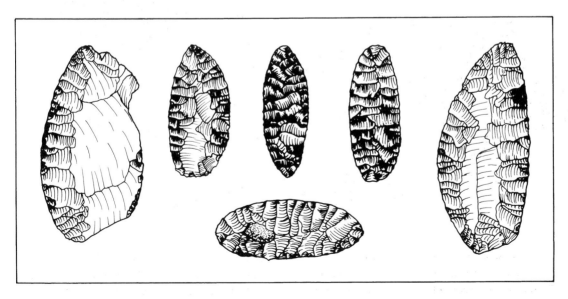

117 Plano-convex knives.

been worn on the lower arm and are another element in many Beaker funerary assemblages. Given these consistent themes, it is possible that the threat of violent confrontation was a common and important concern. Tensions arising between communities may have been endemic and varied in their scale and intensity. Small, local skirmishes, raids and even ritualized combat may have remained an important feature of social life and male rhetoric.

Two other categories of stone tool display a close association with Beaker and Early Bronze Age contexts. Like the long and regular flakes upon which they were often made, plano-convex knives reflect structured routines of flaking and

invasive retouch apparent in many earlier assemblages (fig. 117). Examples from Dalladies in Grampian, Port Charlotte on Islay and Giants Graves on Arran suggest that knives of this general form were probably made from a relatively early stage in the Neolithic. Moreover, the plethora of knives in Later Neolithic contexts include many variations on the same basic theme, from small 'slug-forms' through to larger examples with extensive flake scars on their dorsal surface. There is little evidence for a clear progression of 'types', but the delicate patterns of flaking traced on the surfaces of many later plano-convex knives suggest a heightened concern with the definition of a clear and consistent

118 Flint daggers from eastern England (Museum of Archaeology and Anthropology, Cambridge).

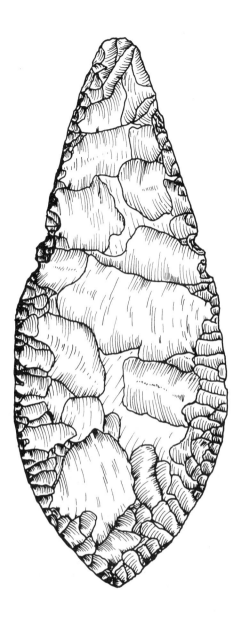

119 The Ffair Rhos dagger. The notches on either side are probably related to the hafting of the blade.

120 Flint dagger from Ronaldsway, Scotland.

form. This is occasionally manifest in patterns of parallel 'ripple-flake' scars running in from both edges. Like earlier discoidal and polished varieties, these knives may have formed a distinctive item of personal gear. Although they occasionally occur with women or children, their strongest funerary associations are with men. They are also found in close association with Collared Urns, a category of vessel that developed during the time that Beakers were in use.

A similar range of associations can be found for daggers, perhaps the most striking expressions of the flintworker's art to appear in later prehistoric Britain (fig. 118). Although it is difficult to identify the precise horizon at which these first appear, daggers have strong links with Beaker contexts and continued to be made and used during the Early Bronze Age. The character and extent of the flake scars that cover the surfaces of these lanceolate tools indicate a high degree of preparation and anticipation. Moreover, while they are characterized by invasive flake scars, grinding seems to have been used to remove irregularities, create sharp platforms and reduce the risk of breakage or loss of control over form. A similar procedure may have occasionally been employed for barbed-and-tanged arrowheads and elaborate knives.

Like these other forms, it is possible to detect variability in the extent to which these different concerns were realized in dagger production. Some daggers display more irregular patterns of scars, and the uniformity and thickness of their cross sections may also vary. Subtle variations in morphology can also be seen. Examples such as the Ffair Rhos dagger have distinctive notches towards their narrowest end, which may be related to the fixing of hafts (fig. 119). Others, such as the dagger from West Cotton, have a pronounced tang which may reflect a similar practical concern. Many are delicately flaked into a fine leaf shape, and it is clear that a number, such as the dagger from Garton Slack in Yorkshire, were never intended for use (fig. 120). Similarly, microwear analysis on the dagger from the Beaker grave at Irthlingborough revealed little evidence of wear or damage (fig. 121). Others do show signs of having been used, and together with morphological variability this may suggest variations in the conditions under which different examples were made and used.

The physical character of daggers has often led us to suppose that they were important prestige goods. Parallels with elaborate Danish and Breton daggers have been drawn, and once again the importation or emulation of exotic forms has been raised as a possibility. Given the nature of the raw materials used and their strong southern and easterly distribution, it is unlikely that daggers were imported. Some were probably passed between different communities as goods or gifts, but many reflect more local patterns of production and consumption, using materials that were ready to hand. It is even possible that massive flake 'blanks' may have been traded, passing into the hands of a relatively small number of skilled stoneworkers. These individuals may have produced daggers for themselves, and perhaps for others, but unlike Denmark, we have yet to find evidence for specialized and clearly demarcated workshops. For that reason, it is difficult to explore the idea that their production may have come under some form of close control or supervision.

Despite the lack of definitive evidence for specialist production, one further aspect of daggers has been taken as evidence that they were caught up in the active negotiation of political authority. Since the end of the last century it has been acknowledged that many bear a close resemblance to the early copper and bronze daggers that begin to appear in graves at this time. This has also been suggested for several daggers carved in bone. Some have argued that these similarities reflect a process of emulation, in which items associated with elites were copied in other materials or in other ways by members of

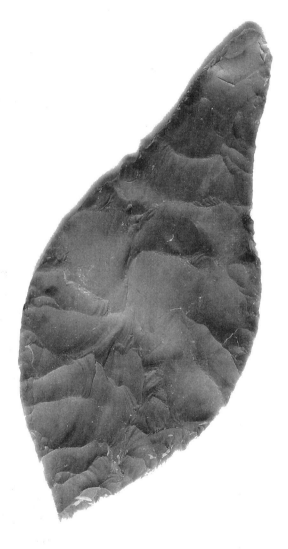

121 Leaf-shaped flint dagger from a Beaker-associated grave at Irthlingborough. Further associations with the man buried in this grave included perforated buttons, bone spatulae and smoothed stones that may have been used for burnishing leather or other materials (courtesy of John Humble).

subordinate groups. It has also been suggested that flint daggers may have been placed in graves instead of metal forms at times when the latter were in limited supply. The same may apply to a small number of stone axes, such as the example from Penicuik, Midlothian, which appear to mimic the form of early copper and bronze axes. These arguments are persuasive; many flint daggers may have been made with a model of metal forms in mind. Yet the purposes that they served probably extended beyond a concern with emulating prestige goods, or making up for a shortfall in the supply of metal daggers. Their display or consumption in different settings may have had as much to do with their capacity to signify rather more basic ideas about the identity of people and their place within the local group.

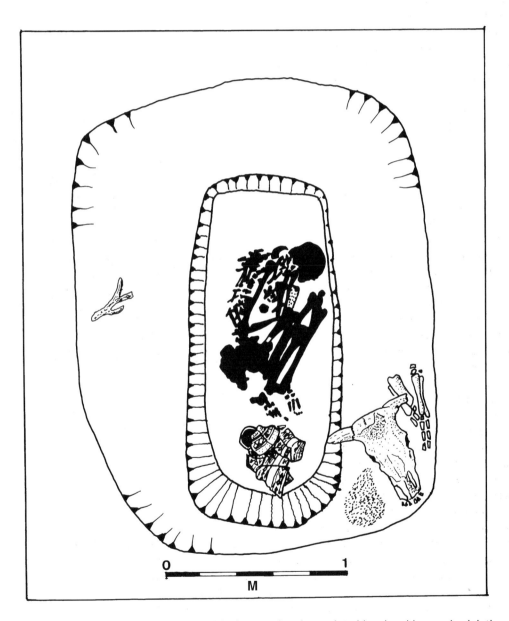

122 Beaker burial at Hemp Knoll. Together with the vessel and associated head and hooves burial, the body was accompanied by an archer's bracer or wristguard (after Asbee 1960).

## Death and definition

Many of these themes appear to have been brought to the fore in death. Beaker and other Early Bronze Age funerary sites take a variety of forms, but generally focus upon the inhumed or cremated bodies of individual people (fig. 122). Ranging from flat graves and small cemeteries through to barrows, Beaker burials occur in an almost bewildering range of contexts – inserted in the ditches of sites up to a thousand years old; in the chambered tombs of the north and west, in more recent henges, and in comparative isolation. Regional differences are also apparent: the use of cists in northern Britain can be contrasted with the greater emphasis upon ring ditches and barrows in the south and east. Ring cairns and stone mounds occur in greater numbers further to the west. This shift towards individual burial was already under way prior to the appearance of Beakers in many areas, and the variety noted above reflects the extent to which they were incorporated into local traditions. In many parts of Britain, their currency may have been broadly contemporary with a decline or change in the use of many Later Neolithic ceremonial monuments.

Although they may be extraordinarily varied, Beaker funerary rites reflect both a shift and perhaps a sharpening of focus. In many earlier tombs, fragments of the human body were no more than elements set within a complex architectural frame. Open and in use for several centuries, the character, content and significance of these ancestral houses was reworked or subtly altered by different generations. Bones

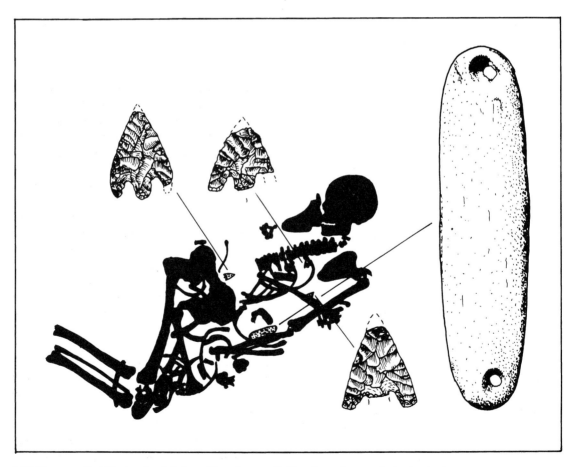

123 The so-called 'Archer burial' from Stonehenge. Unlike the wristguard, the barbed-and-tanged arrows probably entered the grave inside the body and are likely to have been the cause of death.

could be moved around or removed altogether, new assemblages could be added, and the sites themselves appear to have been the focus for other episodes of ceremonial activity. This is one of the reasons why they present so many problems for archaeologists. Many Beaker funerary sites also saw long sequences of use, but the moment of burial appears to have been just that – a specific point in space and time at which the remains of a person were laid down and covered (fig. 123). In other words, the emphasis was shifted from a repetitive and varied encounter with ancestral remains, towards a more limited and clearly defined episode in which a person was buried.

This shift of emphasis is important, but it should not lead us to ignore the considerable lengths of time over which Beaker and other Early Bronze Age burial sites were visited and reused. Single or double graves, occasionally surrounded by circles of posts, were sometimes reopened, and secondary burials were inserted. Perhaps these later events provided access to 'ancient' Beakers and it is not impossible that these provided the models for later copies. Sometimes these secondary burials took the form of articulated individuals, but they could also arrive at the site as cremations or as bundles of selected bones. So-called 'satellite' burials were also inserted in many existing barrows, and mounds were often added to groups of flat graves after many years. Some mounds were stone built, but many others were made entirely of turf stripped from the surrounding area.

The visual impact of this large scar around a newly built mound would have been striking enough, but in many cases, the location of a barrow was enhanced by other cultural features. Cemeteries or clusters of barrows occur in many regions, and in some cases, may be separated by only a handful of miles. High densities of barrows can be found on prominent ridges, as in south Dorset or Cambridgeshire. Others occur at valley heads and on hilltops, or in close proximity to larger ceremonial monuments. That this spatial association was important is suggested by the fact that individual barrow cemeteries sometimes took ancient earthworks as a first point of reference. This practice finds vivid expression at Winterbourne Stoke in Wiltshire, where the ori-

entation of a long barrow provides the principal axis for later round barrows. It is demonstrated in equally dramatic fashion at Kilmartin in Scotland, where concentrations of funerary sites reflect accumulated episodes of activity that spanned many generations.

Although the burial of individual people may have been an event of relatively short duration, these broader patterns suggest that barrow builders often drew upon or otherwise manipulated the historical associations of particular places in the landscape. 'Referencing' archaic sites that may have been abandoned for hundreds of years, many of these barrow concentrations reflect the repeated evocation of links between past and present acts of burial. Real or imagined, these expressions of deep roots and continuity may have been addressed to what was often a relatively local audience. Although the tradition itself is widespread, the construction, use and reuse of barrows and cemeteries – of reinscribing familiar landmarks – may have been closely tied to the renewal of local claims to land and other important resources.

Despite the great numbers of barrows, ring ditches or cairns constructed at this time, it is possible that these rites were often reserved or restricted. Not everybody could be buried in this way, and fragments of human bone from Beaker settlements suggest that other people may have followed different pathways into the afterlife. Although it is difficult to test, it is possible that these differences in treatment may reflect basic differences in position or authority, not just between individuals, but also between groups. Seen on the skyline and in the course of daily life, barrows and cemeteries would have stood as testaments to these distinctions, and to the links that particular groups had with a specific area. These claims to access may have been particularly important where the seasonal pattern of economic life retained a major pastoral component. Ceremonies conducted during funerals may have brought these links into even sharper focus.

This referencing of the past was also important at the level of the individual cemetery and even the single barrow, where new mounds or secondary burials may have occasioned the celebration of earlier generations. This would

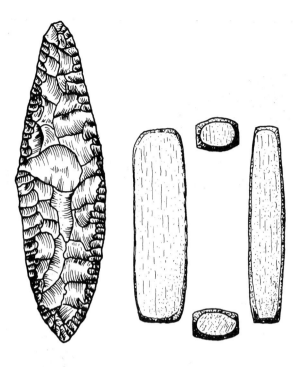

124 Grave goods from Amesbury G54, Wiltshire: a flaked dagger and a ground 'whetstone'.

have been crucial where the inheritance of many authorities and rights could be contested or otherwise questioned. The use of a cemetery or an existing mound may have been an expression of genealogical proximity – not just between the corpse and those who already lay beneath the earth, but also between the corpse and the mourners – though this expression may sometimes have had little basis in fact, as different people attempted to legitimate or assert new claims to local authority. However, many sites must have seen repeated use by the same communities for many generations.

Within this web of social and historical associations lay the moment of burial itself. Occasionally, this moment was marked by acts which retain much of their drama if not their significance. At Irthlingborough in the Nene valley, a mound of over 180 cattle skulls was built over a wooden chamber containing the body of a man, and a grave pit with a second adult. The mound was enlarged on more than one occasion, and became the focus for a series of later burials. In other cases, initial graves may have been marked

with few imposing physical features, but were nevertheless important as a focus for later rites of interment, and for episodes when people gathered to create a covering mound.

If clusters of graves and/or barrows addressed a relatively local audience, the act of burial itself may have been even more closely focused. No doubt some funerals were signal events, involving the coming together of many people, but more may have been undertaken and witnessed by a much smaller group. It has become a truism that the dead do not bury themselves, but it is worth stressing that these sites reflect the actions, perceptions and intentions of mourners. That is why it is not always easy to take the scale, complexity or 'richness' of burials as an index against which to measure the status or political standing of the deceased (fig. 124). Even where no artefacts were interred, the reuse of an existing mound or grave may have made it possible to assert the connections that stretched between different generations, and perhaps even to rank people in terms of their local influence and standing. By the same token, it may be misleading to assume that the distinction between inhumation and cremation was necessarily linked to differences of status or rank. This may have been important in certain cases, but we often forget that the burning of bodies on funeral pyres may have been spectacular events observed by many. While the identity of the corpse was a major concern, that identity – like the body itself – was a resource that could be drawn upon in a number of ways by the living.

Although the details of individual acts of burial vary from one context, site and region to another, it is possible to detect a number of common themes. For example, there is a tendency for cremations and secondary burials to have fewer artefact associations than bodies contained in the central grave, and many graves had no associations at all. At Barnack in Cambridgeshire, only three of the fifteen burials surrounding the central grave were accompanied by artefacts (fig. 125). In the case of cremations, statements concerning the position or persona of the dead may have been made in the context of the pyre, and through the oratory and orchestration of crematory ritual. This may be why they tend to have fewer grave goods than inhumations.

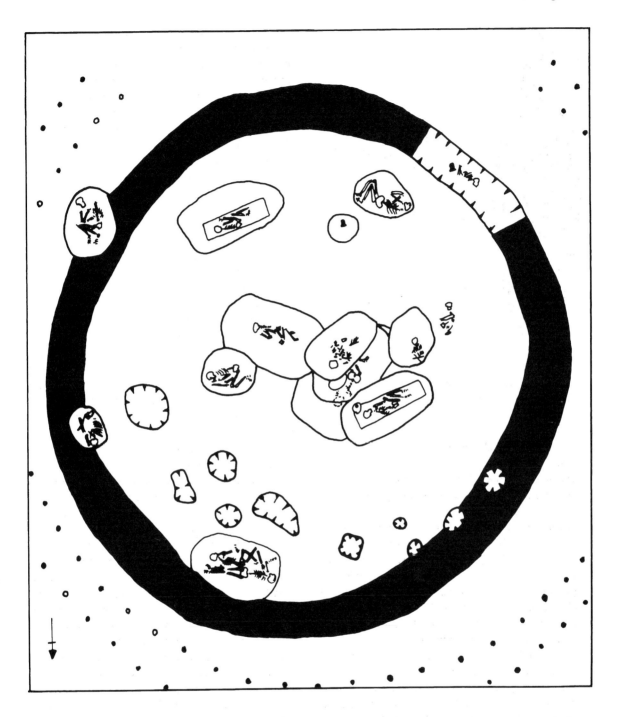

125 Plan of the central area of a cemetery barrow at Barnack, Cambridgeshire. Developing over several generations, sites such as Barnack may have been used repeatedly by members of particular groups.

Apart from artefact associations, the treatment of the body often provided a medium through which statements could be made about the deceased. In Yorkshire, for example, the position and orientation of the body often varied according to age and gender. It has also been suggested that the bodies of women or children were sometimes added to male burial sites as if in keeping with a sense of hierarchical order. This is difficult to establish. There are cases where women or children were the primary interment, and adult males may only form the dominant focus because they were buried in greater numbers.

The importance that gender may have had as an issue during funerals is difficult to determine, and our problems are compounded by the fact that early excavators often based attributions of sex upon indeterminate features or circular arguments from grave goods. What can be said is that, where they have been recognized, female bodies may also be accompanied by elaborate grave goods. The range of associations with women or children is rather more limited than it is with men, but it includes goldwork and jet, and tools such as bronze daggers, knives, pebble hammers and scrapers. Although these scrapers range from irregular retouched flakes through to more circular forms, distinctive thumbnail scrapers are conspicuous by their absence. Where they have any associations at all, they are generally found with men.

The simple fact that few objects have exclusive associations with one or other sex suggests that rigid correlations may have remained more the exception than the rule. If anything, age may have been just as important, and both dimensions may have been blurred in daily life. It was generally in death that these concerns were made more explicit, but even then the evidence is difficult to read. These statements of male influence may have been idealized expressions of divisions of labour and authority which were harnessed to the inheritance or renewal of other resources and powers.

These problems aside, the drawing of distinctions between age and gender categories may account for particular arrangements of grave goods. The so-called 'Beaker package' was by no means rigid, and changed over several centuries, but it is common to find the finest vessels with adult males. The fact that Beakers also occur with women and children suggests that they were not an exclusive item of male gear. But the qualitative distinction that was often drawn may reflect the assertion of a strong link between particular men and the practices in which Beakers were used. Perhaps they had a specific connection with feasting, or with other episodes of ritual consumption undertaken in the company of others. Whatever the case, this association was a guiding principle rather than a strict rule.

Although they only occur in a small number of cases, many of the artefacts recovered from burials demonstrate that grave goods were not so much a package as a series of symbols that could be drawn on in varied ways (fig. 126). The link between men and weapons has already been noted, yet in common with the graves of many women and children, it seems that a rich variety of themes could be evoked. Some artefacts entered graves on the body – clothes' fittings and adornments which may have spoken of the personal history and identity of the deceased. But like the pots themselves, many more artefacts were added to the tableau – a quiver of arrows, a dagger or battle axe; a clutch of scrapers or pins; bone objects and elaborate or exotic items of

126 Grave goods from Garton Slack, Yorkshire.

gold, jet, copper, bronze and amber.

Some of these assemblages reflect the provision of artefacts for use by the dead. Scrapers, knives, blanks for arrowheads, strike-a-lights and cores or flakes may have been interred for use in the tasks that different people were likely to perform in the afterlife. As such, their inclusion may have been in keeping with tacit conventions regarding general divisions of labour. Many tools bear traces of use, and it is possible that they were elements of the personal gear worn and used by particular people. Apart from warfare and the hunt, certain combinations of tools may have highlighted tasks such as leather or metalworking, and in these cases, it is possible that the grave tableau drew attention to a specific link between the deceased and these activities.

Similar purposes may have been served where objects were made specifically for display or burial. Elaborate or finely made variations on everyday themes were probably deposited in keeping with these same conventions. However, their inclusion may have also been geared towards the creation of a more specific expression of the status and influence of the deceased and their relation to the living. Placed by the mourners at different points around the body, these artefacts may have been cues for the interpretation of the dead person, and his or her association with specific concerns. Exotic items may have signalled the existence of distant alliances and the position of particular families within broader social networks. Finely made artefacts such as flint daggers may have carried similar ideas, but may also have been included as material expressions of the standing of particular individuals (and thus their families) within the local area. In cases where a measure of hereditary authority had been established, some of these items may even have been acquired as tributary gifts from subordinates. Their presence may have been an eloquent reminder of existing obligations or a signal that those debts and ties were now broken.

This process of definition would have had important consequences among the living. The act of placing objects with a body may have been seen as a form of exchange, in which a mourner established a lasting relationship with the dead. This may have provided an affirmation of close kinship ties where the right to 'give to the dead' was restricted. Yet it would also have provided a medium through which different mourners could demonstrate their own standing as well as their links to the deceased. Perhaps the burial of eminent elders or even 'Big men' was a time at which people drawn from different communities argued over the reallocation of power and authority in the region.

At the same time, the burial of particular artefacts may have drawn attention to the rights and influence that had been held by a person in life, as means of passing on those rights to particular descendants. Although bodies may have lain in state for a time, these acts of giving to the dead may often have been seen by only a few, and only for a short period. At this specific juncture, the harnessing of objects to a body not only reproduced some of the basic categories of the social world; it also provided a medium through which local networks of political authority could be renewed or redefined.

# 6 The place of stone in Early Bronze Age Britain

The inception of the Early Bronze Age makes little sense as a strictly technical revolution. The first appearance of metal was not marked by the widespread abandonment of stone, and a rich variety of tools continued to be made and used on a day-to-day basis. Some were also incorporated in a variety of formal deposits, and their display, circulation and deposition continued to address important social and political themes. In the case of funerary practices, Beaker-associated graves reflect a sustained concern with genealogy; and with the drawing of basic distinctions between the young and the old, and between women and men. These distinctions would often have been embedded within ceremonies directed towards the inheritance of local rights and resources, and occasionally to the negotiation of political and economic relations within the broader region.

The fact that these varied funerary practices developed when many ceremonial centres were falling out of use has been taken as evidence for a process of social fragmentation. In other words, barrows and cemeteries have often been seen as reflections of an increased emphasis on smaller political units rather than larger corporate or regional social structures. This may well have been the case, but we should be wary of seeing this shift of emphasis in such simple terms. In Wessex, sites such as

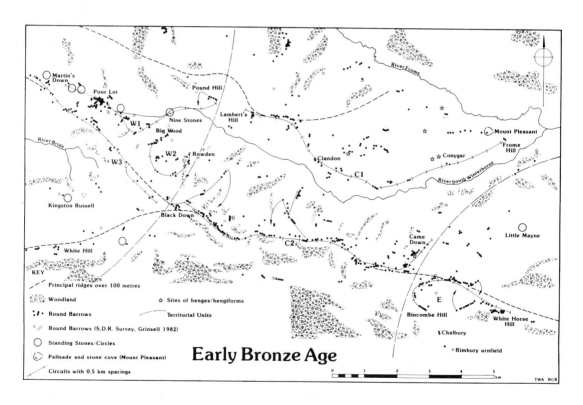

127 Changes in the landscape 3: the Early Bronze Age landscape along the South Dorset Ridgeway (courtesy of Peter Woodward and the Trust for Wessex Archaeology.)

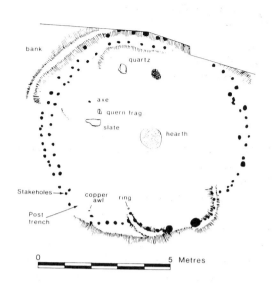

128 Plan of Early Bronze Age house at Gwithian, Cornwall.

Mount Pleasant and Stonehenge persisted as major ceremonial foci throughout the Early Bronze Age, and periodic gatherings probably remained as important events in the lives of many communities throughout Britain. Moreover, as the presence of exotica in burials suggests, these groups were connected through networks of trade, exchange, alliance and obligation which stretched beyond local boundaries (fig. 127).

It was in these contexts that the appearance of metal may have had its most immediate impact, as members of different communities attempted to establish and express authority through the display of portable wealth and the circulation of status items. This authority was probably grounded in a variety of spheres, from the mobilization of surpluses through to the direction of trade and craft production. There may even have been brief periods when particular groups attained a level of hierarchical authority which sanctioned the giving of tributary gifts and services. As with stone, metal objects were probably circulated and consumed in a variety of ways and for a variety of reasons, and there is no reason to suppose that their roles remained constant through time. Indeed, the changing contexts and inventories of Early Bronze Age metalwork assemblages suggest important developments in the practical and social roles played by their constituent elements (fig. 128). What concerns us here is the extent to which the changing roles of metal in the Early Bronze Age had consequences for the ways in which artefacts of stone were perceived, produced and consumed.

## Changing tokens

We can begin to address this question by comparing evidence for the character and treatment of stone and metal axes. Axes of both materials are generally rare in Early Bronze Age graves, and given their traditional links with men, this seems rather puzzling. Copper and bronze axes were introduced to Britain from an early stage, and local production probably developed quite rapidly. Yet in many areas, they were seldom interred with the dead. Axes have, however, been recovered from a small number of graves, such as Edenkilly in Morayshire and Bush Barrow in Wessex, and they appear as carvings on cists at Kilmartin in Argyll. However, their infrequent use as grave goods suggests that subtle conventions surrounded the ways in which different categories of artefact could be treated.

Evidence from the contexts in which axes are more commonly found may indicate that they were kept apart from graves because of their particular associations and roles. The Later Neolithic saw the development of traditions of votive deposition that may have begun rather earlier and these seem to have been maintained and even elaborated during the Early Bronze Age. Hoarding, deposition in pits and the throwing of artefacts into rivers remained as important practices. Unlike daggers, axes are more commonly found in these contexts than in graves. Indeed, they may have been some of the first metal artefacts to be treated in this way and they dominate many hoards. For that reason, it is possible that they were understood and treated in much the same ways as earlier stone forms. While the material had changed, the medium and meaning of these acts of deposition may have retained a measure of continuity with traditional practices.

There is little reason to assume that the decline of stone axes and their replacement in metal had much to do with questions of function or practical efficiency. Although many bronze axes were probably used, others bear few signs of wear and it is by no means clear that this new material conferred a major practical advantage – this is certainly so with copper axes. However, given the broader purposes that these artefacts served, there may have been other dimensions in which metal offered potentials that were not so easily realized in stone. In the first place, metal may have provided a very different scope for control over access to important tokens of value. Native ore sources cluster in the west and north of the country, and the knowledge required to transform these materials may itself have been restricted. This is also suggested by the fact that the earliest metal finds in Britain are imports from Ireland or the Continent.

Constraints upon access to ores or skills were no doubt important at an early stage, just as access to the products of specialist flintworkers may have conferred certain local political advantages. Yet it is unlikely that these basic restrictions persisted for very long, or that they were the only reason that metal came to usurp the place of stone as an important symbolic resource. Equally important may have been the potential that this new material offered for the definition of artefact categories. As many of the earliest axes demonstrate, metal can be decorated or embellished in a variety of ways, and modifications to moulds offer the scope for the reworking of forms (fig. 129). Not only that, metal can be recycled and manipulated in ways which have no counterpart in stone. Apart from the few cases where axes were turned into maceheads, the physical destruction or burial of stone artefacts effectively removed them from systems of circulation. This also happened with many metal objects, but they could also be turned back into liquid and rendered into new and varied forms.

This greater scope for reworking would have introduced a new factor into established traditions of circulation and deposition. In particular, it would have allowed for the manipulation or transformation of the physical characteristics of artefacts as they circulated in different settings, and moved from one 'regime

129 Decorated bronze axes (National Museum of Scotland).

of value' to another. This may have lent itself to the process by which the significance and role of certain items was also transformed. Traded goods may have been turned into appropriate gifts, and artefacts could be refashioned in keeping with local custom or with reference to exotic forms. That this potential was exploited is suggested by the fact that many continental axes seem to have been recast into local forms soon after their arrival in Britain.

Where this process involved items which played an important part in the expression or negotiation of political authority, it is possible that the act of metalworking was surrounded by local proscription and taboo. Whether this was in the context of patronage or trading agreements remains difficult to establish, but it is possible that particular sources may have been closely associated with specific communities. This may have been the case at the extensive Great Orme mines in Wales. The complex networks of shafts and galleries at this site were used over several centuries, and as with flint mines, estimates of the scale of working need to be tempered by this fact. However, it is possible that here too, the people who extracted or processed the ores were caught up in broader networks of trade and exchange which carried the fruits of their labour into different social settings. As yet, we have a limited understanding of the conditions under which these new sources were exploited. The small scale of some of the galleries at Great Orme has been taken as evidence for the use of children in the process of extraction. This might indicate that entire communities were engaged in these tasks, but it is difficult to take this speculation any further.

Superimposed on these potentials in the material itself were the associations and biographies carried by different categories of artefact. Analysis of bronze, jet, shale, gold and amber has shown that objects were traded or exchanged over extraordinary distances from the end of the third millennium onwards, and the orientation of these broad networks may have changed through time. For example, many Beaker assemblages reflect connections with the Rhineland and the Low Countries. Daggers in slightly later graves in Wessex indicate contact with Brittany, and some of the latest Early Bronze Age burials in this area contain objects and materials which signal communication with Central Europe and the Baltic.

As with Beakers, it is open to question how far these exotica represent direct connections between dominant communities in Britain and similar groups abroad. A variety of different mechanisms probably brought Irish gold, Baltic amber or Breton bronze into the country. What is perhaps more important is that some of these objects carried with them ideas or conventions about the media through which authority could be established or expressed. These were probably elaborated or reinterpreted from one local tradition to another, and as with stone axes, we should not assume that people necessarily had a complete understanding of what we often perceive as a system on continental proportions. Such a birds' eye view is only possible from the vantage point of the present. Nevertheless, the existence of trading partnerships, or extensive networks of contact and alliance would have played a crucial part in shaping the flow of goods and important tokens of value and identity in different regions of Britain. The display, circulation and deposition of some of these items would have had important consequences for many dimensions of social and economic life. Apart from the mainte-

nance of rights to land and other resources, networks of kinship may have been extended through marriages, and debts may have been called upon at festivals and times of harvest, or in the face of conflict between communities.

If the production, circulation and deposition of metal artefacts raises similar problems to those seen in earlier chapters, it remains to ask what happened at the sources of stone axes. Unfortunately, this is a question that has yet to be addressed in any detail, and there is a great deal that we do not know. Established sources in Cumbria and Wales saw the production of maceheads, but these occur in relatively small numbers. At Creag na Caillich in Perthshire, much of the debris reflects small-scale axe production, but some of the crude blanks that left the site may have been worked into the maceheads identified through petrological studies. Only in Cornwall were larger numbers of maceheads produced from an established source and even here, little is understood about the conditions under which they were made. Sources in the Midlands and along the Whin Sill saw consistent use for the production of perforated implements such as battle axes and axe hammers throughout the Early Bronze Age. These were probably traded between neighbouring communities, and the evidence suggests that some were passed beyond the regional horizon. Whether they generally made this journey as goods or gifts remains unclear.

It is difficult to imagine that axe production came to a dramatic end or that people abruptly turned their backs on an important source of raw material. Just as the introduction of metalwork encouraged changes in local networks of rank and obligation, and in the very media of authority, so the products of particular sources may have undergone quite gradual changes in their significance or value. Perhaps they became more freely available with the passage of time, and were produced and circulated in a wider range of contexts than before. Perhaps certain raw materials lost some of their exclusive associations prior to the arrival of metal in the source areas. The first appearance of metal may have contributed to a shift of emphasis that was already in progress, and we should not assume that one material simply replaced the other. Whatever the

157

case, there is little evidence to suggest that systematic stone axe production continued long after the appearance of Beakers.

What is also clear is that potential answers will not be found at the sources alone. In areas like Cumbria, East Anglia, County Antrim or north Wales, regions that saw the development of some of the largest mine and quarry complexes, we know little about the manner in which raw material was treated or used away from the source, still less how this may have changed through time. Shafts continued to be sunk at Grimes Graves for the first few centuries of the second millennium, and the working of surface deposits may have continued for even longer. The area was also the focus for Later Bronze Age settlement, as will be discussed further in chapter 7. Work by Frances Healy and others has shown that chalk flint is most frequently found on Later Neolithic and Early Bronze Age sites in the region, but as yet we know very little about the conditions under which this later material was obtained or used.

The picture is even more confused in Cumbria. Here the lack of evidence from settlements or other contemporary contexts prevents us from tracing the later history of the volcanic tuff that had long been used for axe production. In this case at least, where production for exchange may have gained in importance during the course of the Neolithic, the last centuries of the third millennium may have witnessed changes in the political geography of the region. If certain communities had come to occupy a privileged position in the social networks that carried axes out of the area, changes in the nature of demand may have had important repercussions for the order of local relations. It may also have had consequences for the manner in which the raw material was regarded and used. This shift of emphasis may also have been felt at the source, where the general character and organization of production may have reverted to the arrangements that had been followed over a millennium before. The outcrop of tuff may have seen the slow erosion of its symbolic importance. Perhaps it gradually lost its significance as a place where people travelled to make markers of identity and media for exchange. The

imposing peaks of the Langdale Fells may have remained an important point of geographical and historical reference for many generations. But where the quarries had once stood as testaments to the importance of the stone axe, they may now have taken on the patina of an archaic order.

Despite these grey areas, broad continuities in the treatment of stone and metal axes suggest that there may also have been some continuity in the matter of their use. What may have kept axes of both materials out of many graves was their association with specific practices. Other items, such as daggers or goldwork, were undoubtedly circulated between different groups, and some may have carried associations and values accrued through gift exchange. Some may even have been given as a form of tribute, and their inclusion in graves may have been a medium through which mourners were reminded of the status of the deceased and their descendants. By contrast, axes may have derived some of their significance from their use in particular exchanges or competitive displays, and this might have influenced the manner of their deposition. If their passage was commonly directed towards the negotiation of broader political relations, they might have been out of place in burials, where other facets of a person's identity were given greater emphasis.

It is unlikely that every category of artefact singled out for votive deposition served the same purpose. The disposal of axes and other metal items may have been directed towards different ends, and their uses may have cut across the typological boundaries that we construct. A number of these artefacts were in pristine condition when they were released from the hand and a few may have been sheathed or wrapped in cloth. Others show considerable signs of wear, and many appear to have been deliberately bent or broken. Some may have found their way into hoards and rivers in the context of funerary rituals; others may have entered the earth or the water to mark the end of certain relationships or to forge new ties of obligation and authority. Although it is difficult to distinguish between these different roles, the evidence does suggest that it was in these spheres that metal first usurped the place of stone.

## The living and the dead

Although metal axes may have taken on some of the roles played by their stone counterparts over the course of one or two centuries, stone artefacts remained important as practical and symbolic resources for a much longer period. Nowhere is this clearer than in Early Bronze Age funerary practices. Many of the themes highlighted in Beaker graves are evident in later burials associated with Collared Urns and Food Vessels. Beakers remained in use for some time, but they may have gradually come to lose their exclusive associations with particular practices or sections of the community. This may be why they were no longer regarded as suitable for inclusion in graves. This gradual loss of exclusivity did not apply to other artefacts. Flint daggers, plano-convex knives (fig. 130), maceheads and barbed-and-tanged arrowheads were deposited in later graves together with new forms such as the battle axe. In short, the Early Bronze Age saw the continued use of these and other objects as media through which to shape the interpretation of the dead and relations among the living.

The concerns which guided the selection of these artefacts are best illustrated by a brief comparison between battle axes (fig. 131) and another category of perforated implement: the axe hammer. Both categories made their first appearance during the time of Beakers, but are most closely associated with Early Bronze Age contexts. Like earlier maceheads, battle axes may have had a close association with warfare or fighting, and they share a broadly similar distribution, with notable concentrations in Yorkshire (fig. 132). In addition, battle axes have close counterparts on the Continent and a few were actually imported. Many others were locally made from stone from a wide variety of sources. These ranged from cobbles and naturally rounded stones occurring in streams or other deposits, through to larger exposures of raw material in areas such as the Whin Sill in north-eastern

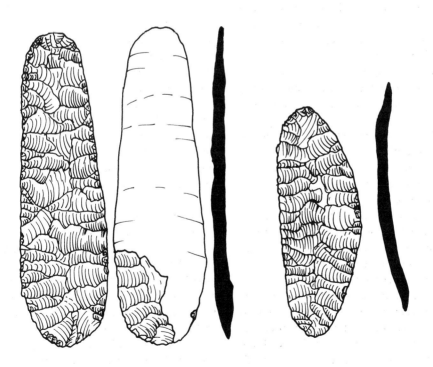

130 Plano-convex knives such as these have been found in Early Bronze Age settlement contexts and in graves associated with Collared Urns.

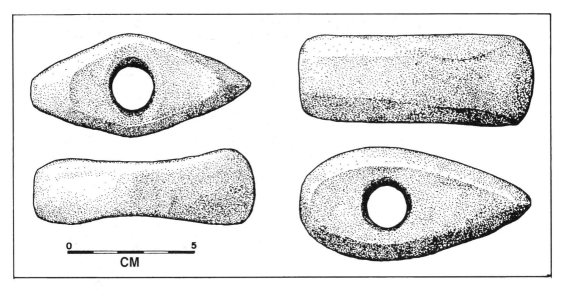

131 Stone battle axes from Yorkshire.

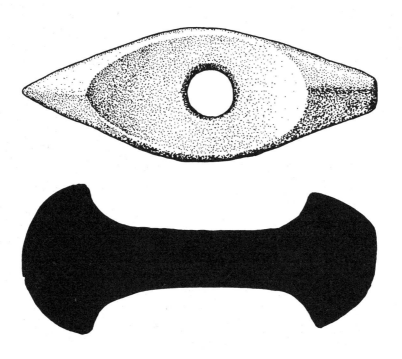

132 Stone battle axe with expanded blade.

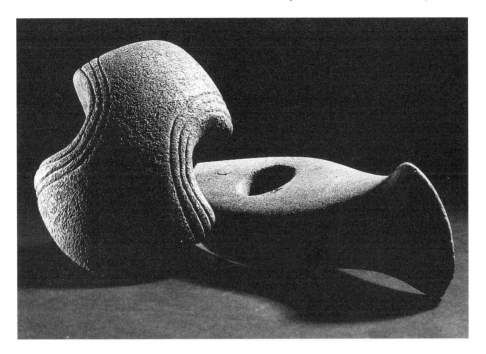

133 Elaborate battle axes from Scotland (National Museum of Scotland).

134 Battle axes from Broomend of Crichie, Aberdeenshire; Chapelton, Lanarkshire; and Longniddry, East Lothian (National Museum of Scotland).

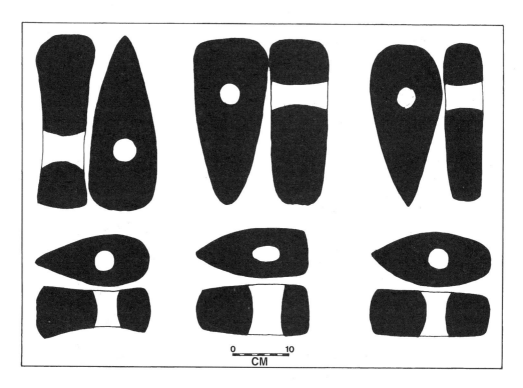

135 Simplified drawings of stone axe hammers.

136 Axe hammers from eastern England (Museum of Archaeology and Antropology, Cambridge).

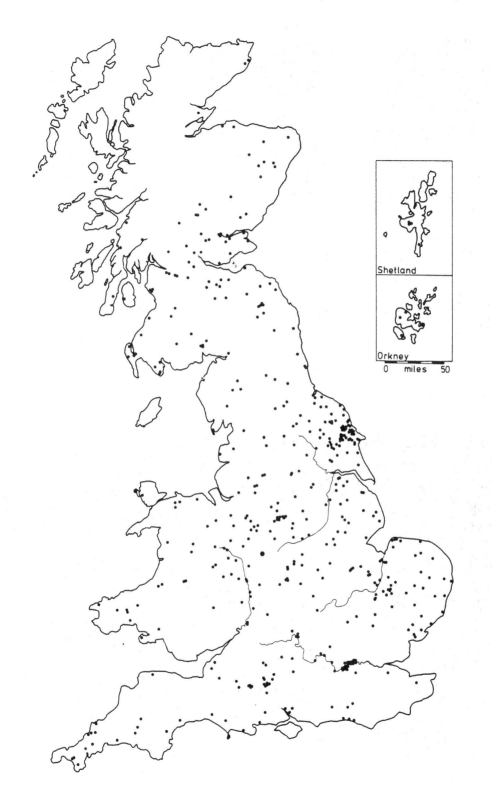

137 Distribution of battle axes in Britain (after Roe 1979).

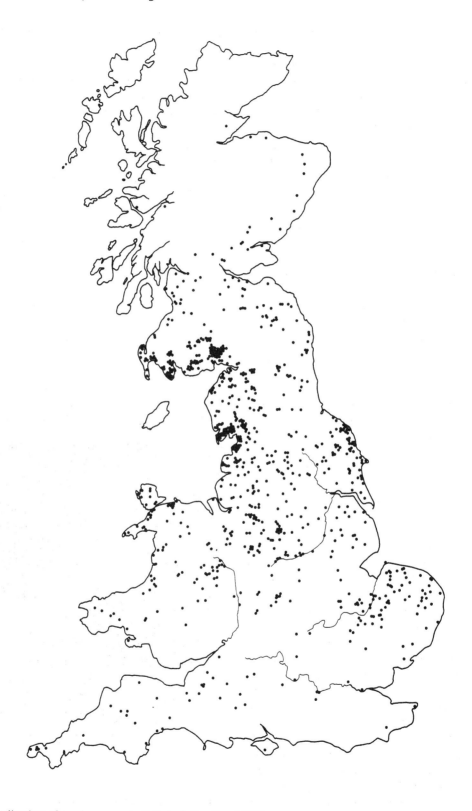

138 Distribution of axe hammers in Britain (after Roe 1979).

England. A similar level of variation has been documented in Scotland, where materials including dolerite, greywacke and amphibolite were exploited. There is little evidence to suggest that battle-axe production was restricted to discrete sources or specialized workshops. Even the more elaborate and decorated examples (figs 133–4) that appear during the period are not generally distinguished by the use of exotic or otherwise restricted raw materials.

The same general picture emerges in the case of axe hammers (fig. 135). Found in many parts of Britain, their distribution is rather more weighted towards the west, but they do occur in the same areas as battle axes. These more massive tools again appear to have been made widely, and petrological analysis suggests that many were probably made, used and perhaps even traded at a relatively local scale. Various suggestions have been made regarding their function, and at the smaller end of the size range a similar role to battle axes is possible. Larger forms were probably used in the splitting of timbers and the working of other materials and it has been suggested that some may even have served as simple ard points.

Despite several points of similarity, one major distinction between battle axes and axe hammers can be seen. Echoing a pattern found on the Continent, the former have a strong association with funerary contexts, where they generally occur as male grave goods. By contrast, axe hammers are virtually absent from these contexts, and there is little evidence for formal or votive deposition (fig. 136). The same appears to be the case for shaft-hole adzes, which were often made of materials such as quartzite, the greywackes of Cumbria or the quartz dolerite of the Whin Sill. This brief comparison suggests that the inclusion of artefacts as grave goods depended upon the roles that they played among the living, and their capacity to signal ideas about particular social practices (figs 137–8). As both practical weapons and as symbols, the production and consumption of battle axes may have helped to sustain the identity and authority of 'those who fought'. In keeping with traditions established on the Continent, it may have been these dimensions of a man's social identity that were brought into focus when items such as battle

axes and barbed-and-tanged arrowheads were included with burials.

Further changes can be seen in the ceramic associations of Early Bronze Age funerary sites. Food Vessels and Collared Urns (figs 139–40) were used in increasing numbers as accompaniments or containers for the dead during the first half of the second millennium. The forms of these vessels display a strong regional aspect, and unlike Beakers they probably reflect the development of indigenous Later Neolithic ceramic traditions. Although it is tempting to take this increased regionalization of ceramic styles as evidence for the existence of cultural groupings, it remains difficult to draw a neat equation between pots and people. Different styles are found on the same site, and it is possible that what separated them was their association with specific practices, or with different sections of the community. This is difficult to demonstrate, and our problems are compounded by the fact that the associations of these vessels probably changed from one area to another as well as through time. In many regions, Food Vessels are often associated with

139 Collared Urns (Museum of Archaeology and Anthropology, Cambridge).

140 Food Vessels (Museum of Archaeology and Anthropology, Cambridge).

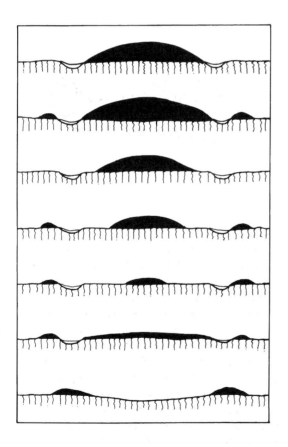

141 Cross-sections of specialized barrow forms from Early Bronze Age cemeteries.

inhumations, while Collared Urns tend to be found more commonly as the containers for cremations. In Yorkshire, burials with Collared Urns are often secondary to those with Food Vessels, and it is tempting to suggest that in this case at least, pots were used to differentiate between the dead.

Rather rarer, but exclusively associated with funerary contexts, were a series of smaller vessels sometimes referred to as 'Pygmy' or 'Accessory' Cups. These have been recognized in a number of regions, from Wessex and western Britain to the north-east. They are often found in association with more elaborately furnished burials, as at Stancombe Downs in Berkshire, where a cup accompanied a bronze razor, an antler hammer and a battle axe. They also occur in some of the more well-provisioned burials in Wessex, although these are massively outnumbered by interments with few material associations.

Alongside the rise to dominance of new vessel categories, many of the barrow cemeteries of southern Britain continued to grow, and in many areas, the monuments that we see today reflect several episodes of activity. Burials in grave pits, cists or wooden coffins may have lain beneath diminutive turf stacks, chalk rubble or timber structures for some time. The construction of a covering mound may not have been undertaken immediately, and barrows could also be enlarged or modified at a later date. These temporal distinctions suggest differences in the significance that was ascribed to various stages in the process of treating the dead. Perhaps the first stage of interment took place soon after the moment of death, supervised by only a small number of immediate kin. The throwing up of a covering mound may have involved the participation of larger numbers of people and may have required elaborate planning, co-operation and agreement before broader rites could be undertaken.

Some of the largest Early Bronze Age cemeteries also contain evidence for the elaboration or reworking of traditions of barrow construction. The simple mounds of earlier generations were augmented by more distinctive forms such as bell, disc and bowl barrows (fig. 141). These are often found in some of the larger cemeteries, and it is in these same contexts that many of the richest

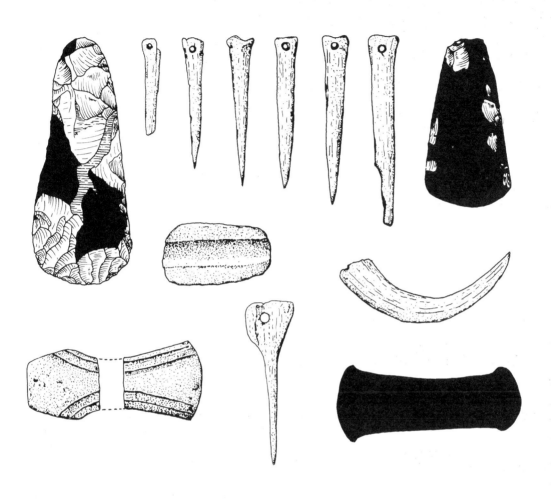

142 Selected artefacts from Upton Lovell G.2, a barrow in Wiltshire excavated in the last century. Although it is difficult to establish the character and condition of the burials located beneath this mound, it does seem that two bodies were identified. What is remarkable about the site is the character and range of grave goods that were placed with the dead. These included over three dozen perforated bone points; a necklace made from the teeth of a wolf and a dog; bone pendants; boar's tusks; perforated battle axes, stone rubbers that were probably used for grinding a variety of materials, and a series of hollow flint pebbles that may have served as containers. At least one of the individuals buried beneath this mound may have been some form of shaman; an individual who had the authority to undertake important rites and ceremonies. What is most surprising is the presence of a number of polished and partially polished flint axes, two of which are shown above. Although it is difficult to test, current ideas about the chronology of these implements would suggest that they were probably made at a much earlier date in the Neolithic than many of the other grave goods. Were these tokens that had been handed down over many generations, or were they artefacts that had been found in the fields or in already ancient features? Whatever the case, their character and antiquity may have meant that they took on the qualities of cult objects.

burials are found. In other areas, distinctions within cemeteries also seem to have been drawn through the size of mounds, the depth of grave pits, or the elaboration of cists. At Towthorpe in Yorkshire for example, a massive barrow covered the extended body of a man equipped with a limestone macehead and a large plano-convex knife.

These developments can be seen in a number of regions, but they find their most striking expression in Wessex (fig. 142). Here the traditional inventory of grave goods was augmented by new forms which signalled close connections with the Continent. Sites such as Bush Barrow in the Wilsford cemetery near Stonehenge are diffi-

cult to interpret as anything other than the resting places of people who occupied a pre-eminent position within the region (fig. 143). In the case of Bush Barrow itself, it is tempting to take the stone macehead, daggers, bronze axe and gold ornaments as reflections of the authority accorded to the man who was buried beneath the mound. Whether all of these artefacts were the possessions or trappings of this man during his life is open to question. Some may have been buried as offerings or gifts by mourners, and their inclusion may have been geared towards goals other than the celebration of the status of the deceased. Similar ideas may have been carried

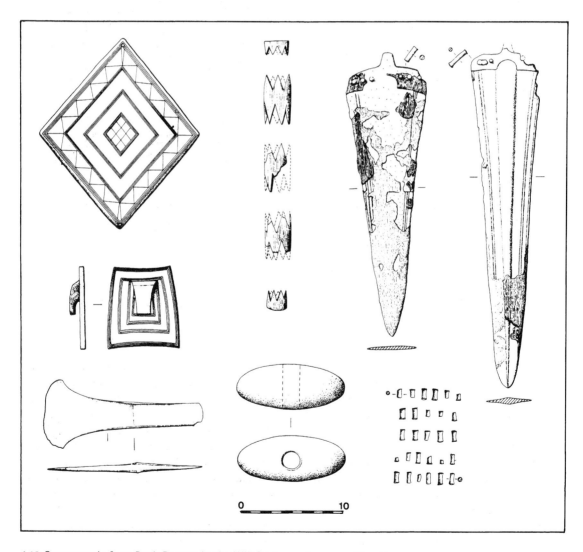

143 Grave goods from Bush Barrow in the Wilsford cemetery near Stonehenge.

144 Funeral at an Early Bronze Age barrow cemetery. The audience at the moment of burial may often have been relatively small, comprising immediate family members and other related individuals responsible for the preparation of the body and the provision of grave goods. This more intimate event may have been followed at a later date by the construction of a barrow involving the participation of a larger number of people. Other acts of burial may have been larger and more spectacular affairs at which the giving of gifts to the dead became an instrument of competition between the mourners and a medium through which the inheritance of certain rights and obligations could be contested (drawn by Judith Dobie; copyright English Heritage).

by the pins, awls and gold and amber objects interred with other burials in the area. Some of these objects had travelled considerable distances, and many reflect the labour of highly skilled specialists.

These trends in the form, context and contents of Wessex barrows suggest that funerary practices continued to play an important part in the definition of genealogies and in the renewal of claims to authority. Here again, we are likely to be dealing with the rites that were accorded to no more than a section of the population. Successive episodes of burial and the throwing

up of mounds may have stressed the continuity of the local order (fig. 144). These acts reaffirmed established lines of inheritance and the ties that bound particular communities to the land. At the same time, the elaboration of barrows and the disparity of grave goods within existing cemeteries may reflect a process of 'differentiation within association'. In other words, the first half of the second millennium may have seen an increased concern with the drawing of distinctions within the groups who customarily used a particular burial ground.

Similar themes may have dominated the lives

145 Shale and gold macehead from Clandon, Dorset (National Museum of Scotland).

of communities in other parts of Britain, although they were not always expressed through the same media. Ostentatious burials have been recognized in many areas, from Rillaton in Cornwall or Mold in Wales, through to Barnhill and the Knowes of Trotty in Scotland. The daggers, goldwork, jet and other jewellery found in these graves indicate that for some groups at least, identity and authority was expressed in much the same way as it was in Wessex (figs 145–7). Indeed, the use of similar symbols may have been one of the means by which people attempted to assert their position in broader networks of contact and communication. These ostentatious burials were undoubtedly signal events, but they were by no means the only ways in which people attempted to negotiate or maintain their position within the local order. Evidence for the deliberate destruction or disposal of wealth is well attested in northern Britain. The creation of hoards such as that from Migdale

in Sutherland, which contained an axe and jet and bronze jewellery, may have played an equally important political role to the burial of wealth with the dead.

## Changes in the landscape

The Early Bronze Age also witnessed broader developments in the character of landscape use. In many areas, the mid second millennium saw further clearance of woodland, and the expansion of settlement onto today's moorlands and uplands. In Derbyshire, settlement on the limestone of the White Peak was augmented by expansion onto the millstone grit of the Dark Peak, where barrows, cairns and settlement traces mark an increased human presence. Similar developments can be traced on the North Yorkshire Moors, in central Scotland, and on the uplands of the south-west such as Dartmoor. Expansion into the uplands also

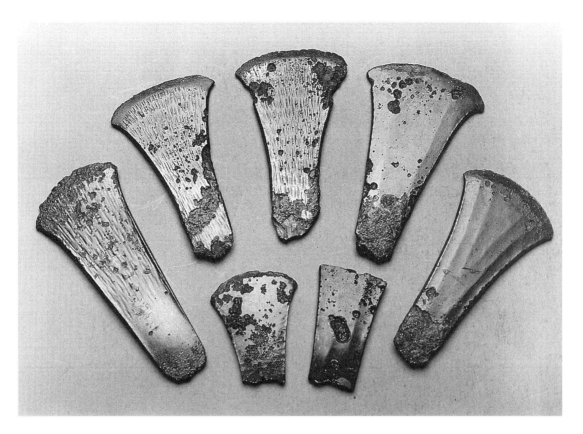

146 Metalwork hoard from Colleonard, Banffshire (National Museum of Scotland).

seems to have taken place in Cumbria, where some of the earliest huts and cairns in the Fells probably date to this period. By this time, the stone sources of the central fells were no longer set apart from the paths and routines of many day-to-day activities. Regularly encountered by many people, this may have contributed to the change in their significance.

As with earlier Beaker settlements, the scale of domestic sites seems to have remained relatively small throughout the Early Bronze Age. However, it is with this period of expansion into more marginal land that some of the details of the physical nature of individual settlements can begin to be identified. Many are characterized by small clusters of round houses of timber or stone, occasionally demarcated by small enclosing banks and associated with small field systems. The vast majority were small homesteads of no more than two or three houses, while others, such as Shaugh Moor on Dartmoor, comprised up to ten structures contained within a stone or earthen boundary. It is unlikely that all of these new settlements were permanently occupied. Some areas may have been exploited on a seasonal basis and may represent no more than an extension of the land routinely used by established communities in the heartlands (fig. 148).

Few of these settlements would have been entirely self-sufficient. Individual communities were probably bound together in complex networks of trade, kinship and alliance, and the annual cycle may have been marked by junctures at which members of different communities assisted each other in the gathering and processing of crops and other resources. As we have seen, funerary rites may have provided another context in which different communities came together. There may also have been periods where different groups co-operated in the clearance of land and in the creation and

171

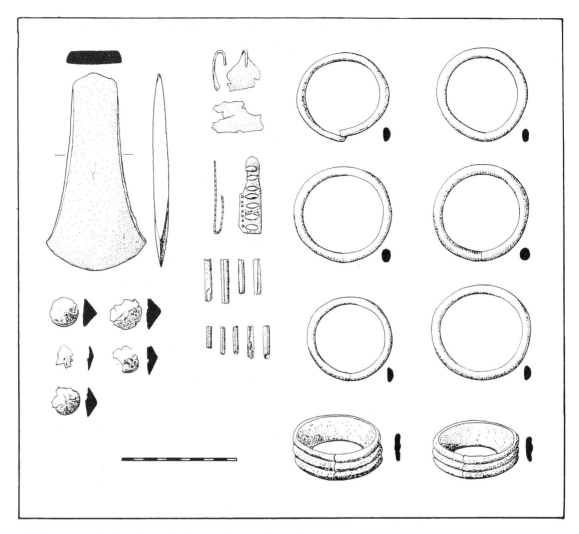

147 Selected artefacts from the Migdale hoard, Sutherland.

maintenance of fields. A physical expression of these themes can be seen on Dartmoor. People walking across the moor today can still see the lines of the stone-built field boundaries and land divisions that date to this time. These 'reaves' occasionally follow earlier lines of wooden fences or hedges and reflect the division of large tracts of land into 'territories' which were themselves subdivided by parallel reaves and individual fields (fig. 149).

Archaeologists have presented a variety of arguments to account for this phase of expansion. Some have interpreted these patterns as a response to the impoverishment of soils in the heartlands although this is not always easy to demonstrate. Others have placed a greater emphasis upon internal social processes, seeing expansion in terms of the inevitable fission or 'budding-off' of new communities from existing social groups. One interesting extension to this argument is that the increased use of marginal land was tied to the negotiation of social and political relations and in particular to the need to generate surpluses for use in feasting and trade. Persuasive though this argument may be, it is difficult to determine the nature of the bonds which linked these communities to those who remained in the traditional core areas. On the basis of differences in the relative 'richness' of graves, it has been suggested that these new communities were

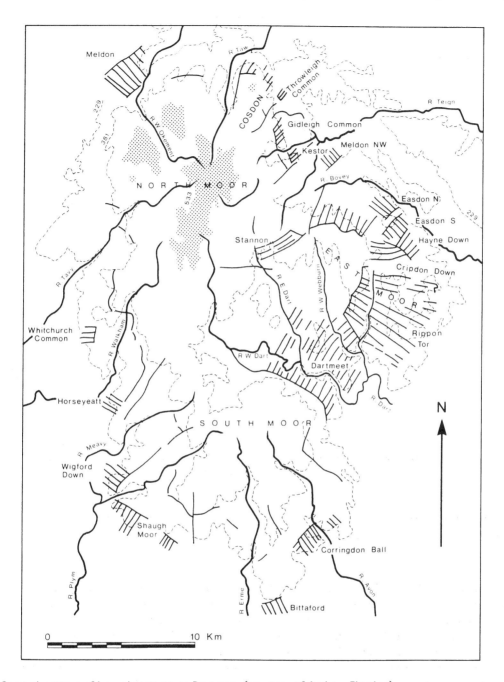

148 General pattern of 'reave' systems on Dartmoor (courtesy of Andrew Fleming).

both physically marginal and politically subordinate to established groups. However, the evidence is equivocal, and it may be that the flow of goods and services was structured by bonds of kinship and affiliation rather than through the imposition of a dominant political will.

These difficulties of interpretation again find an interesting expression on Dartmoor. As Andrew Fleming has pointed out, it is one thing to be able to document or describe the physical nature of the reaves and coaxial field systems which cut across the moor, but quite another to

173

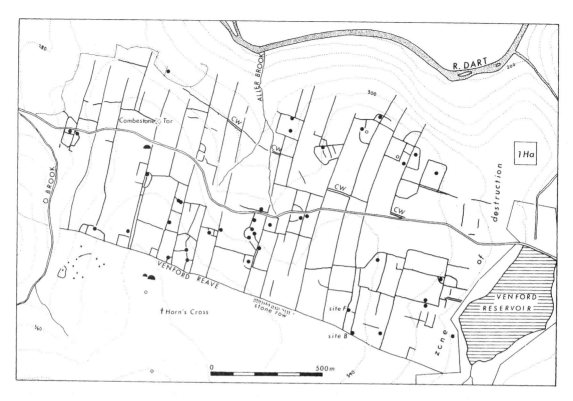

149 Distribution of houses and other structures in relation to field boundaries on Dartmoor (courtesy of Andrew Fleming).

150 Alongside barrows, cairns and cists, the landscape of the Early Bronze Age was also inscribed through the decoration or marking of natural outcrops of rock. Rock art is a predominantly northern phenomenon, which may have first appeared during the Later Neolithic. Commonly comprising cup-and-ring marks, spirals and other simple forms, rock art also occurs on a number of stone circles in north-eastern Scotland. As yet we know relatively little about the purposes that were served by these acts of inscription. Recent work suggests that the carving of prominent outcrops may have been tied to the seasonal use of the uplands by herders and hunters. Placed on important pathways or access routes, many rock art sites may have been important vantage points, as well as markers which reminded people of their place within the social landscape (photo of rock art on Weetwood Moor, Northumberland, courtesy of Richard Bradley).

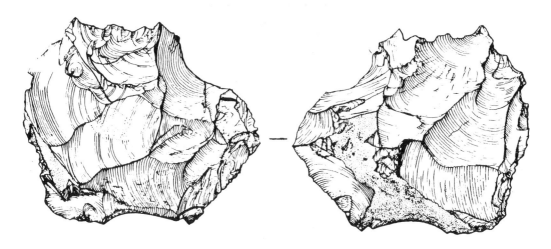

151 Early Bronze Age flint core.

establish the conditions which gave rise to their construction. Some have argued that the patterns we see today reflect the slow, progressive enclosure of land, while others see a more grand design behind the pattern. They suggest that a system of such large proportions must have been planned from the outset, and move from this observation to infer the existence of leaders capable of mobilizing the necessary labour. As with earlier communal monuments, the likelihood is that the answer lies somewhere between these two models. Decisions may have been taken by the senior members of different communities and the physical act of construction may again have been the result of co-operative effort. What is perhaps more interesting here is that these developments on Dartmoor reflect an important sea change in the nature of the activities which drew different communities together. Where the emphasis had once been placed upon the construction of specialized ceremonial monuments, now the greater investment was placed upon the marking or 'monumentalizing' of the agricultural landscape itself (fig. 150).

## Working stone

The first appearance of metal may have had relatively little impact on basic patterns of stone tool production and use. However, when the focus is extended to encompass the course of the Early Bronze Age, a series of more gradual trends can be discerned (fig. 151). These trends take a number of forms, but we can begin by considering the basic manner in which many communities selected and worked different raw materials.

Notwithstanding the occasional selection of exotic stone artefacts for inclusion in graves, the majority of Early Bronze Age assemblages reflect the use of raw materials that were ready to hand. In eastern England, for example, it is not uncommon to find assemblages containing flint from a variety of secondary sources, such as river gravels, together with artefacts made in flint from primary chalk deposits. There is also evidence for the retrieval and reuse of stone discarded during earlier periods. We might imagine that these moments when forgotten cores or flaked nodules were encountered and reused were also moments of reflection. The recognition of a worked surface patinated with age and the action of the soil may have provided quiet confirmation that even the most mundane of activities had a long history. However, these 'relics' were generally accorded no more significance than pieces of unworked but otherwise useful stone. A similar measure of raw material variability can be seen in parts of Scotland. In the north, pebbles of flint derived from rivers and beaches were used alongside quartz. This pattern was already well established during the Later Neolithic, but as recent work by Ann Clarke has shown, the Early Bronze Age sees an increase in the use that was made of other coarse stones. An equally broad range of raw

175

152 Crude knife made on a large flint flake.

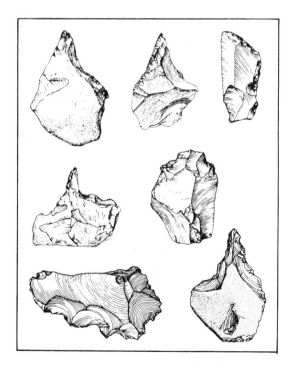

176    153 Early Bronze Age borers and retouched flakes.

materials is represented in assemblages from the Western Isles, central Scotland, and north-western England.

The first half of the second millennium also witnessed changes in the basic character of stoneworking traditions. In southern Britain, these are manifest in a slow but steady decline in the level of control, precision and formality exercised in production (fig. 152). In many areas, the frequency of prepared cores slowly decreased and irregular forms made on flakes became more common. Few assemblages contain evidence for the careful preparation of working edges or for the anticipation and avoidance of errors during core reduction. Moreover, the frequency of rejuvenation or recovery flakes is generally low and this suggests a general lack of concern with the definition of clear flaking routines or the maintenance of control over the form of flakes or cores. Similar patterns are found in the waste generated during the making of many tools and here it is interesting that there is a gradual decline in the range of formal tools that were made and used in many areas. A variety of scrapers, notches and borers remained as the backbone of most assemblages, reflecting the modification of a flake or irregular piece of flint to create a usable edge (fig. 153). Many appear to have been made, used and even discarded relatively rapidly. Fabricators, chisels and simple retouched knives also continued to be made, and in northern Scotland these were augmented by a range of coarse stone tools including ard points.

There is little reason to doubt that stone tool production and use remained a common practice for most members of individual communities. Excavations on Early Bronze Age settlements often produce large quantities of debitage, broken tools and burnt flint scattered around structures and trampled into the floors of houses. The widespread distribution of many artefacts and the ubiquity of cores and unretouched flakes on these sites suggests that many of these activities were unrestricted in either spatial or social terms. Whether this applied to all artefacts remains open to question, and here it is worth considering the case of barbed-and-tanged arrowheads. Some of the finest examples may have been made by individuals with enhanced stoneworking skills and it is possible that some passed between members of different communities as goods or gifts. However, there is no evidence to suggest that the bulk of arrowhead production was necessarily in the hands of specialists. The widespread distribution of these artefacts suggests that, as in earlier times, the making of arrowheads was probably a common feature on many settlements, the majority being made by the people who used them. There is no evidence for specialist workshops, or for the concentration of arrowhead production in spatially discrete zones within or away from settlements.

Further changes can be detected when we consider the contexts within which many of these artefacts have been found. In chapters 4 and 5, we saw how even the simplest of tools and unretouched flakes could be harnessed in acts of formal deposition or in otherwise structured deposits. In the case of the Later Neolithic, it was also suggested that a series of conventions may have guided the association of different stone tools with Peterborough and Grooved Wares. Putting to one side the assemblages from funerary sites, one of the most striking features of Early Bronze Age assemblages is the general lack of evidence for similar conventions. Only rarely do we find evidence for the formal deposition of lithic artefacts in or close to settlements. Put simply, stone tool assemblages were neither as complex nor as diverse as they had been a few centuries before. By the mid second millennium there is little evidence to suggest that stone tools were customarily selected for inclusion in acts of formal deposition, or that complex conventions surrounded their routine use and disposal.

How are we to understand these developments? The evidence certainly indicates that stone continued to play an important role in many day-to-day tasks, and there is no reason to suppose that the practical details of these tasks were very different from those undertaken by earlier generations. So we must ask why it is that patterns of production and deposition should have changed, and why there should be a decrease in the range of tools that were routinely used?

One argument might be that these changes can be attributed to the spread of metal artefacts and metalworking into further areas of social and economic life. While the first appearance of copper and bronze may have had its most dramatic impact on those stone tools that were also important symbolic resources, the passage of time saw this process extend to encompass a wider range of more prosaic artefacts. This is an interesting idea, but it finds little support in the evidence. For much of the Early Bronze Age, the range of metal items in circulation remained relatively restricted. Alongside axes, daggers and pins, the most common forms are rapiers, armlets and other jewellery. A similar emphasis on display or decoration is suggested by most of the goldwork that has been recovered. Given these patterns, it is difficult to see the changes in stone technology and assemblage structure as reflections of a purely utilitarian process. Many metal artefacts were undoubtedly used, but there is little evidence to suggest that these items took over the practical roles of most stone tools at this time. Here again then, it may be that these changes have their roots in the social or symbolic dimensions of stone.

In short, the passage of the Early Bronze Age seems to have witnessed a gradual decline in the extent to which the act of working and using stone was caught up in the reproduction of social relations within communities. At least some of the boundaries and classifications of everyday life may have been expressed or renewed through artefacts made of different materials such as gold, bronze, jet and amber. This process was by no means clear-cut or abrupt – artefacts of stone probably continued to play a part in the classification of people throughout the period though the importance of stone as a medium for the creation of tokens of value and identity did decline. There was also a general decrease in the range of tools that were commonly made and used. If strong conventions no longer surrounded what particular stone tools 'stood for', there may have been less of a concern with the definition of varied and distinctive forms. Equally, if stone tools were no longer one of the principal media through which ideas about the qualities and roles of people were expressed, they may have lost some of their potential to 'presence' those qualities in acts of formal deposition. While many stone artefacts remained important as practical tools, the Early Bronze Age saw the gradual diminution of their role as technologies of remembrance.

# The end of the Early Bronze Age

As we shall see in chapter 7, there is a wealth of evidence to suggest that stone remained an important practical resource for many centuries – perhaps for as much as a thousand years. It is also clear that the use of stone persisted across another of the major thresholds in later British prehistory. The onset of what we define as the Middle Bronze Age is widely recognized as the point at which many of the landmarks of Later Neolithic and Early Bronze Age social life seem to disappear from view. By the end of the second millennium, a landscape that had once been dominated by the dead and by ceremonial monuments was now shaped by permanent settlements, field boundaries and other features of an agricultural regime. Given the nature of archaeological evidence, it is all too easy to view this transition, like many others, as a sudden and dramatic event – a distinct horizon at which many aspects of society were simultaneously transformed. This may be a little misleading. Evidence from many parts of Britain suggests that this process may have been more fragmented.

The gradual and piecemeal nature of these changes can be seen in the development of Early Bronze Age funerary practices. Elaborate barrows and the occasional glittering array of grave goods have tended to capture our attention with the result that a more pervasive trend is sometimes overlooked. The course of the Early Bronze Age saw a steady shift in the nature of funerary rites: in particular an increasing emphasis upon cremations accompanied by or contained within urns. This became increasingly widespread in the centuries after many of the 'rich' burials of Wessex were placed in the earth. These cremations were often inserted into older barrows or on their margins, and this reuse of earlier mounds became a common theme, particularly in northern and western Britain.

As mentioned above, it may be wrong to view cremation as a rite which is necessarily lower in status than inhumation. The presence of heat-shattered flints in a number of cremations suggests that artefacts may have occasionally been burnt with the body. Moreover, a few cremation burials were accompanied by an impressive

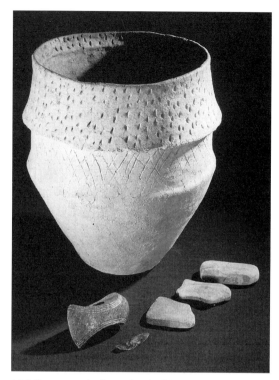

154 Grave goods from Sandmill, Wigtownshire. Containing the cremated bones and ashes of an adult, and placed upside down in a pit, this Collared Urn was accompanied by a decorated battle axe, several whetstones and a bronze razor (National Museum of Scotland).

array of grave goods, including complex jet necklaces, and this suggests that the social identity of the deceased remained an important concern at the moment of burial (fig. 154). However, the trend towards cremation as a dominant mode of interment does suggest a shift of emphasis in the conditions under which rights, obligations and inheritances were negotiated and reproduced. Although the focus may have fallen on other stages in funerary rituals, this trend may also reflect an increased emphasis upon display and consumption among the living rather than the dead.

By the end of the Early Bronze Age, cremation was the dominant form of treatment accorded to the dead. At Knighton Heath in Dorset for example, approximately sixty cremations, many accompanied by urns, were inserted into the upper horizons of an earlier barrow. These interments included men, women and children, and apart from the urns themselves, there were few additional grave goods. It is at this juncture that we can detect an important change in the physical character and location of burials. From this point on, new barrows were seldom erected to mark the resting places of the dead. In their place, and alongside the reuse of older mounds, we see the emergence of small cemeteries immediately adjacent to enclosed settlements and their associated fields. Where barrows and barrow cemeteries had once been set in commanding positions so that they were highly visible, these new cremation cemeteries were far more closely linked to specific settlements and presumably to specific households. Examples of this shift of emphasis can be seen at South Lodge in Dorset and at Blackpatch and Itford Hill in Sussex (fig. 155).

Whereas earlier barrows may have helped to reaffirm the broad links between people and areas of landscape, these new sites expressed the continuity of the household or community within a much smaller area. The cremated remains of family members lay close to home and were probably an important medium through which the very concept of 'home' was defined. Even the pots that were often buried with the dead may have contributed to this process of definition. From the outset, new regional styles of ceramics such as Trevisker or Deverel-Rimbury Wares were used both as domestic vessels and as accompaniments or containers for the dead (fig. 156). Associated with the home, hearth and day-to-day tasks, the metaphoric qualities of these new vessels may have been very different from the more specialized funerary ceramics of earlier generations (fig. 157).

It is at this horizon that we begin to see the development of a more clearly defined agricultural landscape in many areas. Enclosed and open settlements associated with field systems, clearance cairns and lynchets occur widely, from Bracken Rigg in Northumberland through to Trethellan in Cornwall. Although cattle may have assumed a greater importance in upland areas, sites such as South Lodge or Shearplace Hill in Dorset reflect a mixed agricultural regime which was probably followed on many sites. These changes in the character of settlements and the surrounding land may not reflect an economic transformation so much as a shift in the organization and symbolic importance of subsistence-related activities. Many of these settlements resemble those that had been established in the uplands and moors towards the middle of the second millennium. By the end of the Early Bronze Age, many of these more marginal settlements had been abandoned, and it is at this point that we see the establishment of compounds and

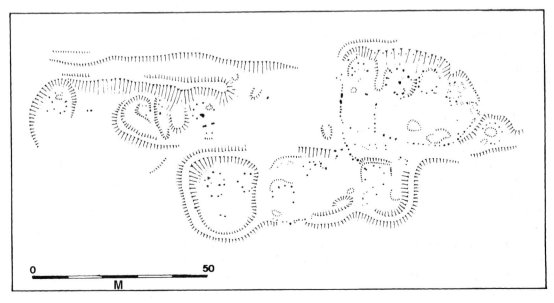

0        50

M

155 Plan of the settlement at Itford Hill, Sussex.

156 Regional traditions of ceramics in use from the end of the Early Bronze Age. Appearing alongside Collared Urns and Food Vessels, Deverel-Rimbury Wares and other regional variants came to dominate Middle Bronze Age assemblages.

157 Examples of Trevisker vessels which became common in the south-west towards the end of the Early Bronze Age (courtesy of Mike Parker Pearson).

around this time. In the wetter conditions that came to prevail, the development of peat bogs and the problem of waterlogging may have contributed to the process of abandonment. Such factors were probably important, but they do not necessarily provide a complete explanation. The abandonment of marginal land was already underway prior to these changes, and it may be that the contraction of settlement, like the earlier phase of expansion, had its roots in broader social and economic relations. Some of these sites may have been exploited on a seasonal basis by communities from the traditional heartlands, while others were linked to the old centres by ties of trade, affiliation and obligation. Under these circumstances, the abandonment of such sites may reflect a more complex process of social change. Where the production of surpluses for use in feasting, exchange and trade had once been achieved by expanding settlement patterns, now the emphasis shifted towards the intensification and reorganization of agricultural production on more fertile soils.

With this shift of emphasis came changes in

hamlets defined by earthworks and fields on more fertile soils (fig. 158).

The reasons for this apparent phase of abandonment remain obscure, and once again a variety of explanations has been offered. It may be that it took only two or three centuries to exhaust this more marginal land and there is evidence that the climate may have deteriorated at

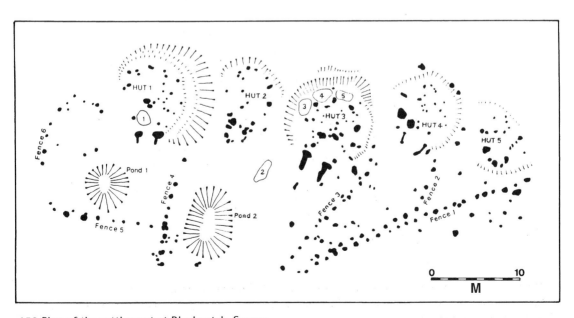

158 Plan of the settlement at Blackpatch, Sussex.

the physical character of the landscape and in the main symbolic resources through which people understood their world and their place within it. Mundane and familiar though they may seem to us, the boundaries, field systems and cairns of this time may have been just as important in defining people's sense of place as earlier ceremonial monuments and tombs. Encountered and maintained in the context of the agricultural cycle, these features would have been an important medium through which the landscape itself was inscribed with social and historical associations. They may have provided physical expressions of the divisions and distinctions that existed between communities. Yet as we saw in the case of the Dartmoor reaves, many of these features may have also played a part in reaffirming the ties that stretched between groups, particularly where they were created through labour organized at an inter-community or broader kinship level.

These changes in the nature of settlement and the physical character of the landscape were accompanied by developments in the character and context of metalwork assemblages. In many areas, the final stages of the Early Bronze Age saw an increased emphasis upon the disposal of individual artefacts such as daggers and rapiers in rivers and other wet places. With the exception of Wessex, this development happened in step with changes in the nature of funerary rites and it may be that the disposal of at least some of these artefacts was linked to the passing of particular individuals into the afterlife. Larger hoards also continued to be deposited during the Middle Bronze Age and there was an increase in the range of metal artefacts that were treated in this manner. This is particularly evident in regions such as East Anglia and the lower Thames valley which emerged as important core areas at around this time.

Many of the new forms in these deposits were weapons and it is likely that their circulation, display and deposition remained as an important medium through which identity and political authority was established or expressed. No longer included on a regular basis in graves and almost unknown on contemporary settlements, the contexts of many of these metalwork assemblages indicate that social and political relations continued to be negotiated outside the domestic sphere. While household cemeteries and the organization of domestic space may have sustained a variety of themes and ideas at a very local level, acts of disposal or conspicuous destruction of metalwork may have often been undertaken in front of a different (and perhaps larger) audience. As such, they may have continued to have important consequences for the realities of social and political life at a broader level.

Only in Wessex do we find developments which run counter to this sequence. In this area, the final centuries of the second millennium saw a return to the tradition of barrow construction and ostentatious burial that had been practised one or two hundred years before. These later barrows lack much of the finer goldwork and some of the exotica associated with earlier graves such as Bush Barrow, but objects such as battle axes and daggers continued to be interred with the dead. Many of the bronzes deposited in these graves were heavily worn. Why people in Wessex returned to this traditional practice after two or three centuries remains the subject of heated debate. One possibility is that these barrows were constructed in the face of broader social and political changes. As such, they may reflect an attempt to draw upon the traditions of the past as a means of legitimating claims to authority and position at a time when that position was increasingly being challenged.

Several archaeologists have pointed to the worn condition of much of the metalwork in these graves, arguing that the artefacts may have been in circulation for lengthy periods. Some have taken this as evidence that the items were worn and displayed as hereditary symbols over several generations. Only when the position of certain groups was coming under threat did it become necessary to return to the ostentatious burial of such items as a means of sanctioning claims to authority. Others have seen these patterns as evidence for fluctuations in the stability of broader exchange networks, and as an indication that certain groups may have progressively lost their pre-eminent position within those networks. As they see it, that position may have been usurped by communities in some of the new core areas of eastern England, who were better placed to maintain contacts and alliances with groups on the Continent. In a sense, these arguments complement each other, and taken together they support the view that this brief period of barrow building and ostentatious burial happened at a time when the broader social and political order was being redefined. How far this process of redefinition was a product of changing networks of exchange and alliance is open to question. Although they were undoubtedly important, it is also possible that the breaking down of these networks was itself an expression of other internal developments.

It was in these final centuries of the second millennium that the last of the major ceremonial centres were also abandoned. Constructed, elaborated and modified over twenty to thirty generations, it is highly unlikely that the meanings or significance attached to sites like Mount Pleasant and Stonehenge remained constant. Indeed, recent arguments over access to Stonehenge remind us that there may always have been differences of opinion and interpretation within the groups who used (or were excluded from) these sites.

Changes in their physical character suggest that the place of these sites in the social landscape, and the roles they played, probably changed over the course of the Later Neolithic and Early Bronze Age. In the case of Stonehenge itself, the final major phase of prehistoric activity that has been detected is represented by the five dressed trilithons and the rough circle of uprights and lintels. The technology involved in the dressing and construction of these features bears many similarities with woodworking, and it may be that these massive stones were designed to evoke a much older tradition associated with the construction and use of timber circles. As Richard Bradley has pointed out, it is surely significant that the last period of prehistoric activity on this site should also be the most monumental. Like the return to the old ways of placing people in the earth, this remodelling of Stonehenge may have been undertaken to sustain a social and political order that was beginning to dissolve. The eventual abandonment of this site suggests that like its rather more mundane counterparts, this massive 'stone tool' was no longer recruited in the reproduction of social and political authority.

# 7 The erosion of stone

Around the beginning of the first millennium bc on what we now call the Sussex Downs, someone stepped out through the low earthworks and fences which defined the margins of their settlement. Walking along the edge of the fields which skirted their home, they occasionally bent to pull out the weeds which grew in great profusion among the newly seeded corn. Tossing them to one side, they finally came to the low flint cairn which stood at the point where the boundaries of two fields ran into each other. The cairn had always been there. Like the sherds of strange pottery and the white stone tools that were sometimes found in the surrounding fields, this low mound capped with flint nodules belonged to another time and to an older family.

Stepping over the jumbled flakes and shattered nodules which mingled with the grass around the base of the cairn, this person scrambled up to where the cap of larger nodules remained intact. Hammerstone in hand, they tapped a number of the nodules, listening for the distinctive ring which spoke of workable stone. For several minutes their tests were met by the dull crack which signified that the weathered nodule in their hand was fractured and liable to shatter. Then, after several of these uppermost stones had been cast aside, they found a number which 'rang true'. Balancing precariously on the shifting pile of stone, they threw these pieces out from the cairn and onto the surrounding earth, then followed their path until they too returned to more level ground.

It was here with their back to the cairn that they began to work, the reports of the hammer echoing across the fields and around the compound. The first fall of the hammer split the largest nodule into three pieces, each slightly larger than a hand. Retrieving one of these from the ground, they delivered further blows, using the fresh dark surface as a platform from which to strike six flakes which they placed in a pile by their side. Work on this core continued until the edges were crushed and stepped, so a second nodule was selected and the process began again. Discarded and exhausted cores were tossed to one side – thrown back onto the margins of the cairn where they came to rest amidst the remains of earlier episodes of knapping.

Soon there was a mound of flakes and serviceable cores, all of which were gathered up and placed in a small leather bag. To this small assemblage was added the hammerstone and a handful of large flakes that had been made and disregarded at an earlier time. The work complete, the person walked back along the field edge, returning to the compound where the contents of the bag that hung at their shoulder would be used. They retraced their steps without even noticing how their feet pressed burnt and broken flint and other midden material into the soft earth (fig. 159).

The course of the Middle Bronze Age saw further developments in the character of stoneworking and a continuation of the trends established during the earlier phase of the period. Although stone clearly remained an important practical resource, many of these later assemblages suggest a further impoverishment of the techniques and traditions that had persisted for many generations. In raw material terms, there is very little to indicate that people used anything other than stone that was locally available. There is no evidence that raw materials were transported or exchanged over any distance and exotic stone artefacts are conspicuous by their absence in the vast majority of contexts. People simply made use of stone that was ready to hand to a far greater extent than before.

In flint-rich areas, working seems to have been characterized by a simple core-flake technology. Raw material obtained from surface exposures was worked down in a relatively basic manner to produce flakes that could either be used as they were, or modified to create simple tools. These included scrapers, simple awls and other piercing

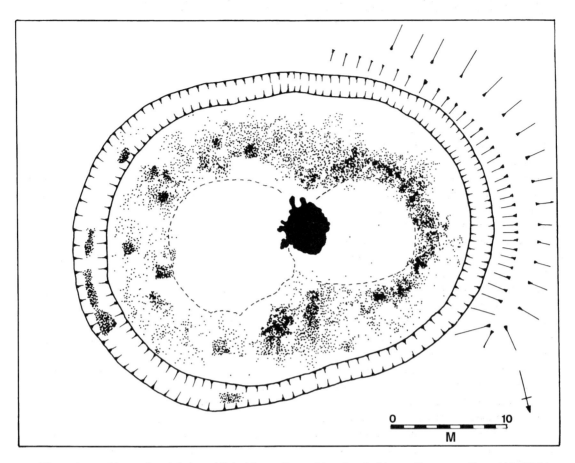

159 Flint cairn and knapping debris at Micheldever, Hampshire. Created by earlier generations, this flint-capped burial cairn became the focus for later episodes of raw material procurement and basic tool production. The dots mark the distribution of waste and discarded tools and cores (after Fasham & Ross 1983).

or graving tools that were probably used in a wide variety of day-to-day tasks. There is little evidence that other more formal retouched artefacts continued to be made on a systematic basis. Similar use was made of raw material obtained from old barrows or cairns that were capped or constructed with flint nodules. Examples of this practice have been noted at Micheldever in Hampshire, on the Berkshire Downs, near Durrington in Wiltshire, and at Blackpatch and Itford Hill in Sussex. There is nothing to indicate that the context of this material influenced either the way in which the stone was worked or the manner in which the tools were used and discarded. These sites were simply good sources that lay close to home, capable of being exploited when needs arose. The many thousands of flakes and

other pieces of waste found around these sites suggest that this pattern of exploitation was a regular feature of life on many settlements.

Much the same patterns are found in areas where stone could only be derived from river gravels and other secondary deposits. In these cases, however, the character of the raw material seems to have had a major impact on basic patterns of working. At sites such as Fengate near Peterborough, usable pieces of stone seem to have been created through the smashing or breaking of flint pebbles. These fractured pieces often possessed edges that were suitable for use as they were, and it seems that this *ad hoc* or unsystematic pattern of reduction was regarded as wholly acceptable. Here again, evidence from middens and other settlement contexts reflects

185

the regular use of a restricted range of retouched tools and unmodified flakes. Many of these simple forms were probably made and used in one place and at one time, and the vast majority were discarded with little formality. Some accumulated in the forgotten corners of settlements – in cooking pits and hearths, around posts or along the line of walls. Many others were gathered up and incorporated in the midden deposits that were a regular feature on many sites. There they may have lain for a considerable period of time before being moved again, either to secondary dumps, or out onto the fields to enrich the soil. There is no evidence to suggest that stone tools were drawn upon to any extent in more formal acts of deposition.

One of the most evocative demonstrations of these changes can be found at Grimes Graves in Norfolk. As discussed in chapter 4, this area had been the focus for the mining of flint and the production of tools and 'blanks' during the final centuries of the Neolithic and the initial stages of the Early Bronze Age. Working on the site over that time was episodic or event-like, and exploitation may have been embedded in broader cycles associated with the seasonal use of the Breckland. It was also shown how there were considerable difficulties in determining the destinations of the many thousands of artefacts which undoubtedly left this source. In certain respects, the 'invisibility' of Grimes Graves products in Later Neolithic and Early Bronze Age contexts is a product of natural processes. The tendency for flint to become patinated or corticated with time creates problems of recognition, and unlike many other raw materials we have yet to develop a secure basis for the characterization of flint. However, it does seem that the distinctive 'floorstone' was relatively rare on contemporary sites in the region, and that many artefacts (and perhaps even quartered nodules of flint) passed into different areas or regimes of value.

These patterns can be contrasted with activities on the site during the Middle Bronze Age. Andrew Herne has shown that although the site remained an important focus, the character of working bore few points of similarity with earlier practices. The traces left by these earlier periods of exploitation would have been even more imposing and impressive than they are today.

Grassland, scrub and trees may have re-established themselves in certain areas, but many of the spoil heaps, infilled shafts and extensive working floors would still have been prominent features, creating an almost 'lunar' landscape that would have been in stark contrast to the environs of the site. Even though these features stood as testaments to the availability of floorstone and to the traditional manner in which material had been obtained and worked, this seems to have had relatively little impact on the people who made use of the area during the Middle Bronze Age.

In the first place, the site was probably exploited by communities who lived on its margins. Small settlements practising cereal cultivation and animal husbandry are known from the area and this marks a significant break with the past. Grimes Graves was no longer physically and seasonally marginal in the way that it had been before. Further changes can be seen at the source itself. There is no evidence for the sinking of deep shafts and the cutting of galleries to obtain the homogeneous black floorstone. Procurement was focused upon material already available on the surface. Some may have been obtained from *in situ* surface exposures, but the vast majority of the flint used at this time was retrieved from the debris that had accumulated on working floors and around shaft-tops many centuries before. This included partially worked blocks of floorstone as well as the more irregular nodules of topstone and wallstone that had been discarded on the surface during earlier episodes of mining. Use was also made of some of the larger decortication flakes and rejects created long before.

The bulk of the Middle Bronze Age assemblages at Grimes Graves were created through two forms of activity. Some of the material reflects the *in situ* knapping of stone for the production of basic cores, flakes and perhaps simple tools. Waste from these activities was probably left where it fell and selected pieces removed from the area for use on nearby sites. In addition, material recovered from the top of one of the earlier shafts reflects the dumping of large quantities of worked, burnt and otherwise discarded stone as elements within midden deposits. Rich in charcoal and bone fragments, these middens were probably accumulated on settlements adjacent to the old mines. Such deposits were periodically gathered up and brought to the site where they were dumped in the tops of long-abandoned shafts.

The inventories from these two contexts confirm many of the patterns found on Middle Bronze Age sites in flint-rich areas. Here again, the assemblages are dominated by a basic core-flake technology, and by simple scrapers, awls and other tools that could be used for piercing or boring. Just as there are few formal types of tools, so there is little evidence for the maintenance of structured routines of flaking in core reduction. Although many nodules and blocks were worked extensively for the production of flakes, it seems that the producers seldom adhered to specific ways of working, or produced clear categories of core.

Given the character of the material from Grimes Graves and from other Middle Bronze Age sites, there is a great temptation to take the absence of structured flaking routines and the limited range of formal tool and core types as evidence that flint was no longer important. This may be an unwarranted assumption. Just because the material does not conform to our elaborate typologies does not mean that stone ceased to play an important part in a variety of tasks. Many of the most basic tools and unmodified flakes that were made and used at this time would have been well suited to most of the activities that characterized life in and around contemporary settlements. What remains to be asked is why we should see such a marked decline in the regularity or formality of technologies and artefact forms. Compared to the Middle Bronze Age, the inventories of Early Bronze Age assemblages seem relatively rich!

For the most part, archaeologists have tended to assume that the disappearance of many formal stone tools in the Middle Bronze Age is a reflection of the spread of metal. Unlike the Early Bronze Age, later metalwork assemblages contain a wider variety of artefacts, many of which would have been suitable for a number of practical tasks. For example, few Middle Bronze Age stone assemblages contain retouched knives; while unretouched flakes may have been used for cutting a variety of materials, it may be that many of these tasks were now performed by metal tools. This argument seems plausible

enough, but it is not sufficient to account for the broader patterns that are discernible. Once again, it may be just as important to consider the broader social contexts in which tools of both materials were produced, obtained and used. If the end of the Early Bronze Age had seen a gradual diminution in the capacity of stone tools to stand for people and practices, the course of the Middle Bronze Age saw a more dramatic erosion of that role.

Despite their continued and widespread use, stone artefacts were no longer caught up in the maintenance or negotiation of social categories and interests. That role was increasingly taken on by artefacts of metal, and through other aspects of material production. As time passed, the definition of personal identity and the negotiation of political authority became more intimately associated with the display, circulation and formal deposition of metal artefacts.

At the same time, the metaphorical qualities of settlements and field systems may have come to play an increasingly important part in shaping people's understanding of their place within the community and within the broader social landscape. In particular, the internal character and layout of many settlements reflects an increasing concern with demarcation and division. Although many activities were probably undertaken communally, different tasks were performed in different locations within many settlements. These distinctions were often stressed by the construction of banks, ditches and fences. While the tools that were used remained important, the Middle Bronze Age saw an increasing emphasis upon the physical context in which tasks were performed as a medium through which people were defined. Taken for granted in the course of day-to-day routines, these spatial arrangements may have been crucial to the reproduction of basic ideas concerning divisions of labour and the social identities of people. Although it may have been ready to hand for a variety of tasks, stone was effectively forgotten as a resource to be drawn upon in the constitution of these ideas about the self and society.

It is this shift of emphasis, rather than any marked change in the nature of subsistence which may account for the treatment of stone during the Middle Bronze Age. As the social dimensions of stone were eroded, so traditional attitudes to procurement, production and consumption were also changed. For the most part, this process was probably gradual, unfolding at a rate which spanned many generations. With each generation, less and less importance may have been attached to the maintenance of traditional patterns of procurement, particularly those which separated the acquisition of tokens of identity and value from day-to-day contexts. The same may even have happened at the more intimate level of attitudes to the working of stone. Where stone tools no longer served as important metaphors for people or their roles and connections, the boundaries between formal artefact categories, and perhaps between different ways of working and finishing stone, may have become increasingly blurred. Indeed, the learning of complex knapping techniques may itself have ceased to be an important feature in the lives of many people.

No doubt there were junctures where these breaks with tradition were more abrupt. The pursuit of particular social and political interests may have involved the conscious transformation of the media used in exchange, display or deposition, and a rejection of aspects of the old order. Just as these junctures are difficult to detect, so we cannot say what interests may have been satisfied by these acts of iconoclasm. Tensions between older and younger adults, and between different groups may all have provided the conditions under which people may have attempted to break with different aspects of the past.

These changes in the practical and social dimensions of stone bring us to the end of this study. Over the course of a few thousand words we have moved from the beginning of the Neolithic and the appearance of new categories of artefact, to a time when formal stone tools ceased to be a regular feature of people's material vocabularies. Although the sound of hammer on flint was probably heard by many later generations, it no longer spoke of the themes and values which had animated communities in earlier times.

In charting the erosion of stone, I have tried to suggest that an exclusive concern with function may place unnecessary limits on our understanding of the tools used by people in the past. At the same time, I have tried to show how it is possible to harness a moment of stoneworking or deposition to broader arguments concerning the character of past social life. Having said that, it should be clear that my use of the evidence has been selective. In emphasising stone, rather less attention has been paid to the part played by other materials in sustaining people's ideas about themselves and in the negotiation of social and political authority. Important as they were, traditions of making, using and depositing stone tools were simply elements within a broader repertoire of activities. Other studies might highlight the role of pottery or the practical and symbolic dimensions of the animals which shaped the character of daily and seasonal routines and ceremonial activities.

It should also be clear that despite the description of moments of stoneworking, this book has sacrificed much that is specific and particular in favour of a more general narrative. More could have been made of the varied sequences of development that unfolded in different parts of the country, and of the very different ways in which stone tools were acquired, used and regarded in particular local contexts. Indeed, it will only be through more detailed local studies that we may hope to capture something of the particular symbolic content of traditions of working and using stone. Equally, the evidence from the major mines and quarries could have been set against a more thorough treatment of minor sources. Many more of these smaller sources remain to be discovered, and current work at sites like the Den of Boddam in Scotland should add much to our understanding. What has been offered here remains a very general account, and in some respects an introduction to themes that would repay closer inspection.

The emphasis here upon stone brings with it other problems. An explicit discussion of the ways in which tools can carry concepts of self and society does little to convey the subtle manner in which this is generally achieved. For the most part, everyday objects are powerful persuaders precisely because they are simply 'ready to hand' – part of the routine trappings of our lives. It is only when they are drawn upon more explicitly that we may become aware of their social, political or even spiritual connotations. If an understanding of these connotations is difficult to achieve in the present, it is even more problematic when our evidence is disentangled from the contexts in which it was originally made and used. That is why we have to emphasise the place of particular tools or ways of working within broader material and historical traditions. Even then, our interpretations will remain to some extent partial and provisional. Models can change, and new data or ways of thinking can stimulate very different attempts to flesh out the patterns that we derive from fieldwalking and excavation. No doubt future studies will lead us to augment, question or reject some of the general assertions made here. The past may well be 'a rock that you cannot move'. But like flint, some of its facets can be worked and reworked into a variety of forms.

# Glossary

As with the references in the bibliography, this glossary is not meant to be exhaustive. Instead, it provides brief definitions for some of the more unusual or specialized terms that appear in this book. For further detail, and a more comprehensive review of both terms and artefact types, readers are advised to consult the journal and the glossary of post-glacial lithic artefacts produced by the Lithics Studies Society.

**bc** The dates given throughout this book are expressed in uncalibrated radiocarbon years as opposed to calibrated dates which are conventionally expressed by BC. For a more detailed discussion of the relationship between calibrated and uncalibrated dates, see Mike Parker Pearson's book *Bronze Age Britain*.

**biface** An artefact with invasive retouch on both of its principal faces, such as a leaf-shaped arrowhead or discoidal knife. The pattern of flaking required to produce these and similar artefacts is sometimes referred to as bifacial working.

**bipolar flaking** A flaking technique commonly employed where workable stone takes the form of small, rounded pebbles. The technique involves striking a core (or unmodified pebble) while it is resting on an anvil stone (see fig. 1). In contrast to more conventional flaking techniques, the use of an anvil creates a 'countershock' which may result in the detachment of a flake from the distal end of the core (the opposite end to that struck by the hammer). It is occasionally referred to as 'scalar flaking', and the cores and flakes created by this process often retain distinctive opposed scars and heavily crushed platforms. A particularly prominent feature in assemblages from western and northern Britain.

**blade** A much-used but often confusing term. As used in this volume, blades are more or less parallel-sided flakes with a length to width ratio of more than 2:1. Although blades may be produced incidentally in the working of a variety of tools and cores, systematic blade production can often be distinguished by the presence of a number of attributes. These include parallel scars or ridges on the dorsal surfaces of flakes and blades or on the faces of blade cores. Other common features include small 'retouch' scars created during the careful trimming and maintenance of core platforms.

**bulb of percussion** One of the more distinctive features on tools and waste created via flaking is the bulb of percussion. This is situated just below the striking platform on the ventral surface of struck flakes, and takes the form of a raised, rounded surface. Although it cannot be taken as a 'hard and fast' rule, large or pronounced bulbs are commonly created in cases where a hard hammer is used, and/or where a large amount of force is applied to a core or tool. Smaller, more diffuse bulbs are more common where soft hammers are used, where the amount of force applied is restricted, and/or where the blow is delivered close to the edge of a platform. The concavities on the facets of flaked tools are sometimes referred to as negative bulbs.

**conchoidal fracture** Many raw materials such as flint and volcanic stones and glasses have a regular crystalline structure. As a result, when force is applied to these materials, they tend to fracture or flake in a relatively regular and predictable manner. A useful analogy for this process is the effect that is created when a pebble is dropped into a pond. When a piece of flint is struck by a hammer, the force travels through the stone in a series of waves. Occasionally, these waves can be seen on a flake or core where they take the form of ripple marks.

**core** In simple terms, a core is a piece of raw material from which flakes have been struck.

Cores may take a wide variety of forms; from well prepared and specialized examples (such as blade cores) through to 'bashed lumps' which have been worked in a more-or-less *ad hoc* and unsystematic manner. Artefacts such as axes or chisels which are not made on flakes are sometimes referred to as 'core tools'.

**core preparation** A term used to describe the initial creation of a striking platform on a core. Often this may involve no more than the removal of a large flake from one end of a nodule. In other cases (blade core production, for instance), core preparation may also involve the modification of the face of a core. Although it is generally regarded as a practice which precedes core working, preparation and maintenance techniques may occur throughout the time that a core is in use. The controlled removal of flakes and the maintenance of a flaking angle (between platform and core face) of less than 90 degrees may require the regular trimming or retouching of platform edges or the more extensive modification of the core face itself (see core rejuvenation).

**core rejuvenation** Effectively a maintenance or recovery technique, core rejuvenation involves the working of a core to extend its use-life, to reduce the angle between platform and core face to 90 degrees or less, or to correct irregularities caused by mis-hits or crushing on platforms. Commonly found in Mesolithic and Earlier Neolithic assemblages, core rejuvenation flakes take a variety of forms. Core rejuvenation tablets are produced when the entire striking platform is removed (and a new platform created) by a lateral blow. Other forms of rejuvenation include the removal of a crushed or irregular platform edge, or the creation of an entirely new striking platform on another part of an existing core.

**cortex** Whether they occur in nodular form, as major outcrops or as glacial erratics, many raw materials possess a distinctive outer surface. In some cases (e.g., volcanic tuffs), this may amount to no more than a generally weathered appearance. In others, most notably flint, this outer surface or cortex may be both thick and distinctive, resulting from the alteration of the flint through water loss and chemical action. The character of cortex on different raw materials can be a useful guide to the geological sources of artefacts found on archaeological sites. For example, a useful distinction is commonly drawn between the thick, chalky 'rind' found on flint from primary chalk deposits, and the thinner more rounded cortex found on flint pebbles from riverine or coastal sources. The presence, position or absence of cortex on flakes and tools often provides a useful indication of the character and range of stoneworking activities conducted in any given context.

**debitage** A term with two related definitions. Originally used to denote the process of working stone to produce flakes and cores, it is now more commonly used to encompass all categories of waste flakes generated during the production of cores and tools made from materials such as flint.

**decortication** The stage in the production of tools and cores at which the outer cortex is removed. Generally associated with the initial stages of production, and with the testing of raw materials, decortication flakes are usually characterized by a more or less completely corticated dorsal surface.

**direct percussion** The direct application of force to a tool or core using a hammer. For much of prehistory, the hammers used to detach flakes or blades from cores and tools were made from either stone or antler. Other materials such as dense bone, hardwood (and possibly metal) may have also been employed (see fig. 1).

**dorsal surface** Term used to describe the outer face of a flake (as opposed to the ventral surface). In the case of materials such as flint, the patterning of scars and ridges on the dorsal surfaces of flakes can provide important information regarding the character of stoneworking in a given context. The presence or absence of cortex and the character, number and orientation of dorsal scars and ridges make it possible to reconstruct 'reduction sequences' – the chain of steps taken in the working of a core or the production, maintenance and reuse of a tool.

**lake** In simple terms, a flake is a piece of stone    191 that has been removed from a core or tool by percussion or pressure. Flakes occur in a bewildering array of forms, a fact that is reflected in the nomenclature developed by stone tool specialists. Perhaps the most important point to be recognized is that the form, size and general characteristics of flakes will vary according to the type of productive activity being undertaken. The close analysis of flake assemblages often allows us to identify what was being made in a given context, and how a particular episode of production was organized in technological terms (see reduction sequence below).

**flake scar** The indentation left when a flake or blade is removed from a tool or core.

**flake termination** The distal end of a flake (opposite to the end with the platform) can take a variety of forms. Feather terminations have a thin, tapering profile, and usually result when the force applied to a core or tool travels through the stone in a regular manner. Hinge or step terminations are created where the force does not travel from one end of the core to the other. Often created as a result of miss-hits, or when a blow is struck too far into the area of a core platform, these irregular terminations can leave deep, irregular scars on the surface of a tool or core which may create problems for further working.

**indirect percussion** Involves the use of a punch or secondary tool between the hammer and the tool or core being worked. Experimental research and ethnographic observation suggests that the use of a punch in tasks such as blade production can increase the level of control and precision exercized by the stoneworker (see fig. 1).

**microlith** Literally 'small stones', microliths are a definitive feature of the Mesolithic period in Britain. Usually made on small blades or bladelets, these minute retouched pieces were commonly mounted and used in a variety of composite tools.

**patination** This is the early stage in the natural formation of cortex on materials such as flint. While freshly worked flint may occur in a variety of colours, the worked surface will – with the passage of time – start to develop a patina or corticated layer. The result of a complex range of factors, including chemical action, weathering, water and even light, corticated surfaces vary in colour from a dull blue-grey through to white. Over the past few years, stone tool analysts have rejected the use of the term patination in favour of 'cortication', seeing this as a more accurate reflection of the processes which lead to the discolouration of flint.

**pecking** In contrast to flint and many volcanic rocks and glasses, basic igneous materials do not display the properties of conchoidal fracture and cannot be flaked in a regular and controlled manner. Pecking involves the pounding of raw material with a dense stone hammer until the desired form is achieved. Often undertaken in conjunction with grinding, this technique was commonly used to fashion battle axes, axe hammers and axes such as those from Cornish sources. Unlike flintworking, which results in the creation of distinctive waste flakes or debitage, the residues of pecking and grinding may amount to little more than a handful of dust.

**polissoir** Stable surface used in the grinding and polishing of stone and flint axes. Although the term is occasionally used to refer to all grinding stones, it is more commonly employed to describe portable grinding slabs such as those found at Gwernvale, Etton and The Trundle. Polissoirs usually possess a bevelled or concave face which has itself become polished or smoothed with use.

**pressure flaking** Although materials such as flint were generally worked through being struck by a variety of hammers, the final shaping or retouching of many artefacts was often achieved through pressure flaking. Commonly associated with the finishing or final shaping of artefacts such as arrowheads or knives, the technique involves the removal of small, thin flakes by a process of pushing against the tool edge with a pointed implement of bone, antler or metal (see fig. 1).

**reduction sequence** A common term in much of the literature, a reduction sequence is simply the series of steps or stages that are followed in the working of a core or the creation, maintenance and reuse of a tool. When dealing with materials such as flint, it is often possible to identify the nature of these steps in some detail. We can often differentiate between the by-products of the primary, secondary and later stages in a particular production process, and can distinguish the definitive signatures that mark different ways of working or the production of different types of tool. The identification of reduction sequences allows us to explore the choices and decisions that were made (or ignored) as a lump of raw material was turned into a cultural artefact.

**refitting** The reassembly or rejoining of flaked material to its parent core or tool. Although it is both laborious and time consuming, refitting can provide important information, not only about the manner in which particular tools were produced, but also on the spatial organization of activities and the genesis of archaeological deposits.

**retouch** The deliberate flaking of the edge of a tool in order to shape, maintain or modify that edge. Retouch traces may take a variety of forms, ranging from small, regular scars which are restricted to the edge of a tool, through to more extensive or invasive scars travelling across much of an artefact's surface. Retouch may be unifacial (e.g., scrapers) or bifacial (e.g., leaf-shaped arrowheads).

**ripple-flaking** A highly distinctive pattern of working which is found on a small number of daggers and arrowheads. The result of skilled pressure flaking, ripple-flaked artefacts possess long, narrow and highly invasive flake scars which often run parallel to each other.

**roughout** An artefact that has been discarded prior to its completion. Commonly used to describe the crude and often irregular pieces found at axe sources.

**scalar flaking** see bipolar flaking.

**spall** Although the working of materials such as flint results in the creation of a wide range of flakes, these are by no means the only by-products. Irregular pieces of shattered material and small chips or spalls are often generated during epsiodes of working. Some of these pieces may be the result of specific acts, such as the creation of small chips during the trimming of a core platform. Others, including small spalls and even quite regular bladelets, may be produced incidentally to the task at hand.

**striking platform** The surface of a core or tool that is struck in order to remove a flake or blade. The nature of striking platforms varies according to the type of core technology being employed, and it is not uncommon for a core to have several platforms.

**tranchet** A term used to describe both a technical act and, by extension, several types of artefact. In essence, a tranchet blow is one delivered close to the cutting edge of a tool and at 90 degrees to its long axis. Usually associated with the creation of cutting edges on so-called 'tranchet blow' axes, the term is also used to describe axes made on large flakes where the cutting edge is formed by the side of the original flake. The term has also been used in the definition of a particular form of arrowhead. First suggested by Graham Clark in 1934, 'petit-tranchet' arrowheads are generally made on a medial segment of a flake or blade, and here again, the cutting edge is formed by the side of the original flake.

**use wear** The use of stone artefacts for different tasks can often be identified by the close inspection of tool edges. At a macroscopic level, use wear traces include small scars and scratches (sometimes referred to as utilization damage). With the aid of a microscope it is also possible to identify microwear traces – alterations to the surface of the tool including striations, polishes and even residues. Experimental research has shown that the character, density and distribution of these traces can be used to identify both how a certain tool was used, and upon what materials.

**ventral surface** The inner (bulbar) face of a struck flake or blade.

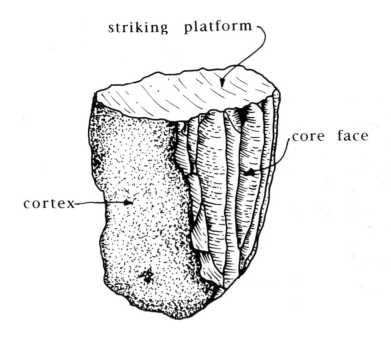

striking platform

core face

cortex

I A single platform core.

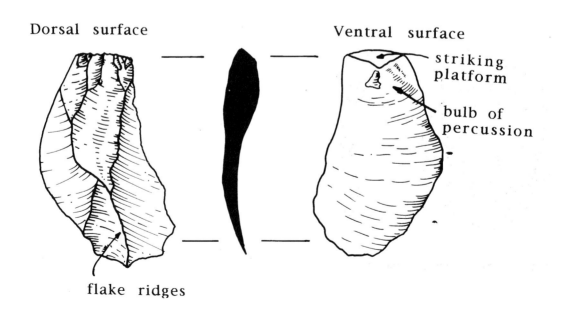

Dorsal surface

Ventral surface

striking platform

bulb of percussion

flake ridges

II Principal features on a struck flake.

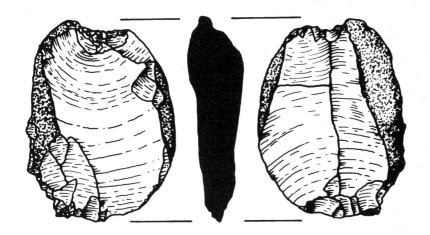

III Bipolar or scalar core.

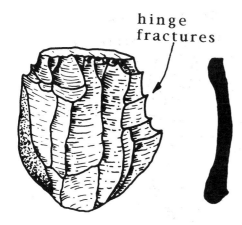

hinge
fractures

IV Hinge fractures on a single platform core.

# Further reading

The references contained in this section serve as an introduction to some of the issues and materials discussed in each chapter of this book. Like the book itself, the bibliography is not designed to cover every issue or aspect of the Neolithic and Early Bronze Age in Britain. However, the texts listed below should provide the reader with a useful starting point for further reading and research.

## Chapter 1

Appadurai, A. (ed.) 1985 *The Social Life of Things*, Cambridge University Press, Cambridge

Archaeological Review from Cambridge 1990 Vol. 9.1 *Technology in the Humanities*, Dept of Archaeology, Cambridge

Barrett, J. 1994 *Fragments of Antiquity*, Blackwells, Oxford

Bloch, M. 1989 *Ritual, History and Power*, LSE monographs on social anthropology 58, Athlone Press, London

Bourdieu, P. 1984 *Distinction: A social critique of the judgement of taste*, Cambridge University Press, Cambridge

Burton, J. 1980 'Making sense of waste flakes: new methods for investigating the technology and economics behind chipped stone assemblages', *Jnl of Archaeological Science* 7, 131–48

Clark, D.L., Cowie, T. & Foxon, A. 1985 *Symbols of Power at the Time of Stonehenge*, National Museum of Scotland, Edinburgh

Connerton, P. 1990 *How Societies Remember*, Cambridge University Press, Cambridge

Douglas, M. 1966 *Purity and Danger*, Routledge & Kegan Paul, London

Godelier, M. 1985 *The Material and the Mental*, Cambridge University Press, Cambridge

Hebdige. D. 1979 *Subcultures: The meaning of style*, Methuen, London

Hodder, I. 1986 *Reading the Past*, Cambridge University Press, Cambridge

Ingold, T. 1986 *Evolution and Social Life*, Cambridge University Press, Cambridge

Larick, R. 1986 'Age grading and ethnicity in Loikop (Samburu) spears', *Jnl of Anthropological Archaeology* 4, 269–83

Larick, R. 1991 'Warriors and blacksmiths: Mediating ethnicity in East African spears', *Jnl of Anthropological Archaeology* 10 (4), 299–331

Lechtman, H. & Steinberg, A. 1979 'The history of technology: an anthropological perspective', in Bugliarello, G. & Doner, D. B. (eds) *History and Philosophy of Technology*, 135–60, University of Illinois Press, Urbana

Lemmonier, P. 1992 *Elements for an Anthropology of Technology*, Anthropological papers of the Museum of Anthropology, University of Michigan, no. 88

Mackenzie, D. & Wajcman, J. 1985 *The Social Shaping of Technology*, Open University Press, Bristol

Mauss, M. 1936 'Les techniques du corps', translated in *Sociology and Psychology: Essays of Marcel Mauss*, Routledge & Kegan Paul, London 1979

Miller, D. 1985 *Artefacts as Categories*, Cambridge University Press, Cambridge

Miller, D. 1987 *Material Culture and Mass Consumption*, Blackwells, Oxford

Moore, H. 1986 *Space, Text and Gender*, Cambridge University Press, Cambridge

Parker Pearson, M. & Richards, C. 1994 *Architecture and Order*, Routledge, London

Patrik, L. 1985 'Is there an archaeological record?', in Schiffer, M.B. (ed.) *Advances in Archaeological Method and Theory*, vol. 8, 27–62, London, Academic

Petrequin, P. & Petrequin, A. 1993 *Ecologie d'un outil: La hache de pierre en Irian Jaya (Indonesie)*, Monograph du CRA 12, CNRS, Paris

Price, S. 1989 *Primitive Art in Civilised Places*, University of Chicago Press, Chicago

Pye, D. 1964 *The nature of Design*, Studio Vista, London

Ricoeur, P. 1984 *The Reality of the Historical Past*,

Marquette University, Milwaukee

Shanks, M. & Tilley, C. 1987 *Re-Constructing Archaeology*, Cambridge University Press, Cambridge

Tacon, P. 1991 'The power of stone: symbolic aspects of stone use and tool development in western Arnhem Land, Australia', *Antiquity* 65 192–207

Thomas, N. 1991 *Entangled Objects*, Harvard University Press, Massachusetts and London

Tilley, C. 1989 'Interpreting Material Culture' in Hodder, I. (ed.) *The Meanings of Things*, 185–94, Unwin Hyman, London

Tilley, C. 1990 *The Art of Ambiguity*, Routledge, London

Torrence, R. 1986 *The Production and Exchange of Stone Tools*, Cambridge University Press, Cambridge

Turner, V. 1967 *The Forest of Symbols*, Cornell University Press, Ithaca

Turner, V. 1969 *The Ritual Process*, Aldine, Chicago

Whittle, A.W.R. 1988a *Problems in Neolithic Archaeology*, Cambridge University Press, Cambridge

Winner, L. 1986 *The Whale and the Reactor: A search for limits in an age of high technology*, University of Chicago Press, Chicago

# Chapter 2

Ashbee, P. 1970 *The Earthen Long Barrow in Britain*, Dent, London

Atkinson, R.J.C. 1968 'Old mortality: some aspects of burial and population in Neolithic England' in Coles, J. & Simpson, D.D.A.(eds) *Studies in Ancient Europe*, 83–94, Edinburgh University Press, Edinburgh

Barker, G.W.W. 1985 *Prehistoric Farming in Europe*, Cambridge University Press, Cambridge

Barrett, J.C. 1988b 'The living, the dead, and the ancestors: Neolithic and Early Bronze Age mortuary practices' in Barrett, J.C.& Kinnes, I.A. (eds) *The Archaeology of Context in the Neolithic and Bronze Age*, 30–41, Department of Archaeology and Prehistory, Sheffield

Bender, B. 1978 'Gatherer-hunter to farmer: a social perspective', *World Archaeology* 10: 204–22

Bloch, M. & Parry, J. (eds) 1982 *Death and the Regeneration of Life*, 211–30, Cambridge University Press, Cambridge

Bonsall, C. 1981 'The coastal factor in the Mesolithic settlement of north-west England' in Gramsch, B. (ed) *Mesolithikum in Europa* 451–72

Bradley, R. 1984 *The Social Foundations of Prehistoric Britain: Themes and variations in the archaeology of power*, Longmans, London

Britnell, W. & Savory, H. 1984 *Gwernvale and Penywyrlod: two Neolithic Long Cairns in the Black Mountains of Brecknock*, Cambrian Archaeological Association, Cardiff

Brown, A. & Edmonds, M. R. (eds) 1987 'Lithic Analysis and Later British Prehistory', 181–6, *British Archaeological Reports* 162

Care, V. 1979 'The production and distribution of Mesolithic axes in southern England', *Proceedings of the Prehistoric Society* 45, 93–102

Care, V. 1982 'The collection and distribution of lithic raw materials during the Mesolithic and Neolithic periods in southern England', *Oxford Jnl of Archaeology* 1, 269–85

Case, H. J. 1969 'Neolithic explanations', *Antiquity* 43: 176–86

Clark, J.G.D., Higgs, E. S. & Longworth, I. 1960 'Excavations at the Neolithic site of Hurst Fen, Mildenhall, Suffolk, 1954, 1957 and 1958', *Proceedings of the Prehistoric Society* 26, 202–45

Cosgrove, D.E. 1984 *Social Formation and Symbolic Landscape*, Croom Helm, London

Darvill, T.C. 1982 *The Megalithic Chambered Tombs of the Cotswold-Severn Region*, Highworth, Vorda

Darvill, T.C. 1987 *Prehistoric Britain*, Batsford, London

Entwistle, R. & Grant, A. 1989 'The evidence for cereal cultivation and animal husbandry in the southern British Neolithic and Bronze Age', in Miles A., Williams D. & Gardner N. (eds.) *The Beginnings of Agriculture*, 203–15, *British Archaeological Reports* S496

Fleming, A. 1973 'Tombs for the living', *Man* 8, 177–93

Frazer, D. 1983 'Land and Society in Neolithic Orkney', *British Archaeological Reports* (British series) 117

Gardiner, J.P. 1984 'Lithic distributions and settlement patterns in central southern England' in Bradley R.J. & Gardiner J.P.(eds) *Neolithic Studies*, 15–40, *British Archaeological Reports* 133

# Further reading

Green, H. S. 1980 'The Flint Arrowheads of the British Isles', *British Archaeological Reports* (British series) 7

Healy, F. 1984 'Farming and field monuments: the Neolithic of Norfolk' in Barringer, C. (ed.) *Aspects of East Anglian Prehistory*, 77–140, Geo, Norwic

Henshall, A. 1963 & 1972 *The Chambered Tombs of Scotland*, (2 vols), Edinburgh University Press, Edinburgh

Herne, A. 1988 'A time and a place for the Grimston bowl' in Barrett, J. & Kinnes, I. (eds) *The Archaeology of Context in the Neolithic and Bronze Age: Recent Trends*, 9–29, Dept of Archaeology and Prehistory, Sheffield

Hodder, I. 1982 *Symbols in Action*, Cambridge University Press, Cambridge

Hodder, I. 1984 'Burials, houses, women and men in the European Neolithic' in Miller, D. & Tilley, C.(eds) *Ideology, Power and Prehistory*, 51–68, Cambridge University Press, Cambridge

Holgate, R. 1988a 'Neolithic Settlement of the Thames Basin', *British Archaeological Reports* 194

Holgate, R. 1988b 'A review of Neolithic domestic activity in Southern Britain' in Barrett, J. & Kinnes, I. (eds) *The Archaeology of Context in the Neolithic and Bronze Age: Recent trends*, 104–12, Dept of Archaeology and Prehistory, Sheffield

Humphreys, S. & King, H. (eds) 1981 *Mortality and Immortality*, 149–59, Academic Press, London

Kinnes, I. 1975 'Monumental function in British Neolithic burial practices', *World Archaeology* 7, 16–28

Kinnes, I. 1985 'Circumstance not context: the Neolithic of Scotland as seen from outside', *Proceedings of the Society of Antiquaries of Scotland*, 115–57

Kinnes, I. 1988 'The Cattleship Potemkin: The first Neolithic in Britain' in Barrett, J. & Kinnes, I. (eds) *The Archaeology of Context in the Neolithic and Bronze Age: Recent Trends*, 2–8, Dept of Archaeology and Prehistory, Sheffield

Lynch, F. & Burgess, C. (eds) 1972 *Prehistoric Man in Wales and the West*, Adams and Dart, Bath

Manby, T. 1988 'The Neolithic in eastern Yorkshire' in Manby, T. (ed.) *Archaeology in Eastern Yorkshire* 35–88, Dept of Archaeology and Prehistory, Sheffield

Mercer, R. 1986, 'The Neolithic in Cornwall' *Cornish Archaeology* 25: 35–80

Moffett, L., Robinson, M.A. & Straker, V. 1989 'Cereals, fruit and nuts: charred plant remains from Neolithic sites in England and Wales and the Neolithic economy' in Milles, A., Williams, D. & Gardner, N. (eds) *The Beginnings of Agriculture*, 243–61, *British Archaeological Reports* 496

Nielsen, P.O. 1986 'The beginning of the Neolithic – assimilation or complex change?', *Jnl of Danish Archaeology* 5, 240–3

Piggott, S. 1962 *The West Kennet Long Barrow*, HMSO, London

Pitts, M. & Jacobi, R. M. 1979 'Some aspects of change in flaked stone industries of the Mesolithic and Neolithic in Southern Britain', *Jnl of Archaeological Science* 6, 163–7

Renfrew, A.C. 1976 'Megaliths, territories and populations' in de Laet, S.(ed.) *Acculturation and Continuity in Atlantic Europe*, 98–220, de Tempel, Bruges

Richards, J. 1984 'The development of the Neolithic landscape in the environs of Stonehenge' in Bradley, R.J. & Gardiner, J. (eds) *Neolithic Studies*, 177–88, *British Archaeological Reports* 133

Saville, A. 1991 *Excavations at Hazelton*, HMSO, London

Shanks, M. & Tilley, C.Y. 1982 'Ideology, symbolic power and ritual communication: a reinterpretation of Neolithic mortuary practices' in Hodder, I. (ed.) *Symbolic and Structural Archaeology*, 129–54, Cambridge University Press, Cambridge

Sharples, N. 1985 'Individual and community: the changing role of megaliths in the Orcadian Neolithic', *Proceedings of the Prehistoric Society* 51, 59–74

Thomas, J.S. 1988 'Neolithic explanations revisited: the Mesolithic–Neolithic transition in Britain and south Scandinavia', *Proceedings of the Prehistoric Society* 54, 59–66

Thomas, J. S. 1991 *Rethinking the Neolithic*, Cambridge University Press, Cambridge

Thomas, J.S. & Whittle, A.W.R. 1986 'Anatomy of a tomb: West Kennet revisited', *Oxford Jnl of Archaeology* 5, 129–56

Thomas, K. 1982 'Neolithic enclosures and woodland habitats on the south Downs in Sussex, England' in Bell, M. & Limbrey, S. (eds) *Archaeological Aspects of Woodland Ecology*, 147–70, *British Archaeological Reports* S146

Thorpe, I.J. 1984 'Ritual, power and ideology: a reconsideration of earlier Neolithic rituals in Wessex' in Bradley, R.J. & Gardiner, J. (eds) *Neolithic Studies*,

41–60, *British Archaeological Reports* 133

Vyner, B. 1984 'The excavation of a Neolithic cairn at Street House, Loftus, Cleveland', *Proceedings of the Prehistoric Society* 50, 151–96

Whittle, A.W.R. 1985 *Neolithic Europe: A survey*, Cambridge University Press, Cambridge

Whittle, A.W.R. 1988a *Problems in Neolithic Archaeology*, Cambridge University Press, Cambridge

Woodman, P. 1978 'The Mesolithic in Ireland', *British Archaeological Reports* **58**

# Chapter 3

Adkins, R. & Jackson, R. 1976 *Neolithic Axes from the River Thames*, British Museum Press, London

Avery, M. 1982 'The Neolithic causewayed enclosure, Abingdon' in Case, H.J. & Whittle, A.W.R.(eds) *Settlement Patterns in the Oxford Region*, 10–50, Council for British Archaeology, London

Bradley, R. 1984 *The Social Foundations of Prehistoric Britain*, Longman, London

Bradley, R. 1993 'The excavation of an oval barrow beside the Abingdon causewayed enclosure, Oxfordshire', *Proceedings of the Prehistoric Society* 58, 127–42

Bradley, R. & Edmonds, M. 1993 *Interpreting the Axe Trade*, Cambridge University Press, Cambridge

Briggs, S. 1976 'Notes on the distribution of some raw materials in later Prehistoric Britain' in Burgess, C. & Miket, R. (eds) *Settlement and economy in the third and second millenia* BC 267–82, *British Archaeological Reports* 33

Burton, J. 1984 'Quarrying in a tribal society', *World Archaeology* 16: 234–47

Bush, P. & de Seiveking, G. 1986 'Geochemistry and the provenance of flint axes' in de Seiveking, G. & Hart, M. (eds) *The scientific study of flint and chert*, 133–40, Cambridge University Press, Cambridge

Clarke, D.V. & Sharples, N. 1985 'Settlements and subsistence in the third millennium B.C.' in Renfrew, A.C. (ed.) *The Prehistory of Orkney*, 54–82, Edinburgh University Press, Edinburgh

Clough, T. & Cummins, W. (eds) 1979 *Stone Axe Studies*, CBA Research Report, London

Clough, T. & Cummins, W. (eds) 1988 *Stone Axe*

*Studies 2*, CBA Research Report 67, London

Curwen, E. & Curwen, E.C. 1926, 'Harrow Hill (Sussex) flint mine excavation, 1924–1925', *Sussex Archaeological Collections* 65, 69–111

Darvill, T. 1987 *Prehistoric Britain*, Batsford, London

David, A. 1989 'Some aspects of the human presence in west Wales during the Mesolithic', in Bonsall, C. (ed.) *The Mesolithic in Europe*, 241–53, John Donald, Edinburgh

Dixon, P. 1988 'The Neolithic settlements on Crickley Hill' in Burgess, C., Topping, P., Mordant, C. & Madison, M. (eds) *Enclosures and Defenses in the Neolithic of Western Europe*, 75–88, *British Archaeological Reports* 403

Edmonds, M. 1994, 'Interpreting causewayed enclosures in the present and the past' in Tilley, C. (ed.) *Interpretative Archaeology*, Berg, London

Ekholm, K. 1977 'External exchange and the transformation of Central African social systems' in Friedman, J. & Rowlands, M. (eds) *The Evolution of Social Systems*, 115–36, London, Duckworth

Ericson, J. & Earle, T.K. 1982 *Contexts for Prehistoric Exchange*, Academic Press, New York

Ericson, J. & Purdy, B. 1984 *Prehistoric Quarries and Lithic Production*, Cambridge University Press, Cambridge

Evans, C. 1988 'Acts of enclosure: a consideration of concentrically organised causewayed enclosures' in Barrett, J. C. & Kinnes, I. A. (eds) *The Archaeology of Context in the Neolithic and Bronze Age: Recent trends*, 85–96, Dept of Archaeology and Prehistory, Sheffield

Fell, C. 1950 'The Great Langdale axe factory', *Transactions of the Cumberland and Westmorland Archaeological Society* 50, 1–13

Gardiner, J. 1990 'Flint procurement and Neolithic axe production on the South Downs: a reassessment', *Oxford Jnl. of Archaeology* 9, 119–40

Godelier, M. 1977 *Perspectives in Marxist Anthropology*, Cambridge University Press, Cambridge

Gregory, C. 1982 *Gifts and Commodities*, Academic Press, London

Hodder, I. & Lane, P. 1982 'A contextual examination of Neolithic axe distributions in Britain' in Ericson, J. & Earle, T. (eds) *Contexts for Prehistoric Exchange*, 213–35, Academic Press, London

Holgate, R. 1990 *Prehistoric Flint Mines*, Shire, Aylesbury

Kinnes, I. 1979 *Round Barrows and Ring Ditches in the British Neolithic*, British Museum, London

Leach, J. & Leach, E. (eds) 1983 *The Kula: New perspectives on Massim exchange*, Cambridge University Press, Cambridge

Lederman, R. 1986 *What Gifts Engender*, Cambridge University Press, Cambridge

LiPuma, E. 1987 *The Gift of Kinship*, Cambridge University Press, Cambridge

Mauss, M. 1954 [1925] *The Gift*, Cohen and West, London

McBryde, I. 1984 'Kulin greenstone quarries: the social contexts of production and distribution for the Mount William site', *World Archaeology* 16, 267–85

Mercer, R.J. 1980 *Hambledon Hill: A Neolithic landscape*, Edinburgh University Press, Edinburgh

Palmer, R. 1976 'Interrupted ditch enclosures in Britain', *Proceedings of the Prehistoric Society* 42, 161–86

Peacock, D.P.S. 1969 'Neolithic pottery production in Cornwall', *Antiquity* 43, 145–9

Pryor, F. 1988 'Etton, near Maxey, Cambridgeshire: a causewayed enclosure on the fen-edge' in Burgess, C., Topping, P., Mordant, C. & Maddison, M.(eds) *Enclosures and Defenses in the Neolithic of Western Europe*,107–26, British Archaeological Reports 403, Oxford

Renfrew, A.C. 1973 'Monuments, mobilisation and social organisation in Neolithic Wessex' in Renfrew, A.C.(ed.) *The Explanation of Culture Change* 539–58, Duckworth, London

Richards, C.C. 1988 'Altered images: a re-examination of Neolithic mortuary practices in Orkney' in Barrett, J.C. & Kinnes, I. A.(eds) *The Archaeology of Context in the Neolithic and Bronze Age: Recent trends*, 42–56, Dept of Archaeology and Prehistory, Sheffield

Robertson-Mackay, R. 1987 'The Neolithic causewayed enclosure at Staines, Surrey; excavations 1961–63', *Proceedings of the Prehistoric Society* 53, 23–128

Shee Twohig, E. 1981 *The Megalithic Art of Western Europe*, Clarendon, Oxford

Smith, I.F. 1965a *Windmill Hill and Avebury*, Clarendon, Oxford

Smith, I.F. 1971 'Causewayed enclosures' in Simpson, D.D.A.(ed.) *Economy and Settlement in Neolithic and Early Bronze Age Britain and Europe*, 89–112, Leicester University Press, Leicester

Strathern, M. 1988 *The Gender of the Gift*, UCLA Press, Berkeley and Los Angeles

Thomas, J. 1991 *Rethinking the Neolithic*, Cambridge University Press, Cambridge

Thomas, J. & Tilley, C. 1994 'The axe and the torso' in Tilley, C. (ed.) *Interpretative archaeology*, Berg, London

Thomas, K. 1982 'Neolithic enclosures and woodland habitats on the south Downs in Sussex, England' in Bell, M. & Limbrey, S. (eds) *Archaeological Aspects of Woodland Ecology*, 147–70, British Archaeological Reports 146, Oxford

Thomas, N. 1991 *Entangled Objects*, Cambridge University Press, Cambridge

Van Gennep, A. 1960 *The Rites of Passage*, Routledge & Kegan Paul, London

Weiner, A. 1985 'Inalienable wealth', *American ethnologist* 12.2, 210–27

Wheeler, R. E. M. 1943 *Maiden Castle, Dorset*, Society of Antiquaries, London

Whittle, A.W. R. 1990 'A pre-enclosure burial at Windmill Hill, Wiltshire', *Oxford Jnl of Archaeology* 9, 25–8

Wilson, D. 1975 '"Causewayed camps" and "interrupted ditch systems"', *Antiquity* 49, 178–86

# Chapter 4

Appadurai, A. 1985 'Introduction: commodities and the politics of value' in Appadurai, A. (ed.) *The Social Life of Things*, 3–63, Cambridge University Press, Cambridge

Atkinson, R. J. C. 1951 'The henge monuments of Great Britain' in Atkinson, R.J.C., Piggott, C.M. & Sandars, N. *Excavations at Dorchester, Oxon*, 81–107, Ashmolean Museum, Oxford

Atkinson, R. J. C., Piggott, C.M. & Sandars, N. 1951 *Excavations at Dorchester, Oxon*, Ashmolean Museum, Oxford

Barrett, J. C. Bradley, R. J., & Green, M. 1991 *Landscape, Monuments and Society: The archaeology of Cranborne Chase*, Cambridge University Press, Cambridge

Bourdieu, P. 1979 'Symbolic power', *Critique of Anthropology* 4, 77–86

Bradley, R. J. 1982 'Position and possession: assemblage variation in the British Neolithic', *Oxford Jnl of Archaeology* 1, 27–38

Bradley, R. J. 1983 'The bank barrows and related monuments of Dorset in the light of recent fieldwork', *Proceedings of the Dorset Natural History and Archaeological Society* 105, 15–20

Bradley, R. J. 1984a *The Social Foundations of Prehistoric Britain*, Longmans, London

Bradley, R. J. 1989 'Deaths and entrances: a contextual analysis of megalithic art', *Current Anthropology* 30, 68–75

Bradley, R. J. 1991 *The Passage of Arms*, Cambridge University Press, Cambridge

Bradley, R.J. & Chambers, R.A. 1988 'A new study of the cursus complex at Dorchester on Thames', *Oxford Jnl of Archaeology* 7, 271–90

Braithwaite, M. 1984 'Ritual and prestige in the prehistory of Wessex *circa* 2000–1400 BC: a new dimension to the archaeological evidence' in Miller, D. & Tilley C.(eds) *Ideology, Power and Prehistory*, 93–110, Cambridge University Press, Cambridge

Brewster, A. 1984 *The Excavation of Whitegrounds Barrow, Burythorpe*, John Gett, Wintringham

Burgess, C. 1980 *The Age of Stonehenge*, Dent, London

Burl, H. A. W. 1969 'Henges: internal structures and regional groups', *Archaeological Jnl* 126, 1–28

Burl, H. A. W. 1976 *Stone Circles of the British Isles*, Yale University Press, Yale

Burl, H. A. W. 1979 *Prehistoric Avebury*, Yale University Press, Yale

Case, H. J, & Whittle, A. W. R. (eds) 1982 *Settlement Patterns in the Oxford Region*, Council for British Archaeology, London

Clare, T. 1987 'Towards a reappraisal of henge monuments: origins, evolution and hierarchies', *Proceedings of the Prehistoric Society* 53, 457–78

Darvill, T. C. 1987 *Prehistoric Britain*, Batsford, London

Davis, D. 1985 'Hereditary emblems: material culture in the context of social change', *Jnl of Anthropological Archaeology* 4: 149–76

Edmonds, M. R. 1992 'Their use is wholly unknown' in Sharples, N. & Sheridan, A. (eds) *Vessels for the Ancestors*, Edinburgh University Press, Edinburgh

Edmonds, M. R. & Thomas, J. S. 1987 'The Archers: an everyday story of country folk' in Brown, A. & Edmonds, M. R.(eds) *Lithic Analysis and Later British Prehistory*, 187–99, *British Archaeological Reports* 162, Oxford

Ford, S. 1987 'Chronological and functional aspects of flint assemblages' in Brown, A. & Edmonds, M. R.(eds) *Lithic Analysis and Later British Prehistory*, 67–86, *British Archaeological Reports* 162, Oxford

Gardiner, J. P. 1984 'Lithic distributions and settlement patterns in central southern England' in Bradley, R.J. & Gardiner, J. P. (eds) *Neolithic Studies*, 15–40, *British Archaeological Reports* 133, Oxford

Harding, A. & Lee, G. 1987 *Henges and Related Monuments in Britain*, *British Archaeological Reports* 190, Oxford

Harding, P. 1988 'The chalk plaque pit, Amesbury', *Proceedings of the Prehistoric Society* 54, 320–6

Healy, F. 1984 'Farming and field monuments: the Neolithic of Norfolk' in Barringer, C. (ed.) *Aspects of East Anglian Prehistory*, 77–140, Geo, Norwich

Healy, F. 1991 'The hunting of the floorstone' in Schofield, A. J. (ed.) *Interpreting Artefact Scatters*, 29–37, Oxbow Monograph 4, Oxford

Hedges, J. & Buckley, D. 1981 *Springfield and The Cursus Problem*, Essex County Council

Helms, M. 1988 *Ulysees' Sail*, Princeton University Press, Princeton

Henson, D. 1989 'Away from the core? A northerner's view of flint exploitation' in Brooks, I. & Phillips, P. (eds) *Breaking the Stony Silence*, 5–31, *British Archaeological Reports* 213, Oxford

Holgate, R. 1988a *Neolithic Settlement of the Thames Basin*, *British Archaeological Reports* 194, Oxford

Houlder, C. 1968 'The henge monuments at Llandegai', *Antiquity* 42, 216–31

Kinnes, I. 1985 'Circumstance not context: the Neolithic of Scotland as seen from outside', *Proceedings of the Society of Antiquaries of Scotland*, 115–57

Kinnes, I., Schadla-Hall, T., Chadwick, P. & Dean, P. 1983 'Duggleby Howe reconsidered', *Archaeological Jnl* 140, 83–108

Kristiansen, K. 1984 'Ideology and material culture: an archaeological perspective' in Spriggs, M. (ed.) *Marxist Perspectives in Archaeology*, Cambridge University Press, Cambridge

Manby, T.G. 1974 *Grooved Ware Sites in Yorkshire and the North of England, British Archaeological Reports* 9, Oxford

Manby, T. 1988 'The Neolithic in eastern Yorkshire' in Manby, T. (ed.) *Archaeology in Eastern Yorkshire*, 35–88, Dept of Archaeology and Prehistory, Sheffield University, Sheffield

Marshall, D. 1977 'Carved stone balls', *Proceedings of the Society of Antiquaries of Scotland* 108, 40–72

Mercer, R.J. 1981a 'The excavation of a late Neolithic henge-type enclosure at Balfarg, Fife, Scotland', *Proceedings of the Society of Antiquaries of Scotland* 111, 63–171

Mercer, 1981b *Grimes Graves, Norfolk. Excavations 1971–72*, HMSO, London

O'Kelly, C. 1969 'Bryn Celli Ddu, Anglesey: a reinterpretation', *Archaeologia Cambrensis* 118, 17–48

Parker Pearson, M. 1992 *The Bronze Age*, Batsford, London

Penny, A. & Wood, J. 1973 'The Dorset Cursus complex – a Neolithic astronomical observatory?' *Archaeological Jnl* 130, 44–76

Pierpoint, S. 1980 *Social Patterns in Yorkshire Prehistory*, British Archaeological Reports 74, Oxford

Powell, T., Corcoran, J.W.X.P., Lynch, F. & Scott, J. 1969 *Megalithic Enquiries in the West of Britain*, Liverpool University Press, Liverpool

Radley, J. 1967 'The York hoard of flint tools', *Yorkshire Archaeological Jnl* 42, 131–2

Renfrew, C. 1973 'Monuments, mobilisation and social organisation in Neolithic Wessex' in Renfrew, C. (ed.) *The Explanation of Culture Change*, 539–58, Duckworth, London

Renfrew, C. & Cherry, J. (eds) 1986 *Peer Polity Interaction and Sociopolitical Change*, Cambridge University Press, Cambridge

Richards, C.C. 1988 'Altered images: a re-examination of Neolithic mortuary practices in Orkney' in Barrett, J. C. & Kinnes, I. A.(eds) *The Archaeology of Context in the Neolithic and Bronze Age: Recent trends*, 42–56, Dept of Archaeology and Prehistory, University of Sheffield, Sheffield

Richards, C. & Thomas, J.S. 1984 'Ritual activity and structured deposition in later Neolithic Wessex' in Bradley, R. J. & Gardiner, J. (eds) *Neolithic Studies*, 189–218, *British Archaeological Reports* 133, Oxford

Richards, J. 1990 *The Stonehenge Environs Project*, English Heritage Monograph, London

Roe, F. 1979 'Typology of implements with shaftholes' in Clough, T. & Cummins, W. (eds) *Stone Axe Studies*, 23–48, CBA Research Report 23, London

Rowlands, M. 1987 'Core and periphery: a review of a concept' in Rowlands, M., Larsen, M. & Kristiansen, K. (eds) *Centre and Periphery in the Ancient World*, 1–11, Cambridge University Press, Cambridge

Sørenson, M. L. 1989 'Ignoring innovation, denying change' in Torrence, R. & Van der Leeuw, S. E. (eds) *What's New?*, 180–203, Unwin Hyman, London

Thomas, J. 1991 *Rethinking the Neolithic*, Cambridge University Press, Cambridge

Wainwright, G.J. 1989 *The Henge Monuments*, Thames & Hudson, London

Whittle, A.W.R. 1981 'Later Neolithic society in Britain: a realignment' in Ruggles, C. & Whittle, A.W.R. (eds) *Astronomy and Society in Britain during the Period 4000–1500 BC*, 297–342, *British Archaeological Reports* 88, Oxford

# Chapter 5

Atkinson, R.J.C. 1970 'Silbury Hill 1969–70', *Antiquity* 44, 313–1

Barrett, J.C. 1988 'The living, the dead, and the ancestors: Neolithic and Early Bronze Age mortuary practices' in Barrett, J.C. & Kinnes, I.A.(eds) *The Archaeology of Context in the Neolithic and Bronze Age*, 30–41, Dept of Archaeology and Prehistory, University of Sheffield, Sheffield

Barrett, J.C. Bradley, R.J., & Green, M. 1991 *Landscape, Monuments and Society: The prehistory of Cranborne Chase*, Cambridge University Press, Cambridge

Bradley, R.J. 1984a *The Social Foundations of Prehistoric Britain*, Longmans, London

Bradley, R.J. 1991 *The Passage of Arms*, Cambridge University Press, Cambridge

Bradley, R.J. & Thomas, J.S. 1984 'Some new information on the henge monument at Maumbury Rings, Dorchester', *Proceedings of the Dorset Natural History and Archaeological Society* 106, 128–32

Braithwaite, M. 1984 'Ritual and prestige in the pre-history of Wessex *circa* 2000–1400 BC: a new dimension to the archaeological evidence' in Miller, D. & Tilley, C.(eds) *Ideology, Power and Prehistory*, 93–110, Cambridge University Press, Cambridge

Burgess, C. 1976 'Meldon Bridge: a Neolithic defended promontory complex near Peebles' in Burgess, C. & Miket, R. (eds) *Settlement and Economy in the Third and Second Millennia BC*, 151–180, *British Archaeological Reports* 33, Oxford

Burgess, C. 1980 *The Age of Stonehenge*, Dent, London

Burgess, C. & Shennan, S. 1978 'The Beaker phenomenon: some suggestions' in Burgess, C. & Miket, R.(eds) *Settlement and Economy in the Second and Third Millennia BC*, 309–31, *British Archaeological Reports* 33, Oxford

Burl, H.A.W. 1976 *Stone Circles of the British Isles*, Yale University Press, Yale

Burl, H.A.W. 1979 *Prehistoric Avebury*, Yale University Press, Yale

Case, H.J. 1977 'The Beaker Culture in Britain and Ireland' in Mercer, R. (ed.) *Beakers in Britain and Europe*, 71–101, *British Archaeological Reports* S26, Oxford

Chippendale, C. 1983 *Stonehenge Complete*, Thames & Hudson, London

Clarke,D.L. 1970 *Beaker Pottery of Great Britain and Ireland*, Cambridge University Press, Cambridge

Clarke, D.V., Cowie, T. & Foxon, A. 1985 *Symbols of Power at the Time of Stonehenge*, National Museum of Scotland, Edinburgh

Cunnington, M.E. 1929 *Woodhenge* , Simpson, Devizes

Darvill, T.C. 1987 *Prehistoric Britain,* Batsford, London

Evans, J.G. 1983 'Stonehenge – the environment in the late Neolithic and Early Bronze Age and a Beaker-Age burial', *Wiltshire Archaeological Magazine* 78, 7–30

Gibson, A. M. 1982 *Beaker Domestic Sites*, British *Archaeological Reports* 107, Oxford

Harrison, R.J. 1980 *The Beaker Folk*, Thames & Hudson, London

Lane, P. 1986 'Past practices in the ritual present: examples from the Welsh Bronze Age', *Archaeological Review from Cambridge* 5, 181–92

Lanting, J. N. & Van der Waals, J.D. 1972 'British Beakers as seen from the continent', *Helenium* 12, 20–46

Parker Pearson, M. 1982 'Mortuary practices, society and ideology: an ethnoarchaeological study' in Hodder, I. (ed.) *Symbolic and Structural Archaeology*, 99–113, Cambridge University Press, Cambridge

Parker Pearson, M. 1992 *The Bronze Age*, Batsford, London

Renfrew, C. & Shennan, S. (eds) 1982 *Ranking, Resource and Exchange*, Cambridge University Press, Cambridge

Richards, C.C. & Thomas, J.S. 1984 'Ritual activity and structured deposition in later Neolithic Wessex' in Bradley, R. J. & Gardiner, J. (eds) *Neolithic Studies*, 189-218, *British Archaeological Reports* 133, Oxford

Richards, J. 1990 *Stonehenge*, Batsford, London

Robertson-Mackay, M.E. 1980 'A head and hooves burial beneath a round barrow, with other Neolithic and Bronze Age sites on Hemp Knoll near Avebury', *Proceedings of the Prehistoric Society* 46, 123–76

Shennan, S. 1982 'Ideology, change and the European Early Bronze Age' in Hodder, I. (ed.) *Symbolic and Structural Archaeology*, 155–61, Cambridge University Press, Cambridge

Shennan, S. 1986 'Interaction and change in third millennium BC western and central Europe' in Renfrew, C. & Cherry, J. (eds) *Peer Polity Interaction and Sociopolitical Change*, 137–48, Cambridge University Press, Cambridge

Shepherd, I.A.G. 1986 *Powerful Pots: beakers in north-east prehistory*, Anthropological Museum, Aberdeen

Thomas, J. 1992 'Reading the body' in Garwood, P., Skeates, R. & Tombs, J. (eds) *Sacred and Profane*, Oxbow Monographs, Oxford

Thorpe, I.J. & Richards, C.C. 1984 'The decline of ritual authority and the introduction of Beakers into Britain' in Bradley, R. J.& Gardiner, J.(eds) *Neolithic Studies*, 67–84, *British Archaeological Reports* 133, Oxford

Wainwright, G.J. 1971 'The excavation of a late Neolithic enclosure at Marden, Wiltshire', *Antiquaries Jnl* 51, 177–239

Wainwright, G.J. 1979a *Mount Pleasant, Dorset: Excavations 1970–71*, Society of Antiquaries, London

Wainwright, G.J. & Longworth, I. 1971 *Durrington Walls: Excavations 1966–1968*, Society of Antiquaries,

London

# Chapters 6–7

Atkinson, R.J.C. 1956 *Stonehenge*, Hamish Hamilton, London

Barrett, J. C. 1980 'The pottery of the later Bronze Age in lowland England', *Proceedings of the Prehistoric Society* 46, 297–319

Barrett, J.C. 1985 'Hoards and related metalwork' in Clarke, D.V. , Cowie, T. & Foxon, A. *Symbols of Power at the Time of Stonehenge*, 93–106, National Museum of Antiquity, Edinburgh

Barrett, J.C. 1994 *Fragments of Antiquity*, Blackwells, Oxford

Barrett, J.C. & Bradley, R. (eds)1980 *Settlement and Society in the British Later Bronze Age*, British Archaeological Reports 83, Oxford

Barrett, J.C. & Kinnes, I. A. (eds)1988 *The Archaeology of Context in the Neolithic and Bronze Age*, 30–41, Department of Archaeology and Prehistory, University of Sheffield, Sheffield

Bowen, H.C. & Fowler, P.J. (eds) 1978 *Early land allotment in the British Isles*, British Archaeological Reports 48, Oxford

Bradley, R. 1981 'Various styles of urn: cemeteries and settlement in southern England *c.* 1400–1000BC' in Chapman, R.W., Kinnes, I. & Randsborg, K. (eds) *The Archaeology of Death*, 93–104, Cambridge University Press, Cambridge

Bradley, R.J. 1984a *The Social Foundations of Prehistoric Britain*, Longmans, London

Bradley, R.J. 1990 *The Passage of Arms*, Cambridge University Press, Cambridge

Burgess, C. 1978 'The background of early metal-working in Ireland and Britain' in Ryan, M. (ed.) *The Origins of Metallurgy in Atlantic Europe*, 258–325, Stationery Office, Dublin

Burgess, C. 1980 *The Age of Stonehenge*. Dent, London

Coles, J. 1969 'Scottish Early Bronze Age metalwork', *Proceedings of the Society of Antiquaries of Scotland* 101, 1–110

Coles, J. M. & Harding, A. F. 1979 *The Bronze Age in Europe*, Methuen, London

Cowie, T. G. 1978 *Bronze Age Food Vessel Urns*, British Archaeological Reports 55 Oxford

Drewett, P. 1982 'Late Bronze Age downland economy and excavations at Black Patch, East Sussex', *Proceedings of the Prehistoric Society* 48, 321–400

Ehrenburg, M. 1980 'The occurrence of Bronze Age metalwork in the Thames: an investigation' *Transactions of the London and Middlesex Archaeological Society* 31, 1–15

Fleming, A. 1971 'Territorial patterns in Bronze Age Wessex', *Proceedings of the Prehistoric Society* 37, 138–66

Fleming, A. 1987 *The Dartmoor Reaves*, Batsford, London

Ford, S., Bradley, R., Hawkes, J. & Fisher, P. 1984 'Flint-working in the metal age', *Oxford Jnl of Archaeology* 3, 157–73

Fowler, P. 1981 'Wildscape to landscape: "enclosure" in prehistoric Britain' in Mercer, R.J. (ed.) *Farming Practice in British Prehistory*, 9–54, Edinburgh University Press, Edinburgh

Grinsell, L.V. 1959 *Dorset Barrows*, Dorset Natural History and Archaeological Society, Dorchester

Herne, A. 1992 'The lithic assemblage' in Longworth, I. (ed.) *Excavations at Grimes Graves, Norfolk*, Fascicule III

Longworth, I. 1984 *Collared Urns of the Bronze Age in Great Britain and Ireland*, Cambridge University Press, Cambridge

Parker Pearson, M. 1992 *The Bronze Age*, Batsford, London

Peterson, F.F. 1981 *The Excavation of a Bronze Age Cemetery on Knighton Heath, Dorset*; British Archaeological Reports 98, Oxford

Rowlands, M.J. 1976 *The Production and Distribution of Metalwork in the Middle Bronze Age in Southern Britain*, British Archaeological Reports 32, Oxford

Shennan, S. 1982 'Ideology, change and the European Early Bronze Age' in Hodder, I. (ed.) *Symbolic and Structural Archaeology*, 155–61, Cambridge University Press, Cambridge

Simpson, D.D.A. 1968 'Food vessels: associations and chronology' in Coles, J. & Dimpson, D.D.A. (eds) *Studies in Ancient Europe*, 197–211, Leicester University Press, Leicester

Taylor, J. 1980 *Bronze Age Goldwork of the British Isles*, Cambridge University Press, Cambridge

# Index